Hiking Yosemite National Park

HELP US KEEP THIS GUIDE UP TO DATE

Every effort has been made by the author and editors to make this guide as accurate and useful as possible. However, many things can change after a guide is published—trails are rerouted, regulations change, techniques evolve, facilities come under new management, and so on.

We would appreciate hearing from you concerning your experiences with this guide and how you feel it could be improved and kept up to date. While we may not be able to respond to all comments and suggestions, we'll take them to heart, and we'll also make certain to share them with the author. Please send your comments and suggestions to the following address:

FalconGuides
Reader Response/Editorial Department
246 Goose Lane, Suite 200
Guilford, CT 06437

Or you may e-mail us at: editorial@falcon.com

Thanks for your input, and happy trails!

Hiking
Yosemite
National Park

A Guide to 61 of the Park's
Greatest Hiking Adventures

Fourth Edition

Suzanne Swedo

FALCONGUIDES

GUILFORD, CONNECTICUT
HELENA, MONTANA

For my sister Jo

FALCONGUIDES®

An imprint of Rowman & Littlefield
Falcon and FalconGuides are registered trademarks and Make Adventure Your Story is a trademark of Rowman & Littlefield.

Distributed by NATIONAL BOOK NETWORK

Copyright © 2005, 2011, 2016 Rowman & Littlefield
A previous edition of this book was published in 2000 by Falcon Publishing, Inc.
Photos by Suzanne Swedo
Maps: XNR Productions, Inc. Updated by Trailhead Graphics Inc. © Rowman & Littlefield

British Library Cataloguing-in-Publication Information available

ISSN 1554-4303
ISBN 978-1-4930-1772-0 (paperback)
ISBN 978-1-4930-1773-7 (e-book)

∞™ The paper used in this publication meets the minimum requirements of American National Standard for Information Sciences—Permanence of Paper for Printed Library Materials, ANSI/NISO Z39.48-1992.

The author and Rowman & Littlefield assume no liability for accidents happening to, or injuries sustained by, readers who engage in the activities described in this book.

Contents

The Hikes

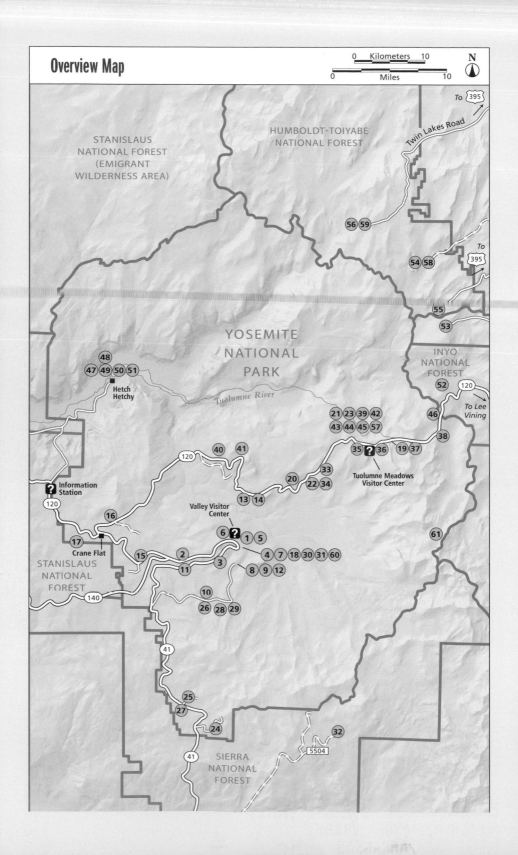

Acknowledgments

Thanks to the many park rangers and other personnel and volunteers of the National Park Service in Yosemite who have been so generous with their time and assistance, especially Laurel Boyers and Dave Gansci, Linda and Alan Estes, and Deanna Petree. All have provided much valuable information and have helped to smooth the way.

The biggest debt of gratitude is owed to wilderness ranger Mark Fincher, who knows everything there is to know about the trails of Yosemite, and to Erin Anders, who builds them. Also deeply appreciated are the support and assistance of June at the USDA Forest Service office in Oakhurst, as well as Pete Devine, Kylie Chappell, Adonia Ripple, and everyone at the Yosemite Conservancy, whose purpose it is to initiate and support interpretation, education, research, and scientific and environmental programs in Yosemite.

For their aid and encouragement, and plain good company in the field, thanks also to Joellyn Acree, Erica Crawford, Ed DeLeonardis, Minh Duong, Melinda Goodwater, Jane Magid, Sally McKinney, Marissa Ortega-Welch, Fumiaki Nakamura, Jeff Nathan, the Nicoletti family, Celia Ronis, Jane Sinclair, and Sandy Steinman.

Introduction

Yosemite National Park occupies the heart of John Muir's "Range of Light" in the Sierra Nevada. The name means "snowy range" in Spanish, and in winter more than 60 feet of snow may accumulate. Yet the Sierra has also been called the gentle wilderness, because extremes of temperature are not great and the hiking days of summer are comparatively dry and sunny. It is a land of amazing diversity. Elevations in Yosemite range from 2,000 to over 13,000 feet, from the rolling oak woodlands of the western slope to the jagged mountain crest, where offspring of the great glaciers that carved the spectacular topography still lie in shady hollows above thousands of lakes. Then, to the east, the land abruptly drops away to the apparently endless sagebrush desert of the Great Basin. There are three groves of giant sequoia trees, the largest living things on earth; miles of forests and meadows; and a rich and varied collection of wildflowers, wildlife, and history galore. Then there is the incomparable valley itself, Yosemite, surrounded by massive granite domes and spires, booming waterfalls, and, in the summer season, teeming with tourists.

As many as 4 million people visit the park each year. Most concentrate their activities in Yosemite Valley, a mere 1-by-7-mile corner of the park. Those who are willing to explore on foot, however, can expect a genuine, uncrowded wilderness experience. Yosemite's borders encompass almost 1,200 square miles, and almost 800 miles of excellent trails travel through some of the most dramatic and beautiful scenery on earth.

This book describes the best of them, how to find them, how to plan and equip yourself to tackle them, and what special, natural wonders to enjoy along the way.

How to Use This Guide

The purpose of this guide is to help you choose and plan a day hike or backpack in Yosemite best suited to your time, energy, experience, and personal preferences. It offers a preview of what you are likely to see and experience along your chosen route: geological features, historical sites, trees, birds, flowers, and mammals. It also helps you anticipate places where the trail is faint, where it is clear, and where and when rivers and streams are special sources of delight, or possible obstacles to travel.

Trail descriptions are intended to be used along with the US Geological Survey topographic maps available at wilderness outfitting and sporting goods stores, at visitor centers and shops in Yosemite, and through the USGS at (888) ASK USGS or www.usgsstore@usgs.gov.

Each trail description opens with a summary of the highlights and expectations for the hike. The statistical section provides a quick reference to the characteristics of the hike.

◀ *The Grizzly Giant is one of the largest trees in the Mariposa Grove.*

The classic view of Yosemite Valley looks to the east.

Within those characteristics, the **Distance** is described in miles. You'll also find out whether the route is a loop, in which you return to the place where you started without retracing your steps; an out-and-back hike, in which you return to the trailhead the same way you came; or a shuttle hike, in which you begin at one trailhead and end at another, requiring two vehicles, a shuttle bus, or another driver to pick you up or deposit you at either end.

The **Difficulty** rating is bound to be interpreted differently by hikers in varying degrees of physical condition, including their adaptability to high elevation. In general, Easy trails can be negotiated by anybody who can walk. Moderate trails are of greater length or involve some elevation gain and loss, and may challenge those who are not accustomed to much physical activity. Moderately strenuous hikes are for experienced hikers or those who are very physically fit. Strenuous hikes will challenge the most experienced and energetic of hikers.

Elevation change will give you some idea of how much climbing and descending you can expect, but don't forget that there may be many ups and downs between the lowest and highest elevations.

Seasons section refers, in most cases, to the only time that trails are open and safe to use at all. The hiking season in Yosemite is all too short. Most trails are passable only on skis, snowshoes, or with special winter climbing equipment for most of the year. More specific times to visit areas especially noteworthy for their seasonal displays of wildflowers, fall colors, or flowing waterfalls will be mentioned here.

Permits for specific hikes are noted in the statistical section of the hike description. For a more general discussion, see the special Wilderness Permits section, starting on page 9.

Important safety or weather information is described in **Special considerations.**

Maps list the relevant names of USGS quads that will be useful for each hike. While our maps give you a great general idea of the hike, it's a good idea to carry these more detailed maps with you for safety.

Miles and Directions are landmarks on the trail, usually trail junctions. The distances are based on the official National Park Service measurements, but the park service cautions hikers to be aware that trails have been rerouted over the years to avoid obstacles like rockslides or washouts or to protect fragile vegetation in boggy meadows. The signs marking these trails have not always been corrected. Sometimes new signs have been added to one end of a trail but not to junctions along the way, so you will find that the miles don't always add up. Still, I have walked every trail in this book and have found none of the stated mileage between points to be inaccurate by more than a quarter mile.

Nearest facilities refers to sources of supplies or contact with emergency services nearest the trailhead.

Life in Yosemite

Yosemite is a hiker's paradise because of its wonderful diversity. The range is only about 400 by 70 miles in extent and is mostly gray, granitic rock, yet every nook and cranny, and every stream drainage or mountain peak, is different from the rest. The main reason for this variety is Yosemite's wide range of elevation. Extremes of topography lead to extremes of weather, temperature, and soil. These in turn provide habitats for a wide variety of plants and animals. More than 1,300 species of flowering plants, 223 kinds of birds, and 77 kinds of mammals are found here. Summer days in the western foothills can reach 100°F; winter nights at the crest of the range may be 30°F below zero. The foothills may receive as little as 15 inches of precipitation in a year while the forests at 8,000 feet may get 65 feet. Still, the Sierra Nevada is a gentle wilderness to hike because 95 percent of its precipitation falls as winter snow. Summers are usually sunny and dry, and though thundershowers can be expected in July and August at higher elevations, they are usually of short duration.

The hiking season can begin as early as April in the western foothills between elevations of 2,000 and 4,000 feet. The rolling hills are covered with a mixture of shrubby chaparral and oak woodland, green and carpeted with flowers usually through May, becoming hotter and drier later in the season. As elevations increase, wispy gray bull pines appear on the hillsides, along with the showy white wands of California buckeye.

At 4,000 to 6,000 feet a mixed coniferous forest of ponderosa pine, Douglas fir, and incense cedar flourishes, along with live oaks, deciduous black oaks, and maples. Warm, moist pockets support three separate groves of giant sequoias. Yosemite Valley, at about 4,000 feet, is at its finest in May and June. Waterfalls pour over the cliffs, and dogwoods and azaleas bloom along the streams. Mule deer, black bears, and several kinds of ground squirrels are active in spring, summer, and fall, along with a great variety of birds.

Lodgepole pine and red fir dominate at 6,500 to 8,000 feet. This is the zone of heaviest snowfall in winter. Moisture from the Pacific Ocean is wrung from the air and piled up here in deep snowdrifts that remain well into July. Forests are dark and deep with fairly open, bare floors because little sunlight reaches the ground. Yet strange little parasitic and saprophytic plants, including several kinds of orchids, thrive here, nourished by dead and decaying material in the soil.

The subalpine zone from 8,000 to 10,000 feet is considered by some to be the beginning of the true High Sierra. The landscape is more open and rocky, and the views are the finest. The sky is intensely blue because the air is thinner. Graceful mountain hemlocks stand tall at the lower end of this zone, but the lodgepole and whitebark pines near timberline are often gnarled and stunted, forced to hunker down to avoid howling winter winds. Belding ground squirrels and marmots whistle in the meadows, and showy black, white, and gray Clark's nutcrackers squawk among the trees.

The region of high peaks and passes above timberline is true arctic-alpine country. The temperature is low, winds high, and the growing season short, so plants keep their heads low. Most of the alpine wildflowers are perennials that wait underground for the few short weeks of sunshine and freedom from snow. Beginning roughly in mid-July and continuing through August, they burst forth to carpet the high meadows and decorate the rock crannies with masses of color. Across the late-lying snowfields, rosy finches chase insects that have been blown upward from below. Pikas scurry among the rock piles, gathering food to see them through the winter.

Then at the crest, all at once, the mountains fall away to the Great Basin. On the steep eastern slope, mountain and desert species mix together. Sagebrush and pinyon pines appear. The very rock is different on the eastern side of the crest. Ancient red and white metamorphics remain above the much younger granite that underlies most of Yosemite. Many points along the crest reveal stupendous views of Mono Lake, the Owens Valley, and the White Mountains.

Geology

Yosemite occupies the central part of the Sierra Nevada, a 400-mile-long active dynamic classroom of geologic forces and features. The range was formed by the collision of vast plates of the earth's crust, lifting what had once been seafloor and offshore volcanic islands to become mountain peaks. Roughly 150 million years ago, huge globs of molten material called magma from beneath the earth's crust forced their way toward the surface, cooking the surrounding and overlying seafloor sediments to a new kind of rock known as metamorphic. Most of the molten material cooled and solidified beneath the surface to become granitic rock. Then, about 80 million years ago, mountain building ended for a time. For millennia rain, wind, and weather washed away almost all of the overlying ancient seafloor to reveal the gray granite that gives Yosemite its distinctive appearance today. A few remnants of the old metamorphic rock can still be seen in a narrow belt low in the western foothills and in another high on the Sierra crest, but more than 95 percent of the Sierra Nevada is granite.

About 25 million years ago, the range began to rise again, this time as a result of movement on the famous San Andreas Fault. North of Yosemite volcanoes erupted, blanketing the land in lava and ash. The entire range broke apart along its eastern border, the Sierra crest thrusting upward, the Owens Valley dropping down, so that the current range slopes gradually upward from west to east, till it reaches the crest, then drops away in a vertical cliff. Eventually the mountains gained enough height to block the flow of the moist winds that blow from the Pacific, which dropped their loads of rain and snow on the western flank of the range, cutting rivers and streams. The sediment washed away to the west, filling the great central valley of California with rich and productive soil. The land to the east, now deprived of water, became desert.

The Royal Arches and North Dome can be seen from the valley floor.

The movement of ice applied the finishing touches to Yosemite's scenery. About 2 to 3 million years ago, the climate of the earth cooled just a bit. Enormous ice caps formed over the poles and spread outward. While they did not reach Yosemite, the snows that did fall accumulated to great depths, then compressed to ice. The ice, under its own weight, began to flow down the previously cut stream courses, gouging them wider and deeper, scraping and polishing their bottoms and sides, sharpening the mountaintops into spires and horns, forming knife-edged ridges called arêtes and amphitheaters called cirques. The ice dug out basins in the rock, and when it melted, it left thousands of sparkling alpine and subalpine lakes, many of which over time filled in with silt to become flower-filled mountain meadows. The glaciers in Yosemite today are not remnants of the original ice flows. The global climate has warmed and cooled in cycles since then, and the glaciers have melted and re-formed in response. The current glaciers are only a few hundred years old, but they lie in the hollows created by their larger predecessors, and the weather processes that created them are still at work. The mountain-building processes are work, too. The mountains are still being steadily, though not smoothly, uplifted. The Sierra is alive and growing. All along the eastern slope, hot springs steam and bubble along numerous faults, and earthquakes rattle local residents. As recently as 1872, an earthquake struck the Sierra to the south of Yosemite, lifting the mountains 15 to 20 feet in that area and devastating the small town of Lone Pine.

In Yosemite we can see the evidence of more than 600 million years of geologic history, and, as the mountains build and erode away, witness the process as it happens.

History

The southern Sierra Miwok people, who hunted, fished, and gathered a rich variety of plant materials, especially acorns, inhabited Yosemite for more than 800 years. They conducted trade with the Piute from the east side of the mountains for obsidian for arrowheads, salt, and various foods. Both made beautiful baskets.

Yosemite was first seen by outsiders in 1851 when the Mariposa battalion chased a band of Indians led by Chief Tenaya into the valley. Shortly thereafter the native people were forced to leave their villages in the area. By 1855 the first tourists had arrived, followed by the first homesteaders. Stagecoach routes, then railroads, were built to reach the valley. Sheep and cattle were turned into the meadows to graze and trample the grasses, and loggers began to cut the trees. Fortunately, a few farsighted individuals recognized the need for protection and set in motion the appropriate political machinery that led to President Abraham Lincoln's signing the bill that placed Yosemite Valley and the Mariposa Grove under the protection of the state of California. In 1868 the legendary John Muir arrived in Yosemite and led the movement for federal protection.

Yosemite National Park was created in 1890. All parks were patrolled by the US Cavalry until 1916, when their function was taken over by the National Park Service. Many trails and other facilities were constructed or expanded by federal agencies like the WPA and the CCC during the Great Depression of the 1930s. After World War II people and cars poured into the park in ever-increasing numbers. Now Yosemite gets 4 million visitors each year, forcing the National Park Service to walk a tightrope between two somewhat contradictory mandates. It must "conserve the scenery and the natural and historic objects and the wildlife therein . . ." and it must "provide for the enjoyment of the same in such manner and by such means as will leave them unimpaired for the enjoyment of future generations."

Providing access to the parks and accommodations within so that everyone can enjoy without disrupting and changing them forever is an ongoing challenge. Roads, trails, campgrounds, other lodging, emergency services, administration, and sources of supply, no matter how carefully planned and constructed, inevitably make an impact on the natural environment. Hikers can do their part by respecting park rules and practicing Leave No Trace principles.

Leave No Trace

While the primary aim of this book is to encourage people to experience and appreciate the beauty of Yosemite up close and on foot, the backcountry is heavily used and the environment is fragile. To prevent further wear and tear on the land, each hiker must accept personal responsibility for his or her impact on the environment by practicing Leave No Trace principles (www.LNT.org). You can do your part by reading and following the suggestions and regulations you receive when you pick up your wilderness permit.

Guidelines for day hikers can be found in the Yosemite Guide, which is given to every park visitor at all entrance stations, and at visitor and wilderness centers.

On the Trail

When traveling on trails, group size is limited to fifteen people (except at a few very heavily used trailheads such as Happy Isles, where the limit is ten). Groups traveling cross-country are limited to eight people. Hiking on trails leaves the least impact on the land, so all the hikes in this book follow established trails. To prevent damage to the trails themselves, do not shortcut switchbacks. They have been built to retard erosion as well as create a more comfortable grade for gaining and losing elevation. When the trail is wet or muddy, try to avoid walking alongside it, trampling vegetation and wearing a parallel trail. Many of Yosemite's meadows are scarred by a series of wide, parallel ruts across the landscape that look like the work of vehicles. On the other hand, if you must cross a meadow with no conspicuous pathway and are part of a group, spread out so that you do not create a new rut by numerous feet passing over the same route.

Good manners and consideration for others, not to mention safety, dictate that foot travelers yield to pack animals on the trail. Step off the trail and stand quietly until the last horse or mule has gone completely past. Bicycles or mechanized travel of any kind is prohibited in the backcountry (as are pets and firearms). Downhill hikers should yield to those heading uphill so that the climbers can maintain rhythm and momentum.

Selecting a Campsite

Camping is prohibited within 4 trail miles of Yosemite Valley, Hetch Hetchy Reservoir, Wawona, Glacier Point, and Tuolumne Meadows, and within 1 mile of any road. Otherwise you may camp anywhere you choose in the Yosemite wilderness so long as you observe a few restrictions designed to reduce your impact on the land and on other campers.

Choose a site at least 100 feet from water and, whenever possible, 100 feet from the trail, or at least out of sight of passers-by. Pitch your tent or spread your tarp on sandy ground or pine duff, never on growing vegetation. In the afternoon sunshine, green meadows are deceptively inviting, but they are cold, damp, and buggy at night. Use an established and designated campsite—one that has been used before—and do not modify the area in any way by digging trenches around tents, building new fire rings, or breaking limbs off trees.

Campfires

Campfires are prohibited above 9,600 feet in Yosemite and are discouraged even at lower elevations. If you must have a fire, keep it small and cozy, and take only firewood that is dead and lying on the ground. Do not remove branches from standing dead trees. They provide homes for dozens of different creatures and are important parts of the ecosystem. High-elevation fires are proscribed not because of wildfire danger, but because the 9,600-foot mark is the average timberline elevation in Yosemite, where vegetation grows slowly and the few trees that manage to hang on to life near timberline are evergreens that do not drop much organic material on the ground. The soil needs protection from the compaction that litter on the forest floor supplies, especially where people are moving around and pitching tents. Compaction prevents the soil from absorbing vital water and oxygen and removes the source of organic material that is returned to the soil as it decomposes.

Harlequin lupine blooms in early season at middle to lower elevations and makes a spectacular show following a fire.

Backpack stoves are so light and efficient, and modern fabrics so warm, that fires are no longer needed for cooking or warmth, but for social atmosphere alone. As attractive as going "back to nature" seems, there are too many of us now, and too little truly wild nature left to afford an extravagant campfire. Keep it small if you must have it, and of course, make sure it is completely out when you leave.

Housekeeping

There is one simple rule for good housekeeping in the wilderness: Do not put anything in the water. That includes soap, food scraps, and fish guts. Biodegradable soap is not the answer. To biodegrade means to decompose, that is, to rot. Biodegradable soap does not poison organisms in the water like detergent can, but it does encourage the growth of bacteria that can upset the chemical balance of the water to the detriment of the organisms that live in it. Hot water and a little sand do fine for washing dishes, but if you must use soap, wash and rinse everything at least 100 feet from any water source. The same goes for your own body. A refreshing swim in a mountain pond won't do any damage, and you can surely survive a few days in the wilderness without contracting some dread disease if you don't use soap, but if you feel you must, wash and rinse at least 100 feet away from water.

Keep your camp clean of crumbs and other edibles. Learn to take just what you need to eat, and pack out your leftovers. At very popular campsites jays, squirrels, mice, and marmots have come to expect human food scraps, and have acquired bad habits like snatching food from your hand or chewing holes in your pack or tent to investigate appetizing smells. In popular camping areas leave pack zippers and flaps open when you are asleep or away from camp so that varmints can crawl in to investigate and crawl back out without gnawing their way through the fabric.

Human waste disposal is one of the most difficult problems in the backcountry. There are simply too many of us concentrated in too few areas to avoid having a serious impact. The park service has constructed solar composting toilets at the most popular campsites in the park and encourages you to use them. Otherwise, find a spot 200 feet from water where there is some organic material on the ground, dig a hole about 6 inches deep, then cover everything. Take extra plastic bags along and pack out your toilet paper. A teaspoon of powdered bleach in the plastic bag will prevent odors. Do not bury it. It is sometimes dug up again by animals, and takes many years to decompose underground. Burning toilet paper is no longer recommended since the practice has started more than one serious fire.

Wilderness Permits

Wilderness permits are required year-round for all overnight trips into the Yosemite backcountry. They are not required for day hikes except for day hikes to Half Dome. The permits are free of charge, though there is a fee for advance reservations.

Permits are issued under a quota system designed to prevent overcrowding and damage from overuse in popular wilderness areas. They are based on trailhead entry, not on final destination. Forty percent of the permits available for each trailhead can be picked up within 24 hours of your trip at wilderness centers throughout Yosemite on a first-come, first-served basis. The Yosemite Valley Wilderness Center, the Tuolumne Meadows Wilderness Center, the Big Oak Flat and Wawona Visitor Centers, and the Hetch Hetchy Entrance Station all issue permits. Reservations for the other 60 percent of the permits are available in advance by mail, fax (preferred), or phone, but you must pick up the permit in person before your hike. There is a per-person charge for advance reservations. Reservations for trips between mid-May and mid-October are accepted up to 26 weeks in advance. Call (209) 372-0740. You can print a reservation form from www.nps.gov/yose, fill it out, and mail it, with your check, to Wilderness Permits, P.O. Box 545, Yosemite, CA 95389. You can fax the completed form to (209) 372-0739. Permit reservations are not accepted online. For more information about permits, call (209) 372-0200. Mail and fax requests are processed before phone requests each day. Rules for obtaining wilderness permits are subject to change. www.nps.gov/yose/planyourvisit/wildpermits.htm is your most up-to-date information source.

If your hike begins outside Yosemite, obtain your permit from the forest service permit station nearest your entry point. All hikes described in this book that originate east of the park begin in the Hoover Wilderness. Trails north of Lundy Canyon are administered by the Bridgeport Ranger District of the Toiyabe National Forest. Permits are available from the USDA Forest Service in Bridgeport. Call (619) 932-7070. Trails south of Lundy Canyon are administered by the Mono Ranger District of the Inyo National Forest. Permits are available from the Mono Basin visitor center at Mono Lake near Lee Vining. Call (619) 647-6525. Hikes that begin to the south of the park are administered by the Sierra National Forest in North Fork and Oakhurst. Call (559) 877-2218 or (559) 297-0706.

If you will be applying for a first-come, first-served permit, you may apply at any wilderness permit station up to 24 hours in advance. You are permitted to camp in a backpack campground one night before and one night after your trip, so that you will be able to apply in person one day in advance. Wilderness center hours are 8:30 a.m. to 4:30 p.m.

The purpose of wilderness permits is not merely to maintain trailhead quotas. They help the National Park Service determine how much use each trail gets so that priorities for trail maintenance and patrols can be established and funds allocated. They also allow a point of contact at which hikers can be informed of current trail conditions or any special regulations that might be in effect due to bear activity, fires, or any other emergency.

Wilderness permits are not a form of trail registration. Your itinerary is on file so that search and rescue teams have some idea of where to begin if you are reported lost. But it is up to you to leave word with someone at home who will contact the park service if you do not return when expected.

Special permit rules are in effect for John Muir Trail and Pacific Crest Trail through-hikers and for those planning to climb Half Dome. See the **Half Dome** and **Two Famous Trails** descriptions for details (hikes 7, 60, and 61).

Bears

Black bear management has become such a serious issue in Yosemite that it deserves special discussion. All of Yosemite's bears are black bears, regardless of their color. The grizzly, the California state mammal, is now extinct in California. Black bears are neither as unpredictable nor as aggressive as grizzlies. No human has ever been killed by a black bear in Yosemite, but there have been numerous injuries, lots of property damage, and many vacations spoiled.

The fault is not with the bears. For many years Yosemite bears were fed scraps from local hotels, to the delight of tourists who came to watch the evening show. When the practice was discontinued, bears resorted to raiding garbage containers all over the park. When bear-resistant garbage containers were installed, bears mastered the art of opening ice chests in campgrounds, and when bear-proof boxes were installed in campgrounds, bears moved into the backcountry to feast on freeze-dried backpack cuisine. At the same time they discovered what culinary delights are to be found in vehicles left in parking lots. The National Park Service has tried tagging, relocating, and even killing hundreds of Yosemite's bears to no avail. Current park policy attempts to change the behavior of the humans, not the bears. After all, we created the problem in the first place.

The best way to help save Yosemite's bears, your expedition, and your vehicle is to carry a bear-proof canister in the backcountry and store any food you must leave behind in the bear-proof boxes located in parking lots and at trailheads. Bear-proof canisters are not perfect; they are bulky, weigh two to three pounds, hold only a few days' food, and cost nearly $100. Still, bears have not figured out how to get into them. *The Park Service now requires the use of bear canisters for overnight stays anywhere in the wilderness.* For more information visit the Yosemite website at www.nps.gov/yose/wilderness. It lists the brands of bear canisters that have been tested and approved. You can rent one in locations all over Yosemite for a small fee for your stay of up to 2 weeks. Once you learn to select and pack your food carefully, you can carry enough food for two people for several days in a single canister.

The counterbalance method of hanging food appears simple on paper, but it is very difficult to find a tree of the proper height with a branch of the proper diameter, and to balance your food sacks perfectly. It was never more than a delaying tactic. Bears are much stronger, more patient, more determined, and much more intelligent than you think. If you could get it up there, they could get it back down again. *Hanging food is no longer permitted in Yosemite.*

Thousands of vehicles have been broken into in parking lots. Bears break windows, tear off doors, and tunnel through upholstery to reach the trunk from the inside. Do not store any food, garbage, anything that smells like food, or any containers that look like they might hold food such as ice chests or paper bags—even if they are empty—in your car. Not even in the trunk. Do not assume that if food is sealed in plastic or foil and has not been opened that a bear cannot smell it. Their sense of smell is extremely acute, and they have learned that food comes in certain kinds of containers even if they can't read the labels or smell what's inside. They have been known to open cans of motor oil just to check. All parking lots, campgrounds, and trailheads in Yosemite have bear-proof food storage boxes nearby. Use them.

The National Park Service considers proper food storage to be your responsibility. Don't expect sympathy if you lose your food. You are liable for a fine for not storing it properly.

A Few Words of Caution

Weather Patterns

While most Sierra summer days are clear and sunny, high mountains create their own weather. Hikers must be prepared for anything. Snow can fall at any time of year, including July and August, though it is not common. Afternoon thundershowers, sometimes accompanied by violent hailstorms, can build with amazing rapidity on summer days that begin without a cloud in the sky. They are usually of short duration, but long enough to drench and chill an unprepared traveler. Never set out without rain gear. Lightning can be a serious hazard on open ridges above timberline. If a storm threatens, head downhill to the cover of timber as quickly as possible. If you're caught in an exposed area with no time to descend, get away from your pack or any metal equipment and squat until the danger passes—do not sit.

Drinking Water

In spite of the clear and sparkling appearance of Yosemite's lakes and streams, water from even the most remote of sources has been found to contain *Giardia lamblia*, a microorganism that causes diarrhea and other intestinal upsets. It is not a life-threatening illness for normal, healthy adults, but it is debilitating and persistent, and must be treated with antibiotics whose side effects may be equally unpleasant. The symptoms do not appear for more than a week after exposure, so victims sometimes do not associate their malady with their wilderness experience. Treat all water with a water filter guaranteed to remove giardia, with iodine or chlorine dioxide tablets, or by boiling. Since the bug is killed at temperatures far below boiling, even at high elevations, just bringing water to a rolling boil is treatment enough. Iodine and chlorine dioxide are lightweight, convenient, and effective if fresh, but some people are allergic and some object to the taste.

Wild Animals

Injuries caused by bears in Yosemite are almost invariably due to human ignorance or carelessness. Take care to avoid moving between a mother and her cubs, and do not try to touch or feed a bear or to reclaim food the bear has already taken from you. More injuries are caused by deer than by bears in the park since people are more likely to approach a deer and risk being sliced by sharp hooves when the animal is startled.

The tiny Belding ground squirrel is prepared to attack when young are nearby.

Mountain lions have been spotted in Yosemite, but they are very shy, and attacks are extremely rare. If you should encounter one, do not run or you might be mistaken for prey. Hold your ground, wave your arms to make yourself appear larger, and shout. Then congratulate yourself on being given the gift of a glimpse of a beautiful animal in its native habitat.

You'll find rattlesnake habitat at lower elevations where there is plenty of brush to provide cover for small animals like rabbits, squirrels, and mice. Rattlers are most active at dawn and dusk and blend beautifully with their surroundings. They prefer to save their venom for catching their prey and do not strike at people unless they feel threatened. Stay alert and watch your step. The chances of being bitten are extremely slim, and snakebites are rarely fatal.

Stream Crossings

This is one hazard that is not exaggerated, unlike perceived threats from wildlife. Most of the larger streams in Yosemite have sturdy bridges across them, but in exceptionally wet years, some of them get washed away. Be sure to research trail conditions in advance if your proposed route involves a major river crossing. More frequently it is the smaller creeks swollen with snowmelt early in the year that are most dangerous. Some have rock or log crossings that must be managed with great care. A stout stick is a great stabilizer if you don't have hiking poles. Be sure to plant it upstream so that rushing water does not grab it and pull it out from under you. Always unbuckle your pack straps so that if you should fall in, you can free yourself from being dragged and held underwater.

If you decide to wade, always overestimate the depth and the strength of the current. Sierra streams are so clear that they are usually deeper and swifter than they seem. Do not wade through water higher than your knees. The recommended method is to remove your socks and cross in your boots, which will give you temporary protection against the numbing cold and more stability on underwater obstacles. Do not try to cross barefooted. Seek out the widest part of the stream, even though the temptation is to pick a narrower spot to make the crossing quicker. The widest spot is usually the shallowest, slowest, and safest. If you are not sure whether you can cross safely, you can try again early in the morning when the snow upstream has begun to melt in the morning sun. Do not take chances. You can always return.

Always overestimate the depth and strength of the current of mountain streams.

Losing the Trail

Yosemite trails are much more defined, well marked, and better maintained than those you will find in most other wilderness areas. Still, some are used more regularly than others and are easier to follow. High water, avalanches, rockslides, and fast-growing meadow vegetation and brush can obscure a clear

Gentians appear in high country meadows in midsummer.

trail in a single season. Watch for trail blazes on the trees, made by cutting away the outer bark, usually in simple geometric shapes at approximately eye level. In open rocky places watch for cairns—piles of rocks also known as ducks—that indicate the presence of a trail. Stay alert for sawed logs, metal tags, sometimes even plastic strips. If you become confused on the trail, go back to a point where you were absolutely certain of your location and start over. If you feel you are hopelessly lost, stay put and wait for help.

Trail blazes mark most of Yosemite's trails.

Trail Finder

	Back-country Lakes	Waterfall	Alpine, Ridges, Passes, Plateaus	No Hills	Day Hikes	Solitude	Early Season	Wild-flowers	Wildlife
The Valley Floor									
1. East Valley Floor (option to waterfalls)		•		•	•		•	•	
2. West Valley Floor				•	•	•	•	•	
3. Glacier Point via the Four Mile Trail					•				
4. Happy Isles to the Top of Nevada Fall		•			•				•
5. Mirror Lake–Tenaya Canyon Loop				•	•		•		•
6. Yosemite Falls		•			•				
7. Half Dome		•							
The South Rim of Yosemite Valley									
8. Taft Point and The Fissures					•				
9. Sentinel Dome		•			•				
10. McGurk Meadow					•	•		•	•
11. The Pohono Trail						•			
12. The Panorama Trail—Glacier Point to Nevada Fall		•			•				

The North Rim of Yosemite Valley

	Back-country Lakes	Waterfall	Alpine, Ridges, Passes, Plateaus	No Hills	Da/ Hikes	Solitude	Early Season	Wild-flowers	Wildlife
13. Tioga Road to the Top of Yosemite Falls and Eagle Peak		•							
14. Porcupine Creek to North Dome					•	•			
15. The North Rim		•				•			
16. Tuolumne Grove					•				
17. Merced Grove				•	•	•	•		

The High Sierra Camps

	Back-country Lakes	Waterfall	Alpine, Ridges, Passes, Plateaus	No Hills	Da/ Hikes	Solitude	Early Season	Wild-flowers	Wildlife
18. Merced Lake High Sierra Camp	•								•
19. Vogelsang High Sierra Camp (options to Vogelsang Lake and Vogelsang Pass)	•		•					•	•
20. May Lake High Sierra Camp	•				•				•
21. Glen Aulin High Sierra Camp (option to the Waterwheels)		•						•	•
22. Sunrise High Sierra Camp	•								•
23. The High Sierra Camp Loop	•	•	•					•	•

The Southern Park

	Back-country Lakes	Waterfall	Alpine, Ridges, Passes, Plateaus	No Hills	Day Hikes	Solitude	Early Season	Wild-flowers	Wildlife
24. Mariposa Grove of Big Trees (options to Wawona Point Vista and Wawona-Mariposa Grove Trail)					•		•		
25. Chilnualna Fall (options to Bridalveil Creek Campground and Chilnualna Lakes)		•				•	•		
26. Buena Vista Crest	•					•			
27. Wawona Meadow				•	•	•	•	•	•
28. Ostrander Lake	•							•	
29. Ottoway Lakes (option to Red Peak Pass)	•		•	•					
30. The Clark Range and Red Peak Pass	•		•			•			
31. Merced River High Trail (option for High Trail Back to the Valley)		•				•			
32. Chain Lakes (options to Fernandez Pass and Breeze Lake)	•					•			

South of Tuolumne Meadows

	Back-country Lakes	Waterfall	Alpine, Ridges, Passes, Plateaus	No Hills	Day Hikes	Solitude	Early Season	Wild-flowers	Wildlife
33. Tenaya Lake				•	•	•			
34. Clouds Rest (option to Half Dome)						•			
35. Cathedral Lakes	•				•			•	•
36. Elizabeth Lake	•				•			•	

	Back-country Lakes	Waterfall	Alpine, Ridges, Passes, Plateaus	No Hills	Day Hikes	Solitude	Early Season	Wild-flowers	Wildlife
37. Lyell Fork of the Tuolumne River (option to Donohue Pass)	•		•		•			•	•
38. Mono Pass (option to Parker Pass)	•		•		•	•			
North of Tuolumne Meadows									
39. Waterwheel Falls and the Grand Canyon of the Tuolumne		•			•	•	•	•	•
40. Lukens Lake	•				•	•		•	
41. Ten Lakes (options for Grand Tour of the Grand Canyon of the Tuolumne)	•		•						•
42. Soda Springs and Parsons Lodge				•	•			•	•
43. Dog Lake	•				•				
44. Lembert Dome					•				
45. Young Lakes	•								
46. Gaylor Lakes	•		•		•			•	
Hetch Hetchy									
47. Wapama Falls		•			•		•	•	•
48. Rancheria Falls (option to top of Rancheria Falls)		•				•	•	•	•
49. Laurel Lake	•						•	•	

The North Boundary Country

	Back-country Lakes	Waterfall	Alpine, Ridges, Passes, Plateaus	No Hills	Day Hikes	Solitude	Early Season	Wild-flowers	Wildlife
50. Lake Vernon and Titill Valley	●								●
51. Jack Main Canyon and Tilden Lake	●	●				●		●	
The North Boundary Country									
52. Saddlebag Lake and 20 Lakes Basin	●		●		●			●	
53. Lundy Canyon		●	●		●	●		●	●
54. Green Creek	●	●			●				
55. Virginia Lakes Basin (option for Green Creek / Virginia Canyon Shuttle)	●		●		●	●			
56. Matterhorn Canyon and the Sawtooth Range	●		●			●			
57. Benson Pass–Northeast Yosemite Grand Tour	●		●			●		●	●
58. McCabe Lakes (option to McCabe Lakes via Tuolumne Meadows)	●		●			●			
59. Piute Mountain–Peeler Lake Loop	●		●						
Two Famous Trails									
60. The John Muir Trail	●	●	●					●	●
61. The Pacific Crest Trail	●	●	●					●	●

Map Legend

Transportation

═〔395〕═	U.S. Highway
═〔120〕═	State Highway/ Major Park Road
───────	Primary Road/ Other Park Road
= = = = =	Unpaved Road
- - - - - - -	Featured Trail
- - - - - - -	Trail

Boundaries

───────	National Park/ Forest Boundary

Hydrology

～～～	Major River
～～	River
·—·—·—	Intermittent Stream
ᴏⸯ	Spring
⩘⩘	Waterfall
∥	Rapids
⬭	Lake
⸚⸚⸚	Marsh

Symbols

⑤	Trailhead
🏚	Ranger Station
▲	Campground
❓	Visitor Center/ Information
▪	Point of Interest/ Structure
🅿	Parking
⛉	Picnic Area
⬕	Overlook
⤳	Bridge
⫯	Gate
←	Direction Arrow

Physiography

⤳	Pass
▲	Peak

The Valley Floor

Yosemite Valley is one of the natural wonders of the world. Almost-vertical walls rise up to 4,733 feet above the valley floor, where the Merced River winds its way through flower-filled meadows and shady forests. The famous profile of Half Dome dominates the east end, and El Capitan the west. Some of the world's highest waterfalls pour from the cliffs. It is a mecca for hikers, climbers, photographers, fishermen, rafters, cyclists, and just plain tourists from everyplace on earth. While it covers only about 7 square miles of a national park that sprawls over 1,200 square miles, the majority of visitors stay in the valley, and indeed, many believe that Yosemite Valley and Yosemite National Park are one and the same. Do not expect a wilderness experience in Yosemite Valley, but don't assume that hiking there is not worthwhile just because it's popular. The valley's attractions draw so many sightseers because they are well worth seeing, but there are also many beautiful, quiet, out-of-the-way corners to enjoy on foot and in solitude.

Spring and fall are the best times to hike the valley. The crowds and traffic are heaviest in summer, and temperatures can be uncomfortably hot for strenuous hiking. Springtime is more pleasant; the waterfalls are full, and the wildflowers are blooming. In fall the air is clear and brisk, and the changing colors of the oaks, dogwoods, maples, and willows are spectacular.

All hikes on the valley floor are day hikes because no camping is allowed outside established campgrounds. Permits are not necessary, but it's a good idea to drop by the visitor center and wilderness center for information about trail conditions and weather reports. You can help reduce traffic and pollution in the valley by parking your car in the lot across Northside Drive from Yosemite Village, or at Camp Curry and using the shuttle buses that run every 10 to 30 minutes and go to most valley trailheads.

If you are planning a backpack that originates in the valley, you can pick up your wilderness permit at the wilderness center, between the Ansel Adams gallery and the post office in Yosemite Village. If you arrive the day before your trip, remember that all accommodations—campgrounds, lodges, and hotels—are usually full and require reservations many months in advance. Camp 4, formerly known as Sunnyside, a walk-in campground used mostly by climbers on the north side west of Yosemite Lodge, is your best bet. Be sure to stow all food, food containers, garbage, and ice chests in the bear-proof containers in the parking lot any time you leave your car. The valley is open year-round and can be reached from the west via CA 41 from Fresno, CA 140 from Merced, and CA 120 from Manteca. In summer CA 120, the Tioga Road, is open all the way through the park to the east side of the Sierra near Lee Vining on US 395. There is a per-car fee to enter the park from any direction. *Remember: There is no gas in Yosemite Valley or at Tuolumne Meadows.*

Contact Yosemite at (209) 372-0200 or e-mail at www.nps.gov/yose for more information.

1 East Valley Floor

This is a leisurely, flat, loop hike with views of North Dome, the Royal Arches, and Yosemite Falls, where you can visit Happy Isles Nature Center and the infamous 1996 rockslide, then stroll along sometimes boisterous, sometimes tranquil stretches of the Merced River.

Start: Hikers parking lot east of Curry Village
Total distance: 1.9-mile loop
Hiking time: 1 to 2 hours
Difficulty: Easy
Elevation change: 100 feet

Seasons: Year-round
Nearest facilities: Curry Village; snacks, water, and toilets at Happy Isles Nature Center
Permits: None
Map: USGS Half Dome quad

Finding the trailhead: Take Southside Drive (one-way, east) almost to its end, passing Curry Village, passing shuttle stop 15, passing the "Do Not Enter" sign, to the turnoff to the right marked "Trailhead Parking." Or board the Yosemite Valley shuttle bus from anyplace in the valley and get off at stop 15, Upper Pines Campground, and continue east along the road to the trailhead parking lot lying in the shadow of Glacier Point. Trailhead GPS: N37 44.09 / W119 33.97

The Hike

After depositing any food in the bear boxes, find the trailhead marked "John Muir Trail, Mist Trail," at the southeast end of the parking lot just beside the big yellow "Bear Warning" sign. Follow the wide dirt path beneath incense cedar, ponderosa pine, Douglas fir, and black oak. You might see other hikers veering left to follow the path that runs alongside the shuttle bus road, but keep right for a quieter, less-traveled route.

Pass a little A-frame structure used for ranger/naturalist talks, and just beyond, at mile 0.5, reach a swampy area known as The Fen. Here a boardwalk runs through a lush growth of water-loving horsetails, sedges, and fragrant mints. An interpretive panel tells about the living things inhabiting soggy places like this one. The trail crosses a paved path and makes a quick left-right-left jog before meeting the Merced River. To the right is the Happy Isles Nature Center at 0.6 mile, with wonderful exhibits and books inside. Behind the building you can see the rubble and smashed trees left by the 1996 rockslide where a hiker was killed. Wooden bridges take you out onto the happy isles themselves, where there are exhibits about interesting creepy-crawlies you'll find there, as well as information about how the islands got to be here in the middle of the Merced River. Now head downstream and follow the riverside path to the Happy Isles shuttle stop (stop 16) on the road, where you will find restrooms and a snack bar.

Swimmers and rafters enjoy the quiet Merced River in summer.

At the paved shuttle bus road, turn right to cross the Happy Isles Bridge, pausing mid-bridge for views of the river, which rushes toward the bridge in noisy whitewater rapids, then emerges more quietly from the other side. The view of North Dome above the river on the downstream side is a photographer's favorite. Now on the north side of the bridge, leave most of the crowd behind and meander along the east bank of the Merced among incense cedar and pine, streamside alder and dogwood, and, in May and June, fragrant, showy white azaleas. The river changes character at every turn, sometimes gurgling busily, sometimes green and placid, occasionally splitting to flow around wooded islands. This section of the trail is shared by horses and mules because it connects their stables to the John Muir Trail. Remember to step off the trail to let them pass, since pack animals always have the right-of-way.

At 1.5 miles the stable area appears across the road on the right, and simultaneously Upper Yosemite Fall comes into view ahead. Turn left here and cross back over the Merced on the road on the Clark Bridge. On hot summer afternoons a colorful collection of rafts and inner tubes drifts down the river. Once over the bridge, turn around to admire Half Dome on the right, North Dome and Washington Column on the left. Pass between the entrances to Upper and Lower Pines Campgrounds, then cross Southside Drive. There are Curry Village tent cabins to the right. Turn left and follow the roadside path back to the trailhead parking lot.

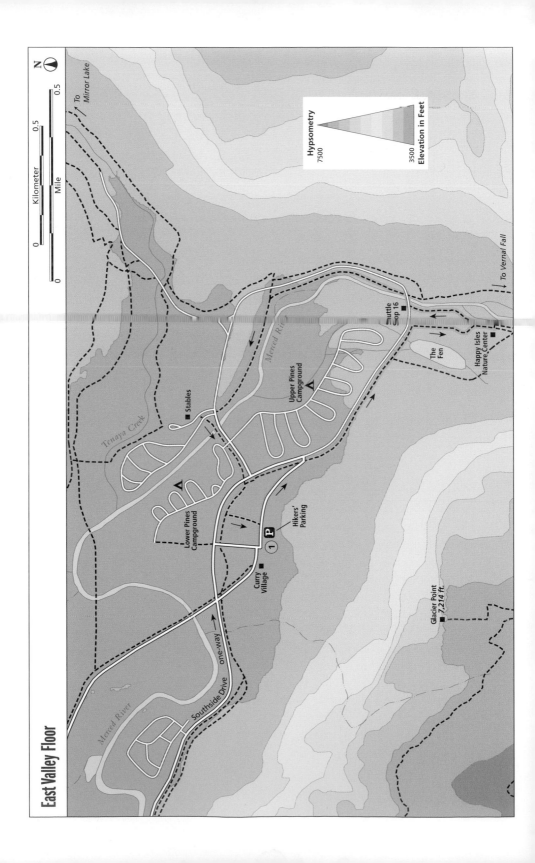

East Valley Floor

N

Kilometer
0   0.5

Mile
0   0.5

Hypsometry
7500

3500
Elevation in Feet

To Mirror Lake

Merced River

Tenaya Creek

Stables ■

Lower Pines Campground ▲

Upper Pines Campground ▲

Merced River

Shuttle Stop 16 ■

The Fen

Happy Isles Nature Center ■

To Vernal Fall

Curry Village ■

① P Hikers' Parking

Southside Drive

one-way

Merced River

Glacier Point
7,214 ft. ■

Miles and Directions

0.0 Trailhead parking lot

0.5 The Fen

0.6 Happy Isles Nature Center

1.0 Happy Isles Bridge on the shuttle bus road

1.5 Stables

1.9 Return to trailhead parking lot

Option: Waterfalls—If you have time and energy to spare, take a short detour out into the open to see two of the valley's finest features and prettiest early springtime waterfalls hidden from view in the parking lot. Walk to the entrance of the parking lot at its west end and go a few dozen yards down the driveway out to Southside Drive, then turn left and walk another 0.1 mile to the corner of the driveway into the Curry Village parking lot. Across the valley are the Royal Arches crowned by North Dome, with Royal Arch Fall trickling down to the west. Behind you, ephemeral Staircase Falls descend to Curry Village in a series of perfect, regular steps.

2 West Valley Floor

This end of Yosemite Valley is surprisingly quiet and unvisited, except near popular attractions like Bridalveil Fall and El Capitan Meadow. If you start fairly early in the morning though, you can have even these busy spots to yourself. Dogwoods and maples are especially beautiful at this end of the valley, blooming and fragrant in spring, blazing with color in fall. The beaches along the Merced River invite sunning and swimming in summer.

Start: El Capitan Bridge near the center of the valley
Total distance: 4.6-mile loop
Hiking time: 3 hours to all day
Difficulty: Easy
Elevation change: 330 feet

Seasons: Spring, summer, and fall
Nearest facilities: Everything you need, except gas, at Curry Village and Yosemite Village
Permits: None
Maps: USGS El Capitan and Half Dome quads

Finding the trailhead: From Yosemite Village take Northside Drive (one-way, west) to El Capitan Drive and turn left (south). From any of the west-side park entrances, take Southside Drive (one-way, east) to a sign that says "To 41, 120, 140," and turn left (west). (**Note:** This is El Capitan Drive, but there is no sign facing this direction to tell you so.) Park along the road on either side of the El Capitan Bridge. In summer take the El Capitan shuttle bus that begins at Yosemite Village to stop E-4, El Capitan Bridge. There are bear boxes at the trailhead. Trailhead GPS: N37 43.45/W119 37.88

The Hike

From the west end of the El Capitan bridge spanning the Merced River, turn right (north) and set off upstream on a path between the river and Northside Drive. A sign at the start says, among other things, "Pohono Bridge 2.8 Miles." You can't miss the 7,569-foot monolith of El Capitan directly ahead, while Cathedral Rocks and Cathedral Spires rise just behind you. Skirt a low fence blocking access to the river as it rounds a curve called the Devil's Elbow. Turn left, cross Northside Drive at the crosswalk, and make a sharp hairpin turn back westward along an old gravel road. There are bear boxes here where El Capitan climbers can leave their food. As you walk westward, the formidable North American wall of El Capitan looms directly overhead. Look for the patch of darker-colored mineral in the granite shaped like the North American continent.

You are close enough here to see the figures clinging to the rock above without binoculars and hear their shouted conversations. As you approach the nose of El Capitan, cross several spur routes used by climbers to reach the base of the wall. Just continue straight ahead. If it's early in the season, you will probably have to hop across

Bridalveil Fall is viewed from across the Merced River.

several little branches of Ribbon Creek flowing down a spot near the Rockslides. In springtime you can get a rare view of Ribbon Fall pouring over the cliff just west of El Capitan. Like Bridalveil across the valley, it dissolves into a mist toward the bottom. It is entirely dry by mid–July.

Your route reaches the Old Big Oak Flat Road, just beyond which is an ugly park service woodlot. Turn left on the road and in just a few steps find the trail again on your right. Follow it beneath the blackened lower trunks of trees that were subjected to prescribed burns. The trail takes you almost all the way out to Northside Drive, where you can look across the road and the valley to see Bridalveil Fall, but there is a better and more easily accessible viewpoint ahead (as well as a restroom). Veer right (north) away from the road and pass around the "back" side of Black Spring through a riotous growth of willows, cattails, horsetails, and ferns.

The trail now angles back down toward the road, where you will soon be able to spot parked cars at Valley View, one of the classic Yosemite Valley postcard portraits of Bridalveil Fall at mile 2.6. Continue westward on the trail and in a few minutes reach a crosswalk across Northside Drive, and cross over the Merced River on the Pohono Bridge at mile 2.7. Now you are heading eastward along the south side of the valley.

Just past the bridge a sign says "Bridalveil Fall 1.6 miles." This is a lovely quiet corner of the valley where dogwoods bloom in spring and maples glow red in fall. There are two little springs across the road, Fern Spring and Moss Spring. This section of the trail can be muddy in springtime, but it hosts a garden of flowers with evocative names like enchanter's nightshade, false Solomon's seal, bleeding heart, and wild

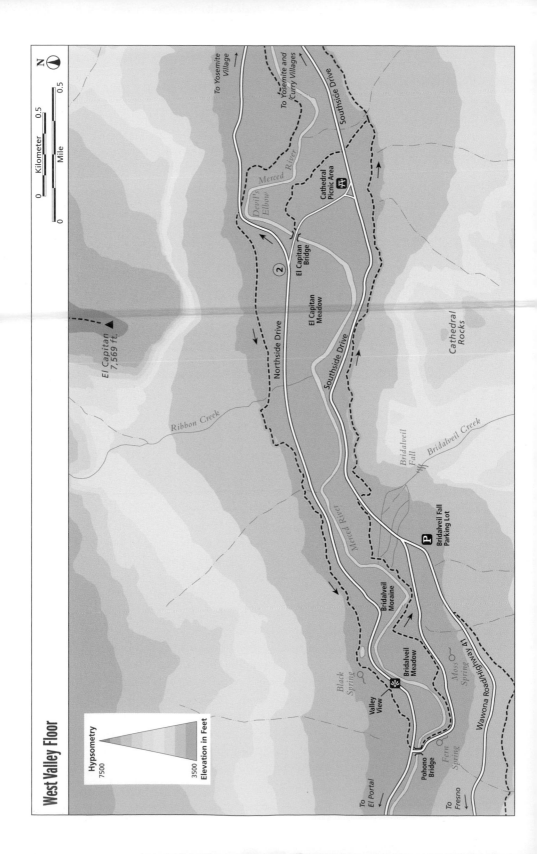

ginger. The trail hugs the riverside for a time, then emerges into sunshine skirting Bridalveil Meadow. Across Southside Drive a sign marks the site of the famous confab between John Muir and Teddy Roosevelt about the importance of protecting places like Yosemite in a national park system.

The "official" trail stays to the left of the road and crosses several branches of Bridalveil Creek, but unless it's very late in the season, you'll stay dryer and safer if you leave the trail and walk along the shoulder of the road. At this point Southside Drive and the Wawona Road and CA 41 come together, so watch for traffic.

Backtrack just a few feet on CA 41 to visit Bridalveil Fall at mile 4.3, which flows over the southern wall of Yosemite Valley through a defile between Cathedral Rocks and the Leaning Tower. Before it reaches the bottom 620 feet below, the wind catches, tatters, and flings the droplets into graceful lacy patterns of spray.

Leave Bridalveil Fall on a wide beaten path and continue east, parallel to Southside Drive. Turn right at the junction that directs you to Curry Village, and climb over the hump of the Bridalveil Moraine a bit above the road amid a tumble of enormous mossy rocks. After the trail flattens out, keep a lookout on the right side of the trail for a low post with a picture of a carabiner on it marking a route for climbers. A few yards beyond, at a second carabiner sign at mile 4.6, find an unmarked but clear trail leading left out of the forest to Southside Drive, and in only a few steps find yourself at a junction marked with the sign "To 41, 120, 140," where you turn sharply left and follow the road for a few minutes more to your starting point.

Miles and Directions

0.0 El Capitan Bridge
0.3 Cross Northside Drive
2.6 Valley View
2.7 Pohono Bridge
4.3 Bridalveil Fall
4.5 Unmarked trail to Southside Drive
4.6 Arrive back at the trailhead

3 Glacier Point via the Four Mile Trail

The Four Mile Trail is really 4.6 miles because it has had to be rerouted since its original construction. It is a steep, steady uphill-and-back pull to Yosemite's most famous viewpoint. It's a great workout where the ever-changing perspective of the valley floor will keep your mind off your thudding heart and straining lungs. You can even reward yourself with a snack and a cold drink at the top.

Start: Four Mile Trailhead at the foot of Sentinel Rock

Total distance: 9.2 miles out and back

Hiking time: 4 to 8 hours

Difficulty: Strenuous if you push yourself

Elevation change: 3,200 feet

Seasons: Late spring, summer, and fall; closed in winter

Nearest facilities: Curry Village and Yosemite Village

Permits: None

Map: USGS Half Dome quad

Finding the trailhead: Drive east on one-way Southside Drive to the parking area on both sides of the road just beyond the Sentinel Beach/Yellow Pine picnic areas. Watch carefully for the trailhead sign on the right—if you miss it, you'll have to drive all the way around the valley to get back. In summer you can take the El Capitan shuttle bus to stop E-5, the Four Mile Trail. Trailhead GPS: N37 44.03/W119 36.06

The Hike

An interpretive panel with historical information about the early days of tourism in Yosemite marks the beginning of the trail. Towering overhead is the vertical flat slab of Sentinel Rock, beneath which the asphalt trail begins its switchback ascent among huge mossy boulders, shady live oaks, laurels, and maples. Mariposa lilies, catchfly, and alum root line the path, which soon crosses a little creek lined with thimbleberry, lupine, and monkey flowers. The route works gradually eastward as it climbs. If you begin your hike by 8 a.m., watch for hang gliders suspended in air right beside the trail on their way to the landing area in Leidig Meadow.

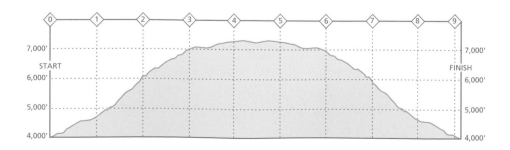

Look down onto Leidig Meadow and the Merced River.

Still climbing, the trail comes even with Yosemite Falls, roaring across the valley in spring and early summer. At about three quarters of the way, you arrive at a short spur trail to Union Point where Tenaya Canyon, North Dome, Clouds Rest, and Half Dome appear briefly, then disappear as the trail heads in a more southerly direction.

The switchbacks become a bit less short and steep and the way becomes sunnier and more open. At last the trail loses a bit of elevation, rounds a shoulder, crosses a tiny rivulet, then makes a short climb to top out at the Glacier Point Snack Bar. Enjoy the stupendous views of the park from Glacier Point, then return the way you came.

On your return, descend carefully. The loose gravel over smooth granite can be slippery.

A FIERY WATERFALL

Until 1968 Glacier Point was the site of the infamous firefall. The bark of hundreds of the magnificent old red firs from the nearby forest was set ablaze just after dark on summer evenings. After an elaborate ceremony of ritual calls between Glacier Point and the valley below, the glowing coals were raked over the cliff to form a fiery waterfall in the dark. It was a popular attraction, of course, but one more suited to an amusement park than to Yosemite. The lichens and other organisms inhabiting the rock face were seared away and the beautiful old forest was threatened. In 1968 the National Park Service ended the practice.

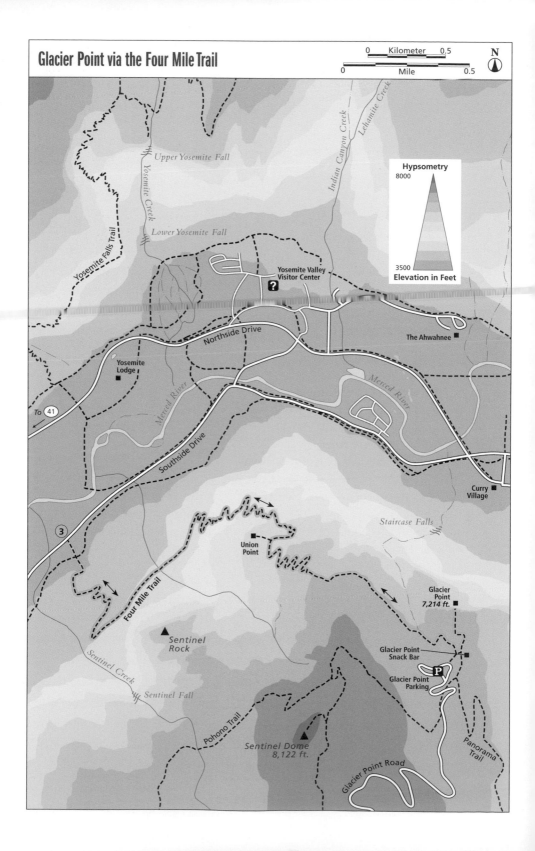

Glacier Point via the Four Mile Trail

Hypsometry
8000

3500
Elevation in Feet

N

0   Kilometer   0.5
0   Mile   0.5

Upper Yosemite Fall

Yosemite Creek

Lower Yosemite Fall

Yosemite Falls Trail

Indian Canyon Creek

Lehamite Creek

Yosemite Valley
Visitor Center

Northside Drive

The Ahwahnee

Yosemite
Lodge

Merced River

Merced River

To 41

Southside Drive

Curry
Village

3

Staircase Falls

Union
Point

Four Mile Trail

Glacier
Point
7,214 ft.

Sentinel
Rock

Glacier Point
Snack Bar

Sentinel Creek

Glacier Point
Parking

P

Pohono Trail

Sentinel Fall

Panorama
Trail

Sentinel Dome
8,122 ft.

Glacier Point Road

Miles and Directions

0.0 Four Mile Trailhead

4.6 Glacier Point Snack Bar

9.2 Return to Four Mile Trailhead

Option: For an easier hike of about 4.5 miles mostly downhill, ride or drive to Glacier Point and hike downhill all the way to Yosemite Valley. To get to the trailhead, drive about 14 miles up CA 41, Wawona Road, to Chinquapin. Turn left onto the Glacier Point Road and continue another 13 miles to its end at Glacier Point. Or you can ride the Glacier Point shuttle bus from Yosemite Lodge to Glacier Point (call 209-372-1240 for a reservation for this bus, which is not part of the free bus system). In summer, when the El Capitan shuttle is running, you can ride back to anyplace in the valley from the Four Mile Trailhead at shuttle stop E-5.

4 Happy Isles to the Top of Nevada Fall

If you have time for only one hike in Yosemite, whether you want to spend the day on the trail or take only a short stroll, this loop (or part of it) is the one. It's what Yosemite is all about: massive granite cliffs, classic glacial features, and views of at least four of the valley's biggest and best waterfalls. It climbs along the course of the Merced River as it plunges over the steps of the Giant Staircase in Nevada Fall, then Vernal Fall, before resuming its flat, meandering course over the floor of Yosemite Valley.

Start: John Muir Trailhead at Happy Isles
Total distance: 5.8-mile lollipop
Hiking time: 3 hours to all day
Difficulty: Moderate
Elevation change: 2,000 feet
Ocasons: May to June for spectacular waterfalls; Oct to early Nov for foliage; closed in winter

Nearest facilities: Snacks, toilets, and water at the trailhead
Permits: None
Map: USGS Half Dome quad
Special considerations: If you'll be hiking the Mist Trail in springtime, carry rain gear or at least choose a warm day. You're sure to be drenched by the spray.

Finding the trailhead: Park in the hikers' lot east of Curry Village. You can take the shuttle bus from Curry Village to Happy Isles (stop 16) or walk from the parking lot, turn right (east) at the entrance, and follow the well-marked path to Happy Isles. This will add 1 mile each way to your hike. From the shuttle bus stop, continue on the paved road over the Happy Isles Bridge, then turn right, following the river upstream to the big sign that marks the beginning of the John Muir Trail. Trailhead GPS: N37 43.51 / W119 33.33

The Hike

The big sign at the trailhead marks the beginning of the John Muir Trail, showing mileage to various points all the way to trail's end at Mount Whitney, about 211 miles to the south. The first part of the trail is asphalt because of the very heavy foot traffic. Don't expect a true wilderness experience here. This is a popular spot for good reasons, but the farther you go, the more solitude you'll find. It's popular not only because it is spectacular, but because it's one of the few routes out of the valley to the high country.

The trail climbs gently through black oak and pine forest among enormous lichen-draped boulders up along the north bank of the Merced. A little spring trickles out of the rocks a few hundred yards up on your left. (**Note:** Don't drink the water without purifying it.) The trail steepens gradually as you climb, but you'll want to stop frequently anyway to enjoy the roaring river through openings in the trees. In about a half mile, across the Merced to your right, tucked back up in Illilouette Gorge, Illilouette Fall pours 370 feet down the Panorama Cliff to meet the Merced River.

Nevada Fall as seen from the Mist Trail in early summer. ▶

The trail suddenly descends to the bridge at 0.8 mile, where dozens of visitors will be taking photos or staring in open-mouthed wonder at 317-foot Vernal Fall upstream. There are restrooms, a water fountain, and dozens of freeloading Steller's jays and ground squirrels near the bridge. For their health and your safety, do not feed them.

▶ **The falls of the Giant Staircase are well named:** *Vernal* **is Latin for "springtime,"** *Nevada* **is Spanish for "snowy."**

Cross the bridge to the south side of the Merced and turn left (upstream). The crowd will soon thin noticeably. At 0.9 mile the Mist Trail leaves the John Muir Trail to the left. To follow the loop clockwise, take the left fork and return on the John Muir Trail. Where a sign says "Foot Trail Only, Top of Vernal Fall Via Mist Trail .3 Miles," get out your rain gear. The Mist Trail climbs steeply over big wet stone blocks. The thunder of the falls is almost deafening in early season; morning sunlight through the spray has a diffuse, mystical quality, and there's always a rainbow or two if the sun is shining. At the top of the falls is an oak-shaded bench where you can shake off excess water. Beside this bench the Merced pauses to collect itself in the deceptively quiet Emerald Pool before crashing over the cliff. A long, slanting ramp called the Silver Apron tempts the sweaty hiker to ride this water slide into the pool. ***Don't do it!*** In an instant you'd be washed over the rim to the rocks 320 feet below. There are several warning signs along the riverbank reminding hikers to keep away from the edge and out of the water. Some who have ignored the warnings have been killed.

At 1.5 miles cross the bridge at the Silver Apron back over the Merced and begin climbing steeply again along its north shore, sometimes through a light mist from Nevada Fall in early season. Another set of switchbacks brings you out onto a sunny bench above the falls where you'll meet the junction with the John Muir Trail; follow the trail, turning right (south) toward Yosemite Valley. There are plenty of viewpoints with protective railings where you can watch Nevada Fall rush over the lip and drop 594 feet. It's a perfect place for sunbathing and picnicking. Keep an eye on your lunch! The local squirrels and jays will make off with it if your attention wanders for even a moment.

After gaping awestruck at the roaring water, cross the bridge and follow the slope upward a short distance to pass the junction with the Panorama Trail at 2.7 miles. It takes off to the left toward Illilouette Fall, Glacier Point, and beyond. Your trail,

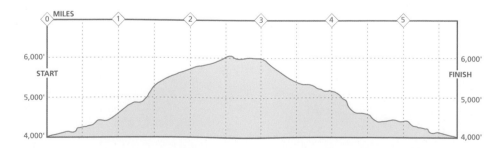

Happy Isles to the Top of Nevada Fall

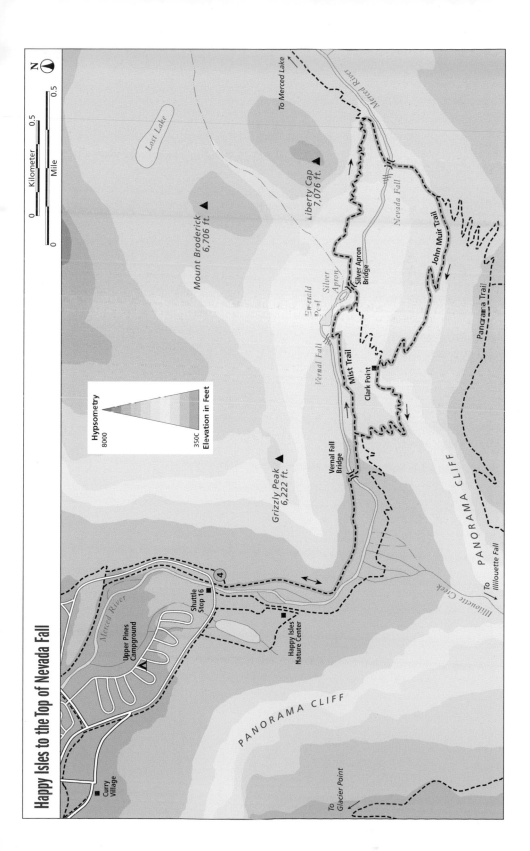

Curry Village

Merced River

Upper Pines Campground

Shuttle Stop 16

Happy Isles Nature Center

PANORAMA CLIFF

To Glacier Point

Grizzly Peak
6,222 ft.

Hypsometry

8000

3500

Elevation in Feet

Vernal Fall Bridge

Mist Trail

Clark Point

John Muir Trail

PANORAMA CLIFF

To Illilouette Fall

Illilouette Creek

Panorama Trail

Vernal Fall

Emerald Pool

Silver Apron

Silver Apron Bridge

Nevada Fall

Mount Broderick
6,706 ft.

Liberty Cap
7,076 ft.

Lost Lake

To Merced Lake

Merced River

N

Kilometer
0   0.5

Mile
0   0.5

to the right, is cut into the side of the cliff beneath a weeping rock overhang that gently drips onto the trail. Delicate ferns and columbines are tucked into the cracks. Continue to descend on well-graded switchbacks, enjoying views of Upper Yosemite Fall across the valley, until you reach Clark Point at mile 3.7. This is where the hiker who is heading upward on the John Muir Trail catches the first jaw-dropping view of Nevada Fall with Mount Broderick and Liberty Cap looming above. There is a lateral trail here that cuts back downhill to the Mist Trail, but if you want to stay dry this time, keep left and stay on the John Muir Trail. Just before you reach the Vernal Fall Bridge again, you'll pass the junction to the Mist Trail at the point where you went up, then another junction for horses only that leads back to the stables. You cross the Vernal Fall Bridge at 5.0 miles and return to Happy Isles Trailhead the way you came.

Miles and Directions

0.0 Happy Isles Trailhead

0.8 Vernal Fall Bridge

0.9 Mist Trail junction

1.5 Silver Apron Bridge

2.5 Top of Nevada Fall

2.7 Panorama Trail junction

3.7 Clark Point

5.0 Vernal Fall Bridge via John Muir Trail

5.8 Return to Happy Isles Trailhead

5 Mirror Lake-Tenaya Canyon Loop

This easy loop day hike leads to one of the most isolated corners of the valley by way of a favorite family picnic and wading spot. If you head out early in the morning, you can complete the entire hike in solitude. If you have come just to splash in the lake or to photograph the famous reflection, your out-and-back hike is less than 2 miles.

Start: Trailhead at Mirror Lake shuttle bus stop 17
Total distance: 4.6-mile loop
Hiking time: 2 to 4 hours
Difficulty: Easy
Elevation change: 100 feet

Seasons: Accessible year-round, but finest May through July
Nearest facilities: Everything you need (except gas) in Yosemite Village and Camp Curry
Permits: None
Maps: USGS Half Dome and Yosemite Falls quads

Finding the trailhead: Board the Yosemite Valley shuttle bus from anyplace in the valley. (Curry Village has parking nearest the trailhead.) Get off at Mirror Lake (stop 17). Trailhead GPS: N37 44.22/W119 33.35

The Hike

To hike the loop in a clockwise direction, skirting the west shore of Tenaya Creek and Mirror Lake and returning along the eastern shore, follow the sign to Mirror Lake along the paved road (no longer in use except for bicycles) across the Tenaya Creek. The path rises slightly as it passes through a quiet forest of ponderosa pine, white fir, Douglas fir, incense cedar, and dogwood. At 1.0 mile the forest opens

A VANISHING LAKE

Mirror Lake was created when a rockslide dammed up a section of Tenaya Creek, which promptly went to work reclaiming its original course. Every spring it washes tons of silt down the canyon to refill the lake basin, extending fingers of earth out into the water. These fingers invite colonization by water-loving plants like sedges and willows, which soon come alive with the songs of redwing blackbirds. Mirror Lake is well on its way to becoming Mirror Meadow. Eventually, as the basin fills in and dries out, trees will move in, and soon the land will again be a conifer forest with Tenaya Creek running through it, perhaps leaving the canyon as though Mirror Lake had never been—at least until the next rockslide. For years the park service periodically dredged the lake, slowing the natural succession from lake to forest in order to preserve the popular reflection, but the practice was finally discontinued in 1971.

Mount Watkins is reflected in Mirror Lake in early season.

Mirror Lake–Tenaya Canyon Loop

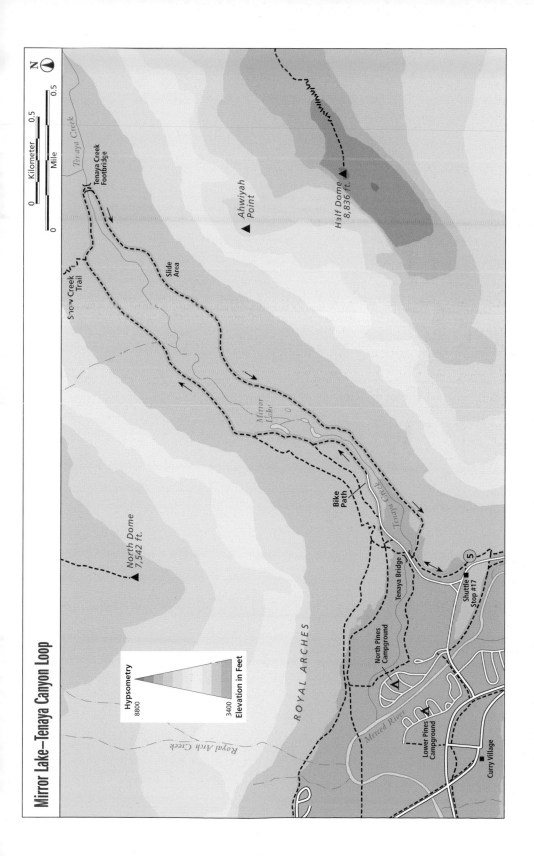

N

Kilometer
0   0.5

Mile
0   0.5

Tenaya Creek

Tenaya Creek Footbridge

Snow Creek Trail

Slide Area

Ahwiyah Point ▲

Half Dome
8,836 ft. ▲

Mirror Lake

Bike Path

North Dome
7,542 ft. ▲

Royal Arch Creek

ROYAL ARCHES

Tenaya Creek

Tenaya Bridge

North Pines Campground

Merced River

Lower Pines Campground

Curry Village

Shuttle Stop #17

5

Hypsometry
8800
3400
Elevation in Feet

to reveal tranquil Mirror Lake, reflecting Mount Watkins above it. There are sandy beaches along the lakeshore for picnics and wading where the majority of visitors stop, but if you continue on upstream, you will discover one of the more isolated, tranquil corners of Yosemite Valley.

The forest floor is deeply carpeted with pine needles and bracken fern. Wild ginger, incongruously tropical looking in this setting, sprawls along the ground. Look for its weird, three-petaled, purplish green flowers hidden beneath the big, shiny, heart-shaped leaves. There are dozens of species of butterflies in patches of sunlight, and you can often hear canyon wren songs echoing off the cliffs upstream. At about 1.5 miles scan the cliff across the canyon to the east to locate a patch of lighter, lichen-free granite above a huge pile of rubble. This is the remains of the Ahwiyah Point rockfall that closed this trail from 2009 to 2012.

A junction appears at 2.1 miles marking the Snow Creek Trail, which climbs steeply up out of Tenaya Canyon to the rim of the valley. Just past the big trail sign, the path swings to the right and crosses a little bridge over a side branch of Tenaya Creek, then crosses the main branch on a bigger bridge and returns downstream along the eastern shore. The trail is mostly above the creek on this side, but you do get an interesting view of bulging Basket Dome, North Dome, and a pretty, unnamed ephemeral waterfall in springtime on the west side of Tenaya Canyon. Pick your way over the new trail that crosses the base of the rockslide, pass several approaches to the western shore of Mirror Lake, and follow the trail to where it meets the road again where it crosses the Tenaya Creek Bridge, within a hundred yards of the shuttle bus stop.

Miles and Directions

0.0   Mirror Lake Trailhead

1.0   West end of Mirror Lake

2.1   Footbridge at far end of Mirror Lake Trail

4.6   Return to Mirror Lake Trailhead

6 Yosemite Falls

You can do this one as a steep up-and-back day hike or spend the night near the top of Yosemite Falls. Although the view back down into Yosemite Valley is a good part of the way up, you don't get more than a glimpse of the falls themselves until you're on top. If you go when Yosemite Creek is full of snowmelt, the experience of standing just beside the very lip of the upper fall as it roars past you out into space is unforgettable and worth almost any amount of hard climbing.

Start: Upper Yosemite Falls Trailhead at Camp 4
Total distance: 7.6 miles out and back
Hiking time: 3 hours to all day as a day hike, or overnight as a backpack
Difficulty: Strenuous
Elevation change: 2,630 feet
Seasons: Late spring and early summer are best

Nearest facilities: Yosemite Lodge and Yosemite Village
Permits: None for a day hike, available for overnights in advance or from the wilderness center in Yosemite Village
Maps: USGS Half Dome and Yosemite Falls quads

Finding the trailhead: Take the shuttle bus from anywhere in Yosemite Valley to Yosemite Lodge (stop 7), then walk to the northwest end of the lodge buildings to Northside Drive. Cross the road to Camp 4 or in summer take the El Capitan shuttle to stop E-2, Camp 4. A sign in front points the way to the Upper Yosemite Fall Trailhead, marked by another, larger sign with information about the history of the trail and mileage to various points. Trailhead GPS: N37 44.30/W119 36.12

The Hike

Begin climbing immediately up rocky switchbacks, winding your way among house-size boulders shaded by canyon live oak, ponderosa pine, and incense cedar. Slowly, more and more of the flat valley floor comes into view through the trees. At 1.0 mile you reach an overlook protected by iron railings known as Columbia Rock, where you'll probably need a breather. The trail ascends a few soft, gravelly switchbacks, then descends for a short distance, crosses several little rivulets, rounds a corner, and suddenly reveals 1,430-foot Upper Yosemite Fall, booming like thunder early in the

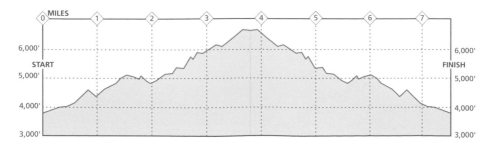

In winter, Upper Yosemite Falls' frozen spray forms a cone of ice at its base.

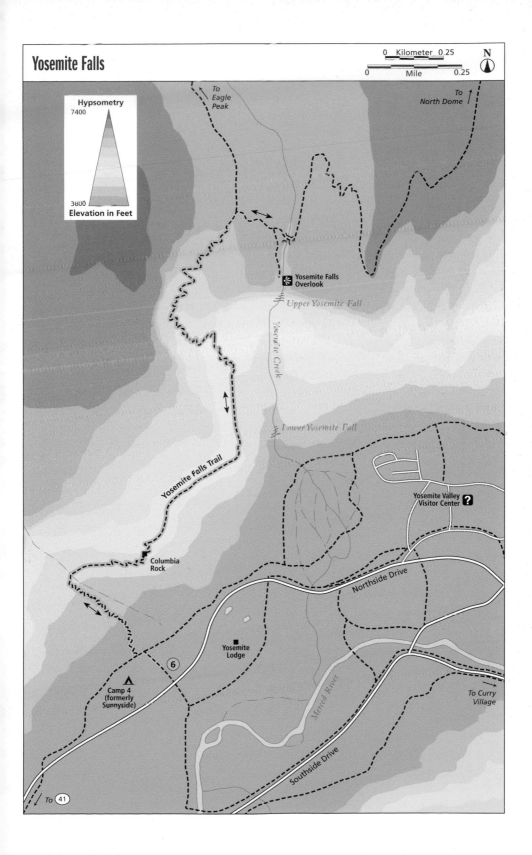

Yosemite Falls

Hypsometry
7400

3800
Elevation in Feet

0 Kilometer 0.25

0 Mile 0.25

N

To Eagle Peak

To North Dome

Yosemite Falls Overlook

Upper Yosemite Fall

Yosemite Creek

Lower Yosemite Fall

Yosemite Falls Trail

Yosemite Valley Visitor Center

Columbia Rock

Northside Drive

Yosemite Lodge

Merced River

6

Camp 4 (formerly Sunnyside)

To Curry Village

Southside Drive

To 41

summer. The refreshing mist supports little moss and fern gardens growing among the rocks. Over the roar of the falls, listen for the sweet, descending notes of the canyon wren's song. The trail now ascends very steep, rough stairsteps past the top of the lower falls and all of the middle falls (675 feet). Notice the trickles of water seeping out of the cracks between the layers of exfoliating (peeling) granite. Partway up the upper falls, the trail ducks behind a ridge, concealing the falls from view until you reach the top. Climb the sunny gully densely clothed in scrub oak, except where a huge pile of talus has spilled into the gully. Above the rock pile you can see a white scar on the cliff above where the darker, lichen-stained rock broke away in 1980 and killed three hikers. This part of the trail can be hot.

As you near the top of the gulch, firs, Jeffrey pines, and a refreshing springtime trickle make a rest at the Yosemite Creek junction at 3.6 miles welcome. Follow the right fork for a few yards, then follow signs to Yosemite Falls Overlook, through sculpted rocks and twisted Jeffrey pines, to an iron railing at 3.8 miles.

Directly across the valley, the upside-down bowl of Sentinel Dome rises alone and to the west of Glacier Point. Farther in the distance is Mount Starr King, also somewhat rounded and isolated from the surrounding ridges. Farther beyond, beautiful Mount Clark and the Clark Range define the horizon. The path now drops down a series of steep and sometimes slippery steps cut into the cliff to a platform protected by more iron railings. The thunderous roar, the drenching spray, and the dizzying drop over the falls are exhilarating, but not for the faint of heart or the acrophobic.

You can return the way you came, or if you are planning to spend the night, follow the left (west) side of the creek upstream for at least 0.25 mile to several good campsites. *Note:* Camping within 0.25 mile of the rim is prohibited.

Miles and Directions

0.0 Upper Yosemite Falls Trailhead
1.0 Columbia Rock Lookout
3.6 Yosemite Creek junction; turn right
3.8 Yosemite Falls Overlook. Turn around to retrace your steps to the trailhead.
3.9 *Option:* Bridge over Yosemite Creek adds about 0.1 mile to hike
7.6 Return to Upper Yosemite Falls Trailhead

Option: For a different perspective, return to the main trail and turn right (southeast), continuing for about 250 feet to a footbridge that spans Yosemite Creek a few yards upstream from the brink.

7 Half Dome

Half Dome is *the* symbol of Yosemite, its summit the goal of just about everybody who has ever donned a pair of hiking boots. It is a grueling workout, especially if you do it in 1 day, but if you spend the night in Little Yosemite Valley and tackle the peak first thing the second morning, you'll have a better chance of avoiding the traffic jams that sometimes build up at the base of the cables. The cables? The last 400 feet is over what feels like nearly vertical (though the angle is probably more like 45 degrees), smooth, exfoliating granite, so a series of horizontal bars about 5 feet apart, flanked by chains with which to pull yourself up, are the only way to get there without technical climbing equipment. It sounds scary but is done by kids and grandmas and everybody in between. Because of its popularity, special rules for obtaining wilderness permits to climb it are in effect and are rigorously enforced (see "Permits" below).

Start: John Muir Trailhead at Happy Isles
Total distance: 16 miles out and back
Hiking time: 1 long day or overnight
Difficulty: Strenuous as a backpack, strenuous as a day hike
Elevation change: 4,842 feet
Seasons: All summer, whenever the cables are up (they are removed when the going gets icy)
Nearest facilities: Everything you need, except gas, in Yosemite Village and Camp Curry
Permits: In 2010 the National Park Service implemented a permit program for day hiking Half Dome because the cables at the top had become so crowded that people there have fallen to their deaths. Day-use permits are now required. Three hundred per day are awarded by lottery, 225 for day hikers and 75 for backpackers. You can apply in advance for a permit between March 1 and March 31. About 50 people per day can apply for permits 2 days in advance. To apply for a permit, go to www.recreation.gov or call (877) 444-6777. For more information visit www.nps.gov/yose/planyourvisit/hdpermitsapps. Rangers are on duty and will impose a fine if you attempt to climb Half Dome without a permit. NPS has changed the page for winter. Just go to www.nps.gov/yose. You should be able to get it from there . . . and probably more directly when summer comes.
Maps: USGS Half Dome and Yosemite Falls quads
Special considerations: This hike is not for acrophobics. Get a weather report before you start. If there is even the slightest chance of a thunderstorm brewing, turn back immediately. There have been several deaths by lightning on the mountain.

Finding the trailhead: Board the Yosemite Valley shuttle bus from anyplace in the valley and get off at stop 16, Happy Isles. If you are backpacking, leave your car in the hikers' lot near Curry Village. Trailhead GPS: N37 43.51/W119 33.33

The Hike

From the big trailhead sign marking the beginning of the John Muir Trail, climb gently on an eroded asphalt path through black oak and ponderosa pine forest among enormous lichen-draped boulders. In about a half mile, across the thundering Merced River on your right, watch for 370-foot Illilouette Fall tucked back in its deeply cut gorge in the Panorama Cliff. The trail steepens briefly, then suddenly descends to the Vernal Fall Bridge at 0.8 mile. Upstream, Vernal Fall is perfectly framed by maple, alder, and various conifers as it drops 317 feet over the lower step of the Giant Staircase. There are restrooms, drinking water, and lots of people here.

Cross the bridge to the south side of the river and turn left, upstream. Just beyond, at mile 0.9, meet the Mist Trail, an alternate route to the top of Nevada Fall, not recommended for backpackers since it is steep, slippery, and wet, but a shorter route to the top. If you are backpacking, stay on the John Muir Trail to the right, passing a lateral trail for horses only that leads back to the stables. Continue climbing on the John Muir Trail as it switchbacks relentlessly uphill. There are plenty of excuses to stop and rest on the way. Across the valley to the northwest you can see Upper Yosemite Fall and to the northeast, across the river gorge, the rounded back side of Half Dome. Shortly beyond, 594-foot Nevada Fall comes into view. This heart-stopping panorama is finest at Clark Point (2.3 miles), where a lateral trail cuts over to the Mist Trail, nearer to the river.

▶ **In earlier days it was possible to camp on the summit of Half Dome, but camping is now prohibited to protect the rare Mount Lyell salamanders that shelter under the rocks on top. This is probably just as well, because there are no sanitary facilities on the summit and you can't dig holes in solid granite.**

Continue to ascend the John Muir Trail on well-graded switchbacks, eventually passing beneath a dripping rock overhang decorated with delicate hanging gardens of ferns, columbines, monkey flowers, and other water-loving species.

At 3.3 miles the Panorama Trail, leading back to Glacier Point, joins this one from the right (south). The trail drops a bit, hops a couple of little creeks, then emerges into a wide sunny expanse of granite at the top of Nevada Fall.

Here, at 3.5 miles, a footbridge crosses the river. Cross the bridge and follow the north shore of the river to a junction with the upper end of the Mist Trail at 3.8 miles. Continue upstream, climbing the well-defined trail over inlaid rocks. The way soon levels out and passes from sunlight into shade, and the Merced changes from a rushing, raging torrent to become quiet, dark, and deep.

At 4.3 miles you reach a turnoff to the Half Dome Trail, but ignore it and keep right, going on to Little Yosemite Valley. If you are backpacking, you'll be going there anyway, and the earlier turnoff is steeper, if shorter, and does not save much time.

Little Yosemite Valley, at 4.8 miles, is a busy place, especially for bears. There are bear-proof boxes in the campground, but you should be carrying a canister anyway. There is also an architecturally elegant two-story solar composting toilet. The

Half Dome has cables to help negotiate the last 400 feet to the summit. ▶

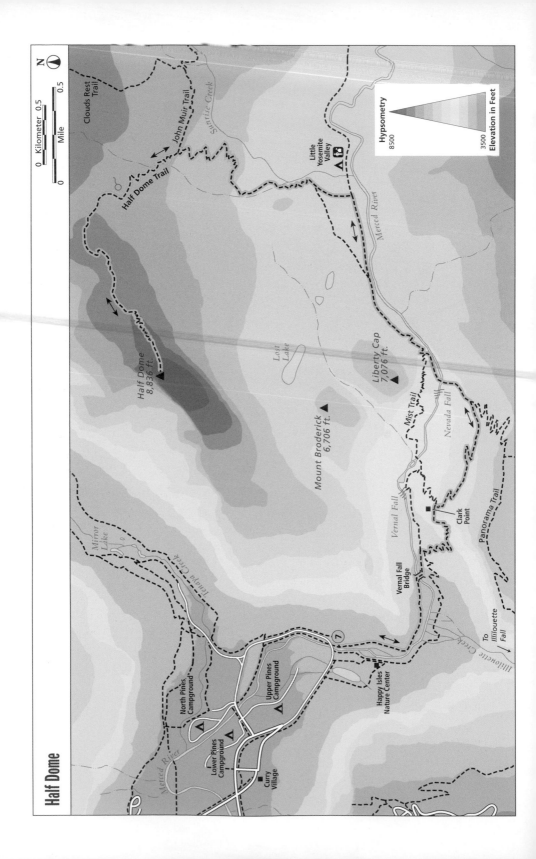

Half Dome

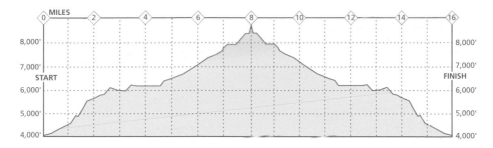

National Park Service has constructed two communal fire rings for campers to share. Please do not scar this already overused area by building another one.

Head north out of Little Yosemite Valley, passing a junction with the shortcut trail and climbing steeply, first along Sunrise Creek, continuing generally northward, and upward to the Half Dome Trail junction at 6.0 miles. Leave the main trail here. About a half mile farther along the wide and dusty path, keep an eye out for a patch of water-loving green plants and a big fallen log on the left, behind which is a little spring. The trail swings west to reveal a view of Half Dome to the left and Clouds Rest to the right. Across the way is Mount Watkins, with Basket Dome and North Dome to the west. The trail swings a little farther south now and faces the huge, sparsely timbered shoulder of Half Dome. A sign warns hikers not to proceed if bad weather threatens. Believe it! Now you switchback steeply on sometimes slippery gravel up and over the crest of a shoulder to at last come face to face with the famous—or infamous—cables. Grab a pair of gloves from the pile there if you haven't brought your own, and haul yourself up the last 400 feet to the summit at 8.0 miles.

The top of Half Dome flattens out considerably and is furnished with flat, irregularly weathered granite slabs. When you have recovered from your climb, wander around to take in the 360-degree panorama. Below, Yosemite Valley is spread out like a map, with El Capitan at its west end. Mount Watkins and Clouds Rest flank smooth, bare Tenaya Canyon. Farther east, Merced Canyon points toward the Cathedral Range, and the colorful Clark Range is visible to the southeast. If you are day hiking, you'll have to tear yourself away after only a short visit to make it back to the valley before dark. You can vary your trip back by taking the Mist Trail down to Happy Isles, but if there is a chance of darkness falling before you get back, stick to the John Muir Trail.

Miles and Directions

0.0 Happy Isles Trailhead
0.8 Vernal Fall Bridge
0.9 Mist Trail junction
2.3 Clark Point
3.3 Panorama Trail junction

3.5 Top of Nevada Fall

3.8 Upper end of Mist Trail

4.3 First Half Dome turnoff

4.8 Little Yosemite Valley

6.0 Half Dome Trail

8.0 Summit

16.0 Return to Happy Isles Trailhead

The South Rim of Yosemite Valley

All of the south rim trails begin along the Glacier Point Road, which cuts off from Wawona Road (CA 41) at Chinquapin, a junction about 14 miles from Yosemite Valley at 6,000 feet. The drive itself is beautiful, beginning among ponderosa and sugar pines, climbing through a red fir forest at almost 8,000 feet, then dropping to 7,200 feet at Glacier Point, 16 miles away. Glacier Point is an extremely popular overlook 3,000 feet above the valley floor; it offers the best views of Half Dome, the valley, and indeed, most of the park of anyplace accessible by road. Almost all of the hikes beginning from this road have spectacular views of the valley, too. There is a snack bar, gift shop, phones, and toilets, along with an amphitheater for ranger talks and nighttime astronomy programs, and an area from which hang gliders are launched before 8 a.m.

It was also the site of the infamous firefall. See the sidebar in hike 3 Glacier Point via the Four Mile Trail.

The only accommodations anywhere on Glacier Point Road are at first-come, first-served Bridalveil Creek Campground. There is no place to stay overnight near the trailhead if you arrive late on the day before your hike, and you must get your wilderness permit for a backpack outing down in Yosemite Valley or at Wawona.

The road is open all the way to Glacier Point spring through fall, but in winter it's plowed only as far as the ski area at Badger Pass. There are plenty of bears around. Do not leave ice chests or food in your car. All trailheads have bear-proof boxes for food storage.

A hiker's shuttle bus runs several times daily from the valley during the summer. You can get a schedule and fares at the visitor center or call (209) 372-1240 or (209) 372-4386. Reservations are necessary.

8 Taft Point and The Fissures

Taft Point is the westernmost of several overlooks into Yosemite Valley from the south rim accessible by only a short hike. Don't miss it, even if you have already been to Glacier Point. In place of rounded domes and polished rocks, this section of the valley wall displays jagged, broken granite crags and soaring spires, as well as a new perspective of Yosemite Falls. On the way you can peek down into the fabulous Fissures, cracks in the cliff that are only inches wide, but thousands of feet deep, through which you can see all the way to the valley floor. One glimpse is as good as a thrill ride.

Start: Taft Point/Sentinel Dome Trailhead
Total distance: 2.2 miles out and back
Hiking time: 2 to 4 hours
Difficulty: Easy
Elevation change: 250 feet
Seasons: Spring, summer, or fall, whenever Glacier Point Road is open
Nearest facilities: Snacks, toilets, phones, and water at Glacier Point

Permits: None
Map: USGS Half Dome quad
Special considerations: The Fissures have not been defaced by protective railings and warning signs; you won't see them until you are very close, so this hike is not recommended for unrestrained small children. It's an upside-down hike, downhill to get there, uphill to get back. Allow extra time for the return trip.

Finding the trailhead: Drive 13 miles up Glacier Point Road from Chinquapin. Parking and the marked trailhead are on the left. (Glacier Point shuttle bus does not stop here.) Trailhead GPS: N37 42.46/W119 35.12

The Hike

The trail begins in a sandy opening in mixed pine and fir forest. Turn left at the trailhead sign. (The right fork goes to Sentinel Dome.) Pass through a flat, fairly open stretch past a big outcrop of almost pure-white quartz on the right, then swing south and start downhill where the forest closes in. At 0.4 mile the Pohono Trail joins yours from the right. Continue straight ahead, now on the Pohono Trail, ignoring the inaccurate trail sign that says you have only come 0.2 mile. The forest deepens and a little creek you will soon hop across nourishes a colorful garden of water-loving cow parsnip, senecio, corn lily, knotweed, and shooting stars. All at once the trail emerges from the shady forest onto open rock and steepens. The flower-filled gully on your right abruptly narrows, deepens, and drops through a notch that sends the little creek plummeting toward the valley floor.

Descend carefully down the rocks past low patches of manzanita and the occasional Jeffrey pine. Stay alert here. At 0.9 mile you will reach the first of several fissures, not visible until you are standing on their rims. They are narrow, deep cracks

Glimpse the Yosemite Valley floor several thousand feet below through one of The Fissures. ▶

Taft Point and The Fissures

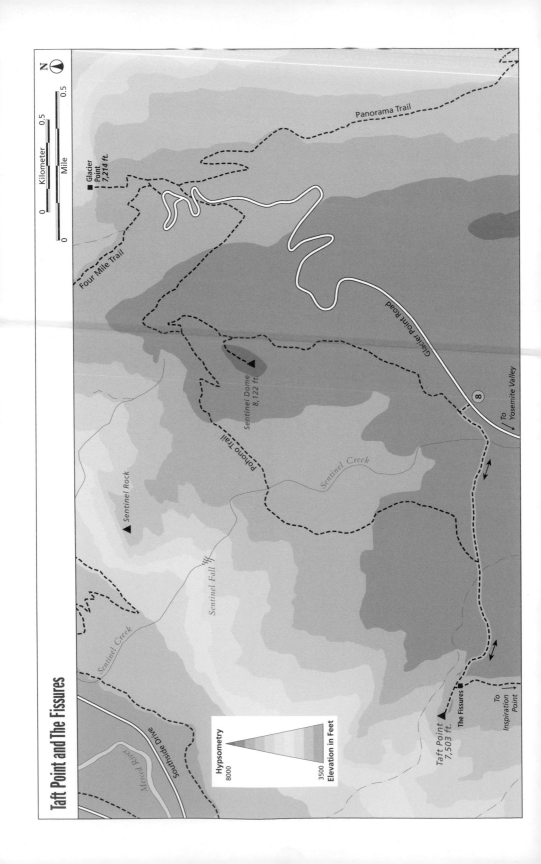

N

Hypsometry

8000

3500

Elevation in Feet

0   Kilometer   0.5

0   Mile   0.5

Glacier Point 7,214 ft.

Panorama Trail

Four Mile Trail

Glacier Point Road

8

To Yosemite Valley

Sentinel Dome 8,122 ft.

Pohono Trail

Sentinel Rock

Sentinel Creek

Sentinel Creek

Sentinel Fall

Sentinel Creek

Merced River

Southside Drive

Taft Point 7,503 ft.

The Fissures

To Inspiration Point

in the granite, perhaps 30 to 40 feet long, extending inward from the edge of the cliff. Peering over the side, you can see that they slice completely through the rock, revealing a stomach-lurching glimpse of the floor of Yosemite Valley several thousand feet below.

Once your internal butterflies have settled, proceed toward a slightly rising point of the cliff that leans out over the valley like the prow of a ship with a protective iron railing around it. This is Taft Point (1.1 miles). A look over the edge is guaranteed to reawaken the butterflies. Directly across from the point are the Three Brothers, the highest of which is Eagle Peak. To the left (west) is the massive face of El Capitan; to the right (east) is Yosemite Falls. Wander westward along the rim to see the dramatic knife edges and needlelike spikes of Cathedral Spires.

When you are ready to return, descend the slight hill to a trail junction. The left fork returns to the trailhead and parking, and the right one heads westward along the Pohono Trail toward Inspiration Point.

Miles and Directions

- **0.0** Taft Point/Sentinel Dome Trailhead
- **0.4** Pohono Trail junction
- **0.9** The Fissures
- **1.1** Taft Point
- **2.2** Return to Taft Point/Sentinel Dome Trailhead

9 Sentinel Dome

Here's your chance to climb one of Yosemite's famous domes with minimal expenditure of time and effort. The view from the summit is everything you would expect—a 360-degree sweep of almost the entire park.

Start: Taft Point/Sentinel Dome Trailhead
Total distance: 2.2 miles out and back
Hiking time: 2 to 4 hours
Difficulty: Moderate
Elevation change: 400 feet
Seasons: Spring, summer, or fall, whenever Glacier Point Road is open

Nearest facilities: Snacks, toilets, phones, and water at Glacier Point
Permits: None
Map: USGS Half Dome quad
Special considerations: The dome is steep and slippery, so wear good sturdy shoes for this one; smooth-soled sandals invite accidents.

Finding the trailhead: Drive 13 miles up Glacier Point Road from Chinquapin. Parking and the marked trailhead are on the left. Trailhead GPS: N37 42.46/W119 35.12

The Hike

The trail begins at a sign in a sandy opening in the forest that directs you to the right (northeast). (The other fork goes to Taft Point and The Fissures.) Follow the rough and rocky path as it crosses a brook, then undulates gradually upward, slowly revealing the top of the dome. Soon it curves to the left (north) and proceeds more steeply over smooth and featureless rock. Stenciled metal signs keep you on course.

California ground squirrels beg for human food, which is detrimental to them, at popular destinations like Sentinel Dome.

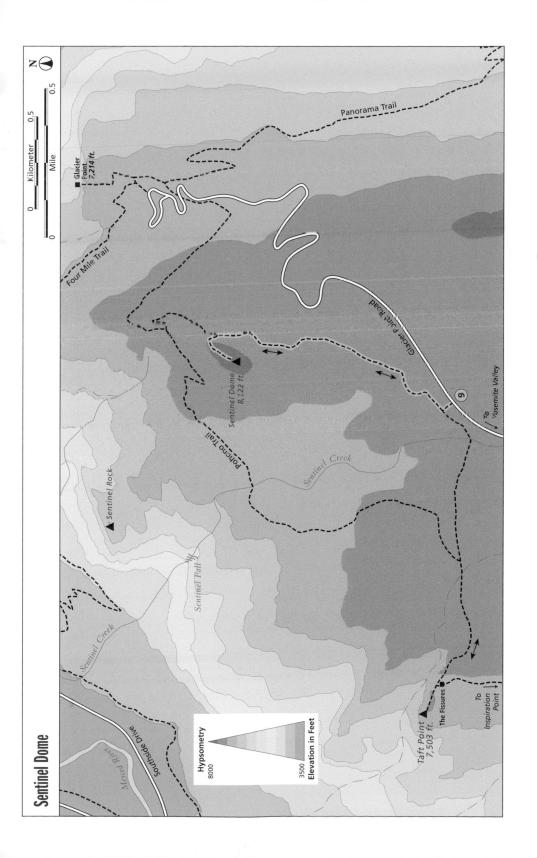

Sentinel Dome

Hypsometry

Elevation in Feet
8000
3500

N

Kilometer
0   0.5

Mile
0   0.5

Four Mile Trail

Glacier
Point
7,214 ft.

Panorama Trail

Glacier Point Road

To
Yosemite Valley

9

Sentinel Dome
8,122 ft.

Pohono Trail

Sentinel Creek

Sentinel Rock

Sentinel Fall

Sentinel Creek

Southside Drive

Merced River

Taft Point
7,503 ft.

The Fissures

To
Inspiration
Point

At 0.4 mile an old, partly paved service road joins the trail from the right. Continue around the base of the dome on your left. When you have reached the "back," or more gradually sloping, side of the dome at 0.6 mile, a trail splits off to the right and heads down to Glacier Point.

Turn left just past this point and head up the steep, open slope on an indistinct trail of sorts. Don't worry if you lose the path; the only way to go is up. At the summit are the remains of the gnarled Jeffrey pine that was once the subject of innumerable photographs and postcards. The tree died in 1977, but remained standing and still beautiful until it toppled in 2003.

When you have caught your breath, make a slow circle around the summit. To the east, Yosemite Valley flanked by the Cathedral Rocks on the left and El Capitan on the right stretches toward the coast. If the Great Central Valley is free of smog (a rare occurrence), you can see all the way to the Coast Ranges. Moving clockwise, the entire length of Yosemite Falls comes into view, and in early summer you can hear its roar from here. Farther east is smoothly rounded Basket Dome and North Dome and, beyond them, Tenaya Canyon with the sheer face of Half Dome glowering over it. Clouds Rest is just beyond Half Dome, and far behind it lies the Cathedral Range. Farther east the Merced River Canyon and Nevada Fall appear, then come Mount Clark and the colorful Clark Range, providing a backdrop for the rounded tops of Mount Starr King. The lower, forested country to the south closes the circle.

When you are ready, descend very slowly and carefully, avoiding loose sand and gravel whenever possible, and return the way you came. Take care to follow the metal signs directing you to the parking lot.

Miles and Directions

0.0 Taft Point/Sentinel Dome Trailhead

0.4 Service road

0.6 Glacier Point Trail junction

1.1 Top of Sentinel Dome

2.2 Return to Taft Point/Sentinel Dome Trailhead

10 McGurk Meadow

A short out-and-back day hike to one of Yosemite's "bloomingest" wildflower meadows.

Start: McGurk Meadow Trailhead on Glacier Point Road
Total distance: 1.6 miles out and back
Hiking time: 1 to 2 hours
Difficulty: Easy
Elevation change: 150 feet

Seasons: All summer, whenever Glacier Point Road is open, but flowers are best in July
Nearest facilities: Food, water, and phones at Glacier Point
Permits: None
Maps: USGS El Capitan and Half Dome quads

Finding the trailhead: Drive about 8.5 miles up Glacier Point Road from Chinquapin. The trailhead is on the left just before you reach the entrance to Bridalveil Creek Campground. It's easy to miss. The campground is on the right (south) side of the road. The easiest way to find the trailhead is to drive to the campground entrance, turn around, and head back the way you came. Park in the first turnout on the right. The trailhead sign is about 100 feet beyond. Trailhead GPS: N37 40.13/W119 37.41

The Hike

The path descends through a quiet lodgepole pine forest where the wildflower show gets under way at once as currants, strawberries, lupines, and larkspur flourish alongside the trail. Just before you emerge from the forest to enter the meadow, watch for an old log cabin on the left. It was built by a Mr. McGurk in the late nineteenth century, but he had to abandon it when it was determined that he did not, in fact, own the land thereabouts.

The meadow is threaded by a little brook and spangled with wildflowers of every kind and color: shooting stars, lungwort, corn lilies, monkey flowers, paintbrush, and dozens of others. This is actually a long, narrow finger that extends eastward from the main part of McGurk Meadow. The larger section of meadow is much too soggy for comfortable hiking, but the path that skirts this section runs along the edge of the forest so that you can enjoy the flowers without getting your feet wet. Such a meeting of forest and meadow as this is the best sort of environment for wildlife watching, especially during morning and evening hours. When meadow once again gives way to forest, retrace your steps to the trailhead. If you want a little more exercise, you can continue your stroll northward downhill for about another half mile to meet the Pohono Trail. Just remember that you'll eventually have to climb back up again.

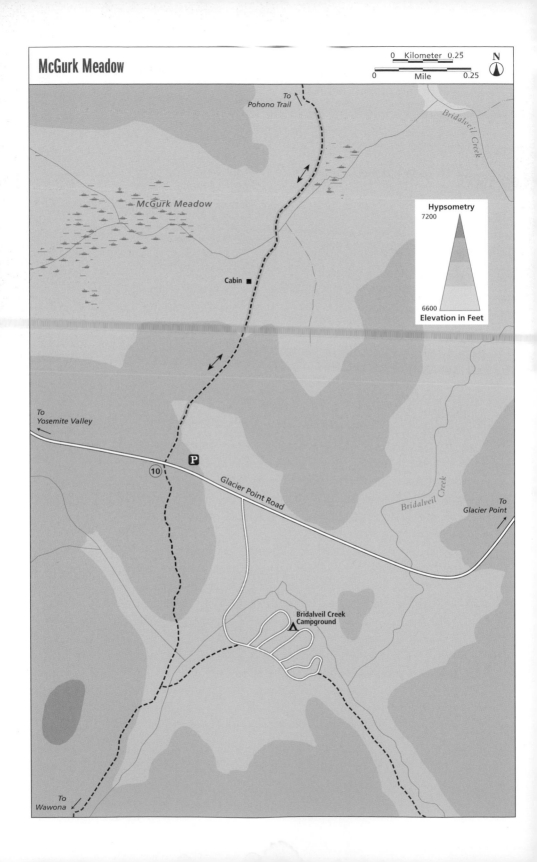

Mr. McGurk's cabin sits on the edge of McGurk Meadow.

Miles and Directions

0.0 McGurk Meadow Trailhead on Glacier Point Road

0.5 Cabin

0.8 Turnaround (*Option:* Continue downhill to the Pohono Trail)

1.6 Return to trailhead

11 The Pohono Trail

The Pohono Trail skirts the entire south rim of Yosemite Valley from Glacier Point to Tunnel View. The rolling, up-and-down route takes you to a series of overlooks—Taft Point, Dewey Point, Crocker Point, Stanford Point, and Old Inspiration Point—that will change the way you perceive familiar landmarks even after you have returned to the valley floor. The view of Bridalveil Fall from above is worth the (nonexistent) price of admission all by itself. Strong hikers could do this one as a day hike, but if you hurry, you're likely to miss the good stuff. It's an easy overnight backpack with camping at Bridalveil Creek, the only really practical spot with reliable water.

Start: Panorama/Pohono Trailhead at Glacier Point

Total distance: 13.8-mile one-way shuttle

Hiking time: Dawn to dinnertime as a day hike (7 to 8 hours), 2 shorter days as a backpack

Difficulty: Strenuous as a day hike, moderate as a backpack

Elevation change: 2,800 feet

Seasons: All summer, though creeks are dry by mid-Aug

Nearest facilities: Everything you need (except gas) in Yosemite Valley; snacks, toilets, and phones at Glacier Point; phones and toilets at Tunnel View

Permits: None required for a day hike; available for overnights in advance or in Yosemite Valley or at Wawona

Maps: USGS El Capitan and Half Dome quads

Special considerations: This is a shuttle hike. You'll need to leave one car at Tunnel View and drive or get a ride to the trailhead at Glacier Point, or you can take the hiker's shuttle bus from the Valley (call 209-372-1240 for reservations).

Finding the trailhead: Follow Glacier Point Road to its end 16 miles from Wawona Road at Chinquapin, or take the shuttle to Glacier Point. If you are driving, park in the upper level of the Glacier Point parking lot, then walk directly toward Half Dome to a spot overlooking an outdoor amphitheater and look to the right to find the trailhead sign. Bear-proof boxes are tucked into the far corner of the upper lot. Trailhead GPS: N37 43.67 / W119 34.40

The Hike

Take a minute to recover from the overwhelming immensity of the panorama at Glacier Point before setting off. To the left is North Dome, capping the graceful Royal Arches; in the center is Half Dome, the monumental symbol of Yosemite. Tenaya Canyon stretches away to the northeast, and to the west runs the Merced River Canyon, down whose Giant Staircase flow Nevada and Vernal Falls.

From the trailhead turn right (east) to find the Panorama and Pohono Trail junction at 0.1 mile. Keep right and at 0.2 mile cross Glacier Point Road, then ascend a few switchbacks beneath white and red firs to 0.4 mile, where a dirt road leads to

Get a different view—from above—of Bridalveil Fall from the Pohono Trail. ▶

a ranger residence on the left. Continue right on the trail that parallels the road for a short time. At 1.0 mile meet the junction with the Sentinel Dome Trail where a half-mile detour (one-way) takes you to the top.

To continue on the Pohono Trail, go straight (southwest) along the valley rim. Watch for Yosemite Falls across the valley as the route climbs, levels, then descends on switchbacks. You can catch occasional glimpses of Sentinel Dome pushing up out of the forest uphill on your left. Cross Sentinel Creek, often dry later in the year, and wind through the forest over gently rolling terrain until you reach a junction at 2.0 miles with a spur trail that goes back to Glacier Point Road. The forest deepens and a little creek you will soon hop across nourishes a colorful garden of water-loving cow parsnip, senecio, corn lily, knotweed, and shooting stars.

All at once the trail emerges from the shady forest onto open rock, and steepens. The flower-filled gully on your right abruptly narrows, deepens, and drops through a notch that sends the little creek plummeting toward the valley floor. Descend carefully down the open rock past low patches of manzanita and the occasional Jeffrey pine. As soon as the path begins to level a bit, watch for The Fissures, cracks in the cliff that are only inches wide but thousands of feet deep. There is a sign, but by the time you reach it, you will already have skirted several of them. They are not visible until you are standing on their rims. Shortly beyond, a short spur trail on your right takes you a few yards uphill to Taft Point, surrounded by an iron railing. This, the first in the series of marvelous valley overlooks, directly faces Eagle Peak and the Three Brothers.

Return to the Pohono Trail and continue west, first over open rock, then into forest, dipping down to meet Bridalveil Creek at mile 4.7. Just across the footbridge are a few small campsites, the best choice for camping on this route. A short distance beyond, at 5.0 miles, go straight ahead at a junction with a trail heading south to meet Glacier Point Road via McGurk Meadow. Another 2 or 3 minutes' walk takes you past a second McGurk Meadow cutoff.

The trail rises and falls through the forest, crossing a few more creeklets that dry out by midsummer, then ascends to Dewey Point at 8.7 miles. You can scramble out to the very top to a granite aerie from which, laid out before you, is a panorama of almost the whole of Yosemite Park. To the west you can see the Wawona Tunnel parking lot, your end point, and beyond it, Cascade Creek Falls. Directly across the valley Ribbon Fall drifts down in early springtime, and just beyond that, El Capitan. You can hear climbers' shouts from here if the wind is blowing in the right direction.

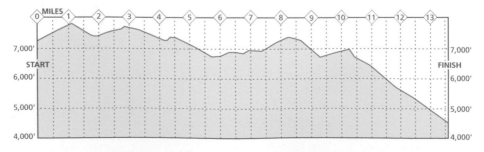

The Pohono Trail

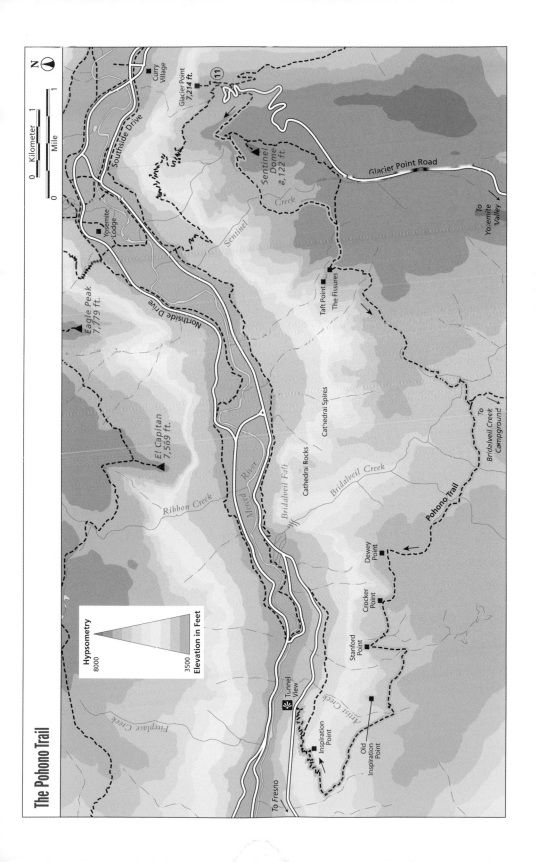

N

0   1   Kilometer
0   1   Mile

Hypsometry
8000
3500
Elevation in Feet

Curry Village

Glacier Point
7,214 ft.

11

Southside Drive

Yosemite
Lodge

Sentinel Dome
8,122 ft.

Sentinel   Creek

Glacier Point Road

To
Yosemite
Valley

Eagle Peak
7,779 ft.

Northside Drive

Taft Point

The Fissures

El Capitan
7,569 ft.

Cathedral Spires

To
Bridalveil Creek
Campground

Ribbon Creek

Merced River

Bridalveil Fall

Cathedral Rocks

Bridalveil Creek

Pohono Trail

Dewey Point

Fireplace Creek

Crocker Point

Stanford Point

Tunnel View

Artist Creek

Inspiration Point

Old
Inspiration Point

To Fresno

Mount Hoffman is on the horizon to the east, marking the geographic center of Yosemite. If the day is clear, you can see Mount Conness on the northern park boundary. Tenaya Canyon, heading straight for the Cathedral Range, cuts the sheer granite at the base of Clouds Rest and Half Dome, partly hidden behind Sentinel Dome.

Return to the trail, which now alternates between forest and open spots with chinquapin, pinemat manzanita, ceanothus, and huckleberry oak—spiny shrubs unfriendly to hikers in shorts. The trail dips to pass Crocker Point at 9.3 miles. Be sure to detour the short distance out to the point, for from here you can look down upon Bridalveil Fall shooting over the cliff between the Leaning Tower and Cathedral Rocks.

The trail dips again and hops an ephemeral creek lined with willow, currant, monkey flower, and wild geranium. It reaches Stanford Point at 10.0 miles, then veers away from the valley rim and climbs a rise through a garden of lupines to reach willow-choked Meadow Brook. This little creek drops over the cliff as delicate Silver Strand Fall, seldom seen past late June. The trail rises, then drops, more steeply now, to Artist Creek, dry in summer, then continues on a knee-pounding descent through shady forest to Old Inspiration Point at 12.7 miles. You can see the remains of the asphalt road that led to this original Inspiration Point years ago. Descend rocky switchbacks to 13.2 miles, where a trail cuts off to the right (east) toward Bridalveil Fall. Continue straight ahead down the rough path to the Wawona Road and the parking lot at Tunnel View.

Miles and Directions

0.0 Panorama/Pohono Trailhead at Glacier Point

0.1 Panorama/Pohono Trail junction; turn right

0.2 Cross Glacier Point Road

0.4 Cross dirt road leading to ranger residence

1.0 Sentinel Dome Trail

2.0 Taft Point Trail

4.7 Bridalveil Creek crossing

5.0 McGurk Meadow/Bridalveil Creek Trail cuts left; continue straight ahead

5.1 Second McGurk Meadow/Bridalveil Creek trail also cuts left; continue straight ahead

8.7 Dewey Point spur

9.3 Crocker Point spur

10.0 Stanford Point spur

12.7 Road to Old Inspiration Point

13.2 Bridalveil Fall turnoff; keep left

13.8 Tunnel View parking lot

12 The Panorama Trail–Glacier Point to Nevada Fall

The name of the trail says it all. It follows the southeastern portion of the valley rim above Happy Isles, crossing Illilouette Creek at the top of Illilouette Fall to the (usually) sunny flat where Nevada Fall launches itself over the cliff into Yosemite Valley. The Giant Staircase is in sight much of the way, as well as occasional glimpses of Yosemite Falls back to the west. You get five famous waterfalls in one hike.

Start: Panorama/Pohono Trailhead at Glacier Point

Total distance: 10.4 miles out and back

Hiking time: 6 to 8 hours

Difficulty: Moderate

Elevation change: 1,500 feet

Seasons: All summer, whenever Glacier Point Road is open, but it's best early in summer when all the falls are flowing

Nearest facilities: Glacier Point has toilets, phones, water, and snacks

Permits: None

Map: USGS Half Dome quad

Finding the trailhead: Follow Glacier Point Road to its end 16 miles from Wawona Road at Chinquapin, or take the Glacier Point shuttle from Yosemite Valley (call 209-372-1240 for reservations). If you are driving, park in the parking lot, then walk directly toward Half Dome to a spot overlooking an outdoor amphitheater and look to the right to find the trailhead sign. There are bear-proof boxes in the far corner of the upper parking lot. Trailhead GPS: N37 43.67/W119 34.40

The Hike

Take a minute to recover from the overwhelming immensity of the panorama from Glacier Point before setting off. To the left is North Dome, capping the graceful Royal Arches; in the center is Half Dome, the monumental symbol of Yosemite. Tenaya Canyon stretches away to the northeast, and to the west runs the Merced River Canyon, down whose Giant Staircase flow Vernal and Nevada Falls.

From the trailhead sign turn right (east) to find the Panorama and Pohono Trail junction at 0.1 mile. The Panorama Trail heads left (south) toward Illilouette Fall. The first mile of trail switchbacks downward through an area burned in 1987. Fragrant ceanothus and

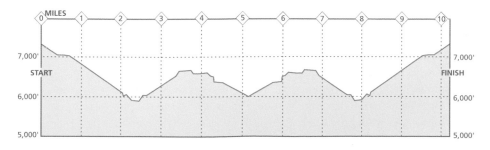

Vernal and Nevada Falls flow down the Giant Staircase through the Merced River Canyon.

chinquapin with its spiny green fruits line the path. This is a good place to listen for the booming call of the blue grouse in spring and early summer.

At 1.2 miles a trail coming from Mono Meadow joins this one from the south. Keep left (northeast) and continue to descend into Illilouette Gorge. Shrubs give way to forest, and the rush of Illilouette Creek becomes audible. Other hikers have worn a little turnout to the left of the trail to get a look at the fall, which is just out of sight from the trail itself. This is the only way to see Illilouette Fall from almost any direction because it is tucked so tightly back into the notch. Just before the trail reaches the bridge over Illilouette Creek, you might spot what appears to be an idyllic campsite on the right, but camping is not permitted here. It's too near the water, too near the trail, and too near the road. It's a nice spot for a rest and a snack, though. Cross the footbridge over the creek at 2.1 miles. The fall is not visible from the footbridge, but the creek cascades down in picturesque wedding cake fashion, and in springtime the blooms of western azaleas lining the banks perfume the air.

Climb steadily from the bridge for about 0.8 mile to an unmarked path heading off to the left to Panorama Point. There is no sign, and you visit at your own risk since the point is no more than a shelf of rock extending out over several thousand feet of thin air. The path to the point winds narrowly through head-high manzanita for 50 yards before opening out to a grand vista that includes the notorious rockslide of 1996 that damaged much of Happy Isles. Yosemite Valley winds off to the left, and Yosemite Falls are just visible on the far side.

The Panorama Trail continues up and around a shoulder to reveal spectacular 584-foot Nevada Fall, and shortly after that reaches a junction at 4.0 miles. Here a trail heads right (south) through a burned area, eventually to rejoin Illilouette Creek several miles upstream from Illilouette Fall. The Panorama Trail stays left and switchbacks down fairly steeply past several little rills and mossy rock gardens to meet the John Muir Trail coming up from Yosemite Valley at 5.0 miles. Follow the signs to the right to the top of Nevada Fall at 5.2 miles.

The Panorama Trail—Glacier Point to Nevada Fall

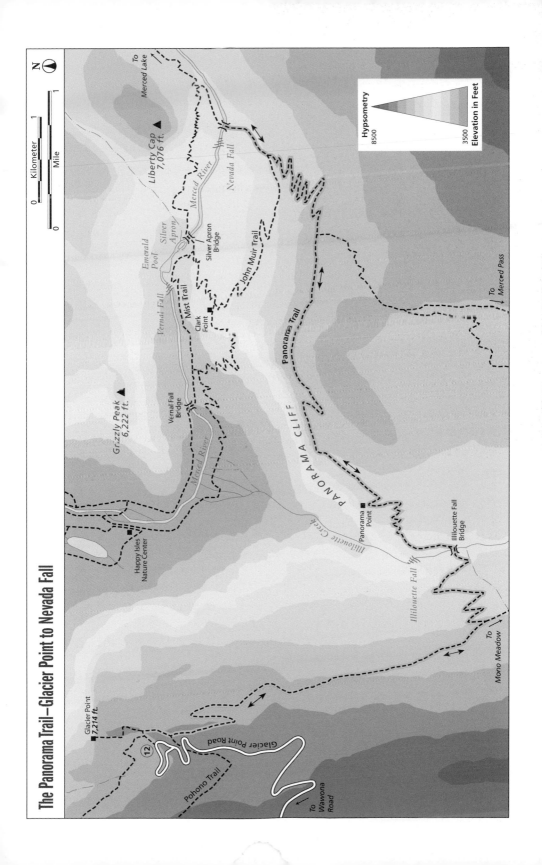

THE BLUE GROUSE

Male blue grouse find a territory to their liking and then sit on a limb and hoot, hour after hour, day after day, sometimes for weeks at a stretch, hoping to encourage a mate and discourage competitors. Their call is like the sound made by blowing over the mouth of a bottle. Later in summer watch for processions of little striped balls of fluff following their mothers (adults are about the size of small chickens) pecking in the duff or crossing the trail. They are visible only when they are moving, blending with the underbrush when they freeze. If you come too close, they explode around you in a flurry of frantic flapping but will wait until the last moment before breaking cover.

Join the crowd there picnicking, sunbathing, and watching the Merced River shoot over the lip of the sheer cliff. Be sure to stay behind the protective rails and away from the slippery edges. The river has claimed several lives here. You can continue on down the John Muir Trail to Yosemite Valley at Happy Isles from here (if you have a ride back up to Glacier Point), or you can return the way you came.

Miles and Directions

0.0 Glacier Point Trailhead

0.1 Panorama/Pohono Trail junction; turn left

1.2 Mono Meadow Trail junction; keep left

2.1 Illilouette Fall Bridge

4.0 Illilouette Creek Trail junction; keep left

5.0 John Muir Trail junction; turn right

5.2 Top of Nevada Fall

10.4 Return to Glacier Point Trailhead

The North Rim of Yosemite Valley

Hikes on this side of the valley start later in the year than those on the south because the snow lasts longer in the shady hollows and valleys, and many of the streams are too fast, too wide, and too deep to cross safely until well into July. Because of the deep gorges cut by these streams, along with differences in the nature of the rock that makes up the cliffs, north rim trails cannot skirt the valley rim as closely as the south rim trails do. There are many breathtaking views from the tops of landmarks like El Capitan and North Dome, but the trails sometimes retreat through forest back toward Tioga Road for several miles between one scenic point and the next. Furthermore, many of the south rim overlooks can be reached in a relatively short day hike, while most of the north rim trails are very strenuous as day hikes and may be more enjoyable as overnighters. For these reasons the north rim is not as heavily used as the south, providing more opportunities for solitude (and for obtaining wilderness permits). The nearest source for permits for these hikes is the Big Oak Flat Entrance Station; they are also available at Tuolumne Meadows and Yosemite Valley.

All of the hikes in this section are reached from CA 120, known as the Big Oak Flat Road west of Crane Flat, and Tioga Road to the east. There are several first-come, first-served campgrounds off the road: Porcupine Flat, Tamarack Flat, Yosemite Creek, and White Wolf. The Hodgdon Meadow Campground at the Big Oak Flat entrance and the Crane Flat Campground require reservations. White Wolf has a High Sierra Camp as well, for which reservations many months in advance are needed.

The nearest (minimal) source of supplies is the gas station at Crane Flat. Both Tuolumne Meadows and Yosemite Valley have more, but the valley is almost an hour away, and Tuolumne Meadows is even farther. There is no gas in Yosemite Valley.

13 Tioga Road to the Top of Yosemite Falls and Eagle Peak

This is an easier but much longer way to reach the top of Yosemite Falls than climbing straight up from the valley floor. The mostly forested up-and-down trail follows along Yosemite Creek, hopping or wading several of its tributaries to where the creek, compressed between narrow walls, gathers speed and force and shoots out over the north rim in a series of steps totaling 2,425 feet into the valley. You can stand very close to the edge where the falls begin and, if the water is high, get soaked and half stunned by the spray and the roar. There is camping nearby.

Start: Yosemite Creek Trailhead on Tioga Road
Total distance: 16.0 miles out and back from Tioga Road (13.0 if you start from Yosemite Creek Campground)
Hiking time: 8 to 14 hours
Difficulty: Moderate
Elevation change: 1,000 feet
Seasons: Summer and fall; best after June when the snow is gone and before August when the falls dry up
Nearest facilities: Crane Flat

Permits: None for a day hike; required for overnights, in advance or from the wilderness center in Yosemite Valley or Tuolumne Meadows
Map: USGS Yosemite Falls quad
Special considerations: You can save 3 miles and some elevation gain and loss as well as one potentially difficult stream crossing by parking in the Yosemite Creek Campground and beginning your hike from there. The road to the campground cuts off to the south from Tioga Road several miles to the east of the parking area. But parking spots are limited.

Finding the trailhead: On Tioga Road (CA 120), drive about 20 miles east of Crane Flat or 26 miles west of Tuolumne Meadows. There is parking on both sides of the highway. The Ten Lakes Trail departs from the north side, the Yosemite Creek Trail from the south. The trail begins at the west end of the parking area. Trailhead GPS: N37 51.07 / W119 34.40

The Hike

From the trailhead sign descend through lodgepole pines to cross Yosemite Creek, which can be difficult in early season when the water is high. Then descend more gradually until you reach the Yosemite Creek Campground at 1.5 miles. Follow the paved road all the way through the campground, over the bridge across Yosemite Creek, and past the campground entrance. Just after crossing another smaller branch of the creek, turn left at a sign marked "Trail Junction" and leave the road and the campground at 2.2 miles.

The trail wanders through fairly flat forest, then climbs over a rocky shoulder marked with ducks where the route is obscure. Some handsome junipers grow from cracks in the rock. Shortly after dropping from this shoulder, a trail cuts back to the

From Yosemite Falls Overlook you get a dizzying view of Yosemite Village.

right (northwest) at 3.7 miles, heading toward Lukens Lake and White Wolf. Continue straight ahead (south) and cross a tributary of Yosemite Creek. There are a few campsites here.

Gradually the smooth rounded granite walls force the trail and the creek into a narrow defile, and the lovely aquamarine water races over the smooth rock in hypnotic swirling patterns. Then the valley widens and the creek and trail meander more slowly through the forest where more good campsites can be found. Cross Blue Jay Creek carefully on rocks that are sometimes slippery, then cross two wide, sandy flats, reenter the forest, and meet the Eagle Peak Trail in a ferny glen at 7.5 miles. (See Option below.) Descend a slot that crosses a couple of bumps to reach the Yosemite Falls junction at 8.0 miles. This is where you will meet a steady stream of sweating, gasping hikers laboring up from the valley floor.

Turn left at this junction for a few yards, then follow signs to the overlook through sculpted rocks and twisted Jeffrey pines to an iron railing. Directly across the valley the upside-down bowl of Sentinel Dome rises alone and to the west of Glacier Point. Farther in the distance is Mount Starr King, also somewhat rounded and isolated from the surrounding ridges. Half Dome is to the left, and the Clark Range is on the horizon. The path now drops down a series of steep and slippery steps cut into the cliff to a platform protected by more iron railings. The thunderous roar, the drenching spray, and the dizzying drop over the falls is exhilarating, but not for the faint of heart or the acrophobic. For a different perspective return to the main trail and turn right

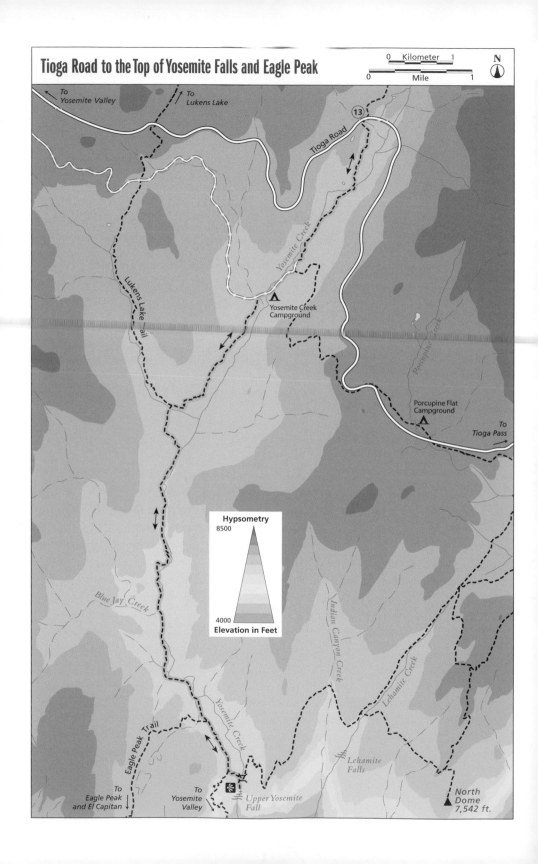

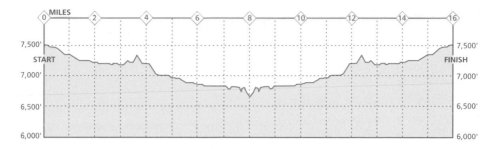

(southeast), continuing on for 0.1 mile to a footbridge that spans Yosemite Creek a few yards upstream from the brink.

You can return the way you came, or if you are planning to spend the night, retrace your steps to the main trail and follow it back upstream along the west side of the creek before pitching your tent. The area just at the top of the falls is trampled and overused, and camping within 0.25 mile of the rim is prohibited anyway.

Miles and Directions

0.0 Yosemite Creek Trailhead

1.5 Yosemite Creek Campground. Follow the paved road through the middle.

2.2 End of campground; leave the road and turn left

3.7 Lukens Lake Trail junction; continue straight ahead

7.5 Eagle Peak Trail junction; continue straight ahead

8.0 Yosemite Falls; turn left to the overlook

16.0 Return to the Yosemite Creek Trailhead

Option: Eagle Peak—At 7,779 feet Eagle Peak is the highest of the Three Brothers. From its summit you can see just about all of the park, from the star attractions of Yosemite Valley to distant landmarks like Mounts Lyell and Maclure, the Clark Range, parts of the Cathedral Range, and all the way to Mount Conness. Beginning at the Eagle Peak Trail junction at the top of Yosemite Falls, head back northwest toward the Tioga Road, climbing up a steep gully in deep shade to top a rise, then turning left at a signed trail fork. You slosh through ferns and soggy ground, climb steeply to an open grove where you cross Eagle Peak Creek, skirting the edge of more damp meadows, then turn left at the fork with the El Capitan Trail. The sign says that Eagle Peak is 0.3 mile ahead, but it's more like 0.6. There's a little scramble up a pile of weathered granite to reach the very top, but you can see almost as much from the ridge just below the summit if you have no head for heights. This option adds about 6.0 miles and more than 1,000 feet gain to the Yosemite Creek hike, but the view is well worth every calorie and drop of sweat you'll expend to get there.

14 Porcupine Creek to North Dome

North Dome is one of the most photographed features of the park, especially from the Happy Isles Bridge with the Merced River in the foreground. It is smooth and rounded, more symmetrical than Half Dome, crowning the exfoliating Royal Arches. This is probably the best full-day outing on the north rim, and it is a popular one. The views are everything you would expect from such a vantage point, and as a bonus you get to see the famous granite arch atop Indian Ridge, accessible only to foot (or horse) travelers.

Start: Porcupine Creek Trailhead
Total distance: 8.8 miles out and back
Hiking time: 6 to 9 hours
Difficulty: Moderate
Elevation change: 900 feet
Seasons: Summer and fall
Nearest facilities: Food, water, phones, and gas in Tuolumne Meadows

Permits: None
Map: USGS Yosemite Falls quad
Special considerations: Allow more time than you think you will need for this hike. There are lots of ups and downs, and the rock is sometimes slippery. Wear good boots and take your time.

Finding the trailhead: On Tioga Road (CA 120), drive 14 miles west of Tuolumne Meadows or 23 miles east of Crane Flat. The trailhead and parking area are on the south side of the road. Trailhead GPS: N37 48.24 / W119 32.43

The Hike

From the trailhead sign at the east end of the parking area, head downhill to meet the eroded remains of an old road and follow it on down until you reach Porcupine Creek at mile 0.7. If the water is high, there is a log crossing just upstream. Continue through red fir and lodgepole pine forest, climbing slightly, to a junction at 1.5 miles. Your trail goes straight ahead.

A few feet beyond this, another sign directs you straight ahead again to North Dome and Yosemite Falls. At yet another fork you keep left toward North Dome. The right fork goes down to Yosemite Valley via Yosemite Falls. (This series of forks shows as a single four-way junction on the topographic map.) Wind steadily uphill, partly through forest, partly over open rock lined with manzanita, until you reach the top of Indian Ridge at mile 2.7. A short detour cuts off to the left (northeast) to a very unusual rock arch, a geologic feature seldom seen in granite. There is nothing else like it in Yosemite, so don't miss it.

The main trail follows the top of Indian Ridge toward the south, drops sharply off to the left, then picks up the ridgeline again. Here in an open rocky space, another short spur trail goes right (south) for a stupendous view and your first look at the

This arch on Indian Ridge is unusual because it's made of granite.

bald, rounded top of North Dome just below. Yosemite Valley stretches away to the right, flanked by Sentinel Rock and El Capitan. To the left Half Dome looms impossibly huge just across the gorge and Clouds Rest rises even higher in smooth curves farther back along the same ridge. The bare dome rising out of the trees behind Half Dome like a whale snout surfacing is Mount Starr King.

Return to the main trail and make your way carefully down the slickrock to a junction at 3.9 miles. Turn left and head southeast down toward North Dome. At first you drop down the east side of the ridge crest, and while it may at first appear that you are heading in the wrong direction, this is the trail. Some people do not return to the main trail, but, following the spur, shortcut straight down the smooth rock face directly above North Dome, but the way is slippery. The trail is safer. It passes to the right of Basket Dome to a timbered saddle, then back up the smooth, exfoliating crown of North Dome, reaching the summit at 4.4 miles. North Dome's position

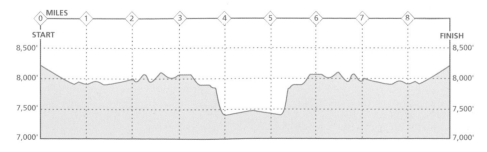

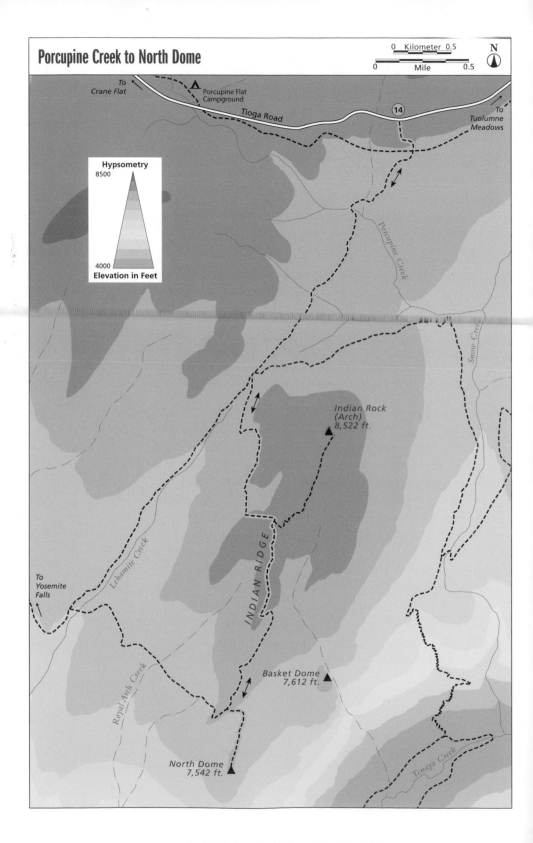

Porcupine Creek to North Dome

Hypsometry

8500

4000

Elevation in Feet

To Crane Flat

Porcupine Flat Campground

Tioga Road

14

To Tuolumne Meadows

Porcupine Creek

Snow Creek

Indian Rock (Arch) 8,522 ft.

INDIAN RIDGE

Lehamite Creek

To Yosemite Falls

Royal Arch Creek

Basket Dome 7,612 ft.

North Dome 7,542 ft.

Tenaya Creek

N

0 Kilometer 0.5

0 Mile 0.5

above the confluence of several major drainages makes it one of the finest viewpoints in Yosemite. From left to right Tenaya Canyon, Merced Canyon, Illilouette Gorge, and Yosemite Valley itself fan out in all directions. When you have run out of time, return the way you came.

Miles and Directions

0.0 Porcupine Creek Trailhead

0.7 Porcupine Creek crossing

1.5 Four-way junction

2.7 Indian Ridge

3.9 North Dome spur trail

4.4 Summit

8.8 Return to Porcupine Creek Trailhead

15 The North Rim

This is an overnight shuttle route that follows the north rim of Yosemite Valley from west to east, beginning near Big Oak Flat Road, skirting the tops of El Capitan, Eagle Peak, Yosemite Falls, and North Dome, and dropping into the valley at Tenaya Canyon above Mirror Lake. It is a cooler, longer, slightly later-season trek than the south-rim route, with breathtaking views of the valley.

Start: Trailhead near the Foresta turnoff on CA 120, Big Oak Flat Road
Total distance: 33.0 miles one way
Hiking time: 3 to 4 days
Difficulty: Moderate to strenuous
Elevation change: 5,400 feet
Seasons: Early summer to fall

Nearest facilities: Everything you need except gas in Yosemite Valley. There is gas at Crane Flat.
Permits: Required; available in advance or from the wilderness center in Yosemite Valley and the Big Oak Flat Entrance Station
Maps: USGS El Capitan, Half Dome, and Yosemite Falls quads

Finding the trailhead: From the junction at the west end of Yosemite Valley, drive 4 miles north on Big Oak Flat Road (CA 120). There is marked trailhead parking on the left (south) side, just beyond the Foresta Road turnoff. The trail begins on the other side of the road. Trailhead GPS: N37 42.85/W119 44.18

The Hike

Climb the formerly chaparral-covered slope now recovering from a prescribed burn that escaped in 2009. Cross to the north side of the ridge where thousands of young ponderosa pines jostle one another for growing space and sunlight. Birding is exceptional here because of the number of desirable nesting sites in the hollow, burned-out trees. Leave the burned area behind in about 1.5 miles and cross several tributaries of Wildcat Creek blooming with dogwood and azaleas and continue on to Tamarack Creek, which might be tricky to cross until midseason. Huge leaves of Indian rhubarb the size of dinner plates line the creek, and when they are in bloom, their flower clusters seem to poke right up through the center of the leaves.

A little farther on, cross a small branch of Cascade Creek and reach the now-abandoned Old Big Oak Flat Road at 4.0 miles. Turn right (south) here. The left fork heads back up to Tamarack Flat Campground and the Tioga Road. Cross the main fork of Cascade Creek on a bridge. There is a campsite on the south side of the creek above the bridge. Be sure to fill your bottles with filtered or treated water at the creek because there is a long, hot climb ahead.

You can see almost all of Yosemite Valley from the summit of Eagle Peak. ▶

Continue down the old road to mile 4.6, where the asphalt has become almost obliterated and the way is blocked by a pile of logs diverting you to the left (north) at a signed but easy-to-miss junction. Begin a stiff climb up a partly forested slope to a ridgeline, which you follow to its highest point. Descend to Ribbon Meadow, thickly forested, boggy, and buggy. Snow often lingers late in this shady section of trail, but red metal trail markers high on the trees help you stay on track. Ribbon Creek itself is so narrow, you might not even notice when you cross it.

The route crosses Ribbon Creek, beyond which there is some camping if the stream is still flowing, then begins to climb again. It cuts back north around the edge of El Capitan Gully, down which there is a stomach-lurching view of the valley. You can see the deceptively flat summit of El Capitan ahead of you now, and soon a junction with the spur trail to the top appears. There is no sign, but if you happen to miss the junction and walk straight ahead, you will find yourself on the summit. The main trail makes a left turn (northeast) at a cairn. The view from here is all you would expect from such a height, but don't go too near the downward-sloping edge. There is a flat-topped, gnarled, old Jeffrey pine beyond which the footing is very steep and slippery.

Return to the main trail, turn right, and descend through forest and over open slabs where you will have to watch for ducks. A very steep pull uphill takes you to the turnoff to Eagle Peak at mile 13. The trail sign says "Eagle Peak 0.3 Miles," but it is actually almost twice that distance. Eagle Peak, at 7,779 feet, is the highest of the Three Brothers, and from the pile of granite boulders at the top you can see almost the entire park.

Back on the North Rim Trail, continue north over mushy ground alongside Eagle Peak Meadow to meet the Yosemite Creek Trail coming from the Tioga Road. There is some camping in the forest to the left of the trail just before you reach this junction. This is a good spot to keep in mind if you want to spend the night near the top of Yosemite Falls since camping within 0.25 mile of the rim is prohibited. Descend to another junction at mile 16.9, where you will meet the sweating, panting hikers toiling up from the valley floor.

To see the upper fall, turn left (southeast) and follow the signs marked "Overlook" through sculpted rocks and twisted Jeffrey pines to an iron railing. Directly across the valley the upside-down bowl of Sentinel Dome rises alone to the left of Glacier Point. Farther in the distance is bullet-shaped Mount Starr King, standing isolated from the surrounding ridges. The path drops down a series of steep and sometimes slippery steps cut into the cliff to a platform protected by more iron railings. The thunderous roar, the drenching spray, and the dizzying drop over the falls are exhilarating but not for the faint of heart or the acrophobic. Return to the main trail and cross Yosemite Creek on a footbridge just above where the creek plunges over the rim. Continue upstream on switchbacks over mostly open rock to Yosemite Point, just a few yards off the trail to the right, where you can gaze directly down onto Yosemite Village.

The North Rim

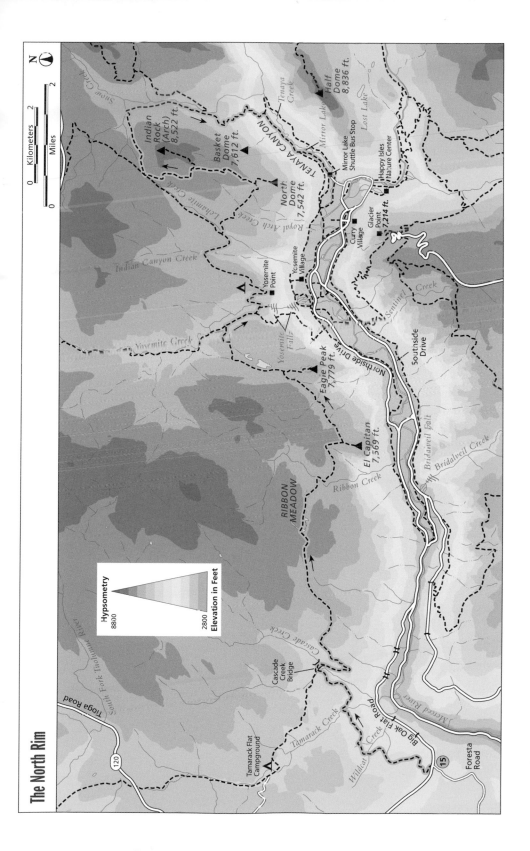

Hypsometry

8800

2800

Elevation in Feet

Tioga Road

120

South Fork Tuolumne River

Snow Creek

Indian Rock (Arch) 8,522 ft.

Basket Dome 7,612 ft.

Lehamite Creek

Royal Arch Creek

North Dome 7,542 ft.

TENAYA CANYON

Tenaya Creek

Half Dome 8,836 ft.

Mirror Lake

Mirror Lake Shuttle Bus Stop

Lost Lake

Happy Isles Nature Center

Glacier Point 7,214 ft.

Curry Village

Yosemite Village

Yosemite Point

Indian Canyon Creek

Yosemite Creek

Yosemite Falls

Eagle Peak 7,779 ft.

Northside Drive

Sentinel Creek

Southside Drive

El Capitan 7,569 ft.

Ribbon Creek

RIBBON MEADOW

Bridalveil Fall

Bridalveil Creek

Cascade Creek

Cascade Creek Bridge

Tamarack Creek

Tamarack Flat Campground

Wildcat Creek Road

Big Oak Flat Road

Merced River

15

Foresta Road

N

0   Kilometers   2

0   Miles   2

To continue your journey along the rim, climb steadily northward at first, then begin a mostly downhill progress through fir forest, crossing Indian Canyon Creek, which may be dry by midseason. Just before reaching more reliable Lehamite Creek, pass a side trail that joins yours coming from the Tioga Road. Your trail continues straight ahead, crossing Lehamite Creek, where you can find some camping spots. The trail now gains elevation gradually at first, then more steeply, on rough switchbacks to Indian Ridge. Half Dome rears up in front of you, impossibly enormous at such close range. You can see the bald pate of North Dome below you as well. Cross over the ridge, following cairns to a signed spur trail to North Dome at 22.1 miles. Don't miss the experience of descending to the top of North Dome, where Yosemite Valley stretches off to the west, Illilouette Gorge heads south, Merced Canyon comes in from the east, and Tenaya Canyon from the northwest.

Back on the North Rim Trail, climb steeply up the slickrock along the east side of the crest of Indian Ridge to a saddle where a short detour to the right (northeast) leads to a very unusual rock arch, a geologic feature seldom seen in granite. There is nothing else like it in Yosemite. Back on the trail, descend through alternating manzanita and forest to a four-way junction. Turn right (east) toward Mirror Lake. As you descend, the trail comes close to beautiful Snow Creek Falls, where you can find campsites not too far away. The route makes a curve to the right, following alongside the stream until mile 27, where yet another trail coming in from the Tioga Road crosses Tenaya Creek on a bridge just below you.

Now begin a long series of very steep switchbacks beside wonderful exfoliating granite with hanging gardens fed by seeps of water trickling from between the layers. On this stretch you must watch your footing, but you will want to stop often to gape at the stupendous, head-on view of Half Dome just across Tenaya Canyon. At last, with knees wobbling, you gratefully find flat ground at mile 30.8. From here turn right (west) and follow Tenaya Creek past Mirror Lake and on to the Mirror Lake shuttle bus stop (stop 17) at mile 33.0. From here you can follow the road for a mile back to the backpack parking lot or ride the shuttle bus back to Curry Village.

Miles and Directions

0.0   Big Oak Flat Road Trailhead

2.7   Cross Tamarack Creek

4.0   Old Big Oak Flat Road; turn right

4.6   Turn left off the road onto trail

8.0   Ribbon Meadow

10.4   Spur trail to El Capitan

13.0   Spur trail to Eagle Peak

16.2   First Yosemite Creek junction

16.9   Second Yosemite Creek junction near top of Yosemite Falls

17.1   Yosemite Overlook

20.6 Lehamite Creek

22.1 North Dome spur

24.3 Indian Rock spur

25.2 Four-way junction; turn right

27.0 Tenaya Creek bridge junction

30.8 Bottom of Tenaya Canyon; turn right

33.0 Mirror Lake shuttle bus stop

16 Tuolumne Grove

The Tuolumne Grove, one of three giant sequoia groves in Yosemite, is not as heavily visited as the Mariposa Grove and does not have a tram tour through it, so you can enjoy the beauty and serenity of the forest away from the sounds of "civilization," especially if you make this easy out-and-back hike early in the morning. The Tuolumne Grove was saved from the 2013 Rim Fire that probably would have destroyed even these fire-resistant sequoias when firefighters set a backfire that stopped the hotter and more aggressive blaze in its tracks. Some of the more vulnerable species in the grove are a bit charred, but the Big Trees have survived the biggest fire in the history of the park.

Start: Tuolumne Grove Trailhead
Total distance: 2.7 miles out and back
Hiking time: 1 to 2 hours
Difficulty: Easy
Elevation change: 500 feet

Seasons: Spring, summer, and fall, whenever Tioga Road is open
Nearest facilities: Gas, phones, and snacks at Crane Flat
Permits: None
Map: USGS Ackerson Mountain quad

Finding the trailhead: From Yosemite Valley drive 16 miles north on Big Oak Flat Road to Crane Flat. Turn right on the Tioga Road (CA 120) and drive less than a mile to the Tuolumne Grove parking area on the left. Trailhead GPS: N37 45.27 / W119 48.15

The Hike

The route through the grove follows an old road now closed to vehicle traffic. It starts at a replica of a slice of a giant sequoia showing how its growth rings can be traced back 2,000 years. The road descends through a beautiful old forest of white fir, Douglas fir, sugar pine, and incense cedar. This last, with its smooth red bark, is often confused with the giant sequoia, but the first of these will not appear for almost a mile. In spring, exquisite white dogwoods bloom in openings in the forest.

At 0.9 mile a sign on your left announces that you are entering the Tuolumne Grove, and in a few minutes Big Red, the first giant sequoia, appears on the left. At mile 1.1 the road splits. Keep right to see—and walk through—the Tunnel Tree. This tree was already

▶ The ancient Tunnel Tree draws visitors to the Tuolumne Grove from all over the world. All giant sequoias are confined to a narrow band in the western United States only 15 miles wide and 260 miles long, between 5,000 and 7,000 feet in elevation along the western slope of the Sierra Nevada. They are clustered together in seventy-five separate groves where conditions of temperature and moisture suit them best. There are three groves in Yosemite.

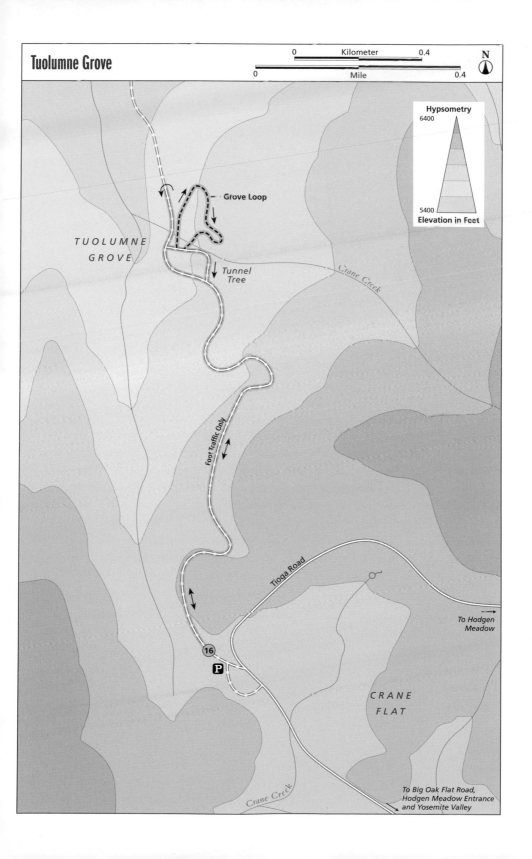

Tuolumne Grove

0   Kilometer   0.4
0   Mile   0.4

N

Hypsometry
6400

5400
Elevation in Feet

Grove Loop

TUOLUMNE
GROVE

Tunnel
Tree

Crane Creek

Foot Traffic Only

Tioga Road

To Hodgen
Meadow

16
P

CRANE
FLAT

Crane Creek

To Big Oak Flat Road,
Hodgen Meadow Entrance
and Yosemite Valley

The ancient Tunnel Tree is the star attraction in the Tuolumne Grove.

only a stump when the tunnel was cut through it in 1878, but dead or alive, it gives you an eerie feeling to look straight up at the sky while you're inside. Just past the Tunnel Tree, follow signs that lead you across a bridge over Crane Creek. This is the beginning of the Grove Loop, a nature trail with a series of excellent interpretive signs explaining the natural history of the trees: how they reach their great ages of 3,000 years; how they have adapted to survive repeated fires; how they depend on fire, insects, and squirrels to reproduce; and more. At mile 1.5, the farthest, and lowest, point on the hike, cross the creek again on a second bridge and head back uphill (south) to a picnic area. Just to the right the nature trail rejoins the road where you turn left, hiking back up past the Tunnel Tree turnoff to the trailhead.

Miles and Directions

- **0.0**   Tuolumne Grove Trailhead
- **0.9**   Enter the grove
- **1.1**   Tunnel Tree
- **1.6**   Picnic area in Tuolumne Grove
- **2.7**   Return to Tuolumne Grove Trailhead

17 Merced Grove

This is the smallest of Yosemite's three groves, but you shouldn't miss it, especially if the Mariposa Grove is still under restoration (expected to be completed in 2017). It's the one you're most likely to have to yourself anytime. It doesn't have as great a number of Big Trees, and many years of fire suppression have prevented the germination of any new seedlings, but the quiet and isolation of this little grove make it especially appealing. The route follows the Old Coulterville Road, the winner of an intense competition among developers to become the first stage road to bring visitors into Yosemite Valley. (It was abandoned almost as soon as it was finished, though, since runner-up routes turned out to be more convenient.)

Start: Merced Grove Trailhead
Total distance: 3.0 miles out and back
Hiking time: 2 to 3 hours
Difficulty: Easy
Elevation change: 600 feet
Seasons: Spring, summer, fall, whenever Big Oak Flat Road is open, and can be used by skiers in winter

Nearest facilities: Gas, store, water, and toilets at Crane Flat. There is a pit toilet but no water at the trailhead.
Permits: None
Maps: USGS Ackerson Mountain and El Portal quads

Finding the trailhead: On the Big Oak Flat Road (CA 120), drive 4 miles east of the Big Oak Flat entrance to the park, or from Tuolumne Meadows or Yosemite Valley, drive about 4 miles west on CA 120 from the junction at Crane Flat. GPS: N37 45.79 / W119 50.50

The Hike

Spend a moment or two at the trailhead sign to learn about the history of this old road and the grove of Big Trees before you set out. Beyond the parking area follow the road south and slightly downhill through a classic mid-elevation forest of Douglas fir, white fir, incense cedar, and sugar pine. The understory supports a rich growth of spring-blooming shrubs like hazelnut, dogwood, and wild rose, and you can hear Moss Creek gurgling down in the gully below you (though you won't be able to reach it from the trail).

In less than 0.5 mile the road forks. Follow the left fork, the one with the gate, and continue a pleasant but unremarkable stroll downhill until all at once, at a turn in the road at mile 1.5, you find yourself amid a gathering of magnificent sequoias. Please enjoy them outside the low railings surrounding them as their roots are shallow and can be damaged by the trampling feet of their countless admirers. Just beyond this little grove are more sequoias larger than the last towering over a little log cabin that looks like a dollhouse in contrast. It was used as a getaway for the park superintendent

A perfect arrangement of giant sequoias marks the beginning of the Merced Grove.

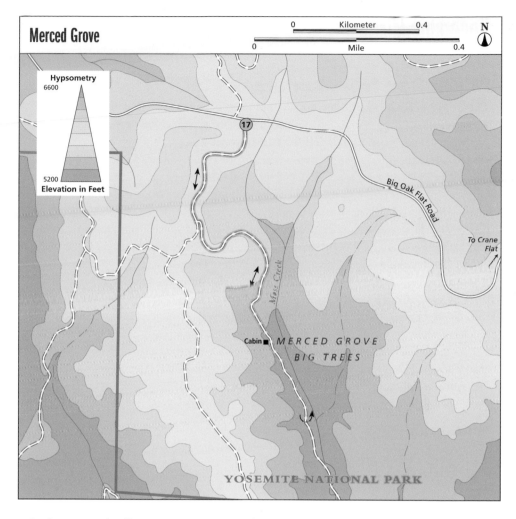

Merced Grove

Hypsometry

6600

5200
Elevation in Feet

17

Big Oak Flat Road

To Crane
Flat

Moss Creek

Cabin ■ *MERCED GROVE*
BIG TREES

YOSEMITE NATIONAL PARK

in the past and still serves as an occasional classroom for outdoor education groups. A short distance beyond the cabin are the biggest and best of all the Big Trees flanking the trail; this is the best place to turn around—the road beyond narrows to overgrown trail, there are only a few younger sequoias on the surrounding hillsides, and it's uphill all the way back.

Miles and Directions

0.0 Merced Grove Trailhead

0.5 Keep left at the junction

1.5 Last of the biggest trees

3.0 Return to the trailhead

Honorable Mention

El Capitan from Tamarack Flat

This route gets you to the top of El Capitan the "easy" way, that is, by trail from Tamarack Flat Campground rather than straight up the face with rope and climbing hardware. It follows an abandoned road down to Cascade Creek, which it crosses on a bridge, then begins a steep, waterless, 1,800-foot climb, followed by a more gradual descent to Ribbon Meadow. After crossing Ribbon Creek and skirting El Capitan Gully, a short spur trail cuts off to the summit. The distance from the trailhead is 8.2 miles. The top of El Cap is more rounded than it appears from below; don't try to get too near the very brink to look down. The views from the safer, higher ground are thrilling enough. If the views of the Valley are your main objective, Eagle Peak, about 2 miles along the trail to the east, is better. The distance there, at least from Yosemite Valley, is shorter too, only 6.4 miles. The only place you can camp along the El Capitan Trail is near Ribbon Creek, which dries out early in the year, so make sure to check with the park service about availability of water before setting out on an overnight trip.

To get to the trailhead, find the Tamarack Flat Campground turnoff, about 3 miles east of Crane Flat off the Tioga Road on the south side. Follow the campground road for another 3 miles to the trailhead.

The High Sierra Camps

These are a series of five backcountry camps with tent cabins that offer dorm-style sleeping, linens, meals, and showers (except at Vogelsang and Glen Aulin). They are about a day's hike apart, and a popular trip is to make a loop of all of them, though each is within a day's walk of a trailhead and may be visited individually. They range in elevation from 7,200 feet at Merced Lake to 10,100 feet at Vogelsang and occupy some of the most beautiful settings in Yosemite. The largest, Merced Lake, accommodates sixty people; the smallest, Glen Aulin, holds thirty-two. You can hike the camps on your own or as part of an organized, naturalist-led group. The High Sierra Camps offer a wonderful way to see some of Yosemite's finest backcountry without carrying a pack, but of course, they are extremely popular. They are operated by Aramark, the concessionaire, and reservations are granted by lottery. Lottery applications are accepted from September 1 to December 1 for the following summer, and the lottery is held in mid-December. Call (801) 559-5000.

Each of the High Sierra Camps provides good camping with solar toilets for backpackers. Snacks and emergency supplies are available at the camps during limited hours each day, which vary from camp to camp. Even if you are backpacking, these camps are very popular and permit quotas are filled early. The surest way to see them is to go early or late in the season.

This section will describe hikes to each of the camps from their nearest trailhead; then Hike 23, the High Sierra Camp Loop, will describe the multiday hike to all camps in a counterclockwise direction, beginning at Tuolumne Meadows—since the first camp on the loop, Glen Aulin, is downhill from here, you have extra time to adjust to the higher elevations.

Pacific tree frogs change color to match their surroundings.

18 Merced Lake High Sierra Camp

Merced Lake is the site of the largest of the High Sierra Camps and the farthest from any trailhead. The hike up the Giant Staircase along the Merced River allows you to experience the river in its many moods and to appreciate the power of the glaciers that carved and polished the canyon. Expect lots of company; it's a popular route.

Start: Happy Isles/John Muir Trailhead
Total distance: 26.8 miles out and back
Hiking time: 2 to 4 days
Difficulty: Strenuous as a 2-day trip, moderate if you take longer
Elevation change: 3,260 feet
Seasons: Mid-June through Sept
Nearest facilities: Everything you need except gas in Yosemite Valley. There are toilets, water, and snacks at Happy Isles.

Permits: Required. Available in advance or from the wilderness center in Yosemite Valley. *Note:* Because this trailhead gets so much use, group size is limited to ten people rather than the usual fifteen.
Maps: USGS Half Dome and Merced Peak quads

Finding the trailhead: Park in the hikers' lot east of Curry Village. You can take the shuttle bus from Curry Village to Happy Isles (stop 16) or walk from the parking lot, turn right (east) at the entrance, and follow the well-marked path to Happy Isles. This will add 1 mile each way to your hike. From the shuttle bus stop, continue on the paved road over the Happy Isles Bridge, then turn right, following the river upstream to the big sign that marks the beginning of the John Muir Trail. Trailhead GPS: N37 43.51/W119 33.33

The Hike

The sign at the trailhead shows mileage to various points on the John Muir Trail all the way to Mount Whitney, 211 miles to the south. You will have plenty of company, especially at the beginning of this hike, since it is one of the starting points of the High Sierra Camp loop, as well as the jumping-off point for the John Muir Trail and the climb to Half Dome.

The trail climbs gently on an asphalt path through black oak and ponderosa pine forest among enormous lichen-draped boulders. In about a half mile, across the thundering Merced on your right, watch for 370-foot Illilouette Fall tucked back in its deeply cut gorge in the Panorama Cliff. The trail now steepens briefly, then suddenly descends to the Vernal Fall Bridge at 0.8 mile. Upstream, Vernal Fall is perfectly framed by maple, alder, and various conifers as it drops 317 feet over the lower step of the Giant Staircase. There are restrooms, drinking water, and lots of people here.

Cross the bridge to the south side of the river and turn left, upstream. Just beyond, at mile 0.9, meet the Mist Trail, an alternate route to the top of Nevada Fall, not

The Merced River slides over the Bunnell Cascade.

recommended for backpacking since it is steep, slippery, and wet. Shortly beyond this junction, ignore a lateral trail on the right for horses only that leads back to the stables. Continue climbing on the John Muir Trail as it switchbacks relentlessly uphill. There are plenty of excuses to stop and rest on the way. Across the valley to the northwest you can see Upper Yosemite Fall. To the northeast across the river gorge, the rounded back side of Half Dome comes into view, along with Mount Broderick, Liberty Cap, and, finally, 594-foot Nevada Fall. This heart-stopping view is finest at Clark Point (2.3 miles), where a lateral trail cuts over to the Mist Trail, nearer to the river. Continue to ascend the John Muir Trail on well-graded switchbacks, eventually passing beneath a dripping rock overhang decorated with delicate hanging gardens of ferns, columbines, monkey flowers, and other water-loving species.

At 3.3 miles the Panorama Trail, leading back to Glacier Point, joins this one from the right (south). The trail drops a bit, hops a couple of little creeks, then emerges into a wide sunny expanse of smooth granite at the top of Nevada Fall. Here, at 3.5 miles, a footbridge crosses the river. There are plenty of viewpoints with protective railings where you can watch the falls rush over the lip. Please stay behind the railings and heed the warning signs. Hikers have slipped on the slickrock and been washed over the falls. This is a perfect place for lunch or a snack, but please do not share your food with the panhandling squirrels and jays.

Cross the footbridge and follow the north shore of the river to 3.8 miles. There is an outhouse here, and just beyond, the junction with the upper end of the Mist Trail. Continue upstream, climbing the well-defined trail over inlaid rocks. The way

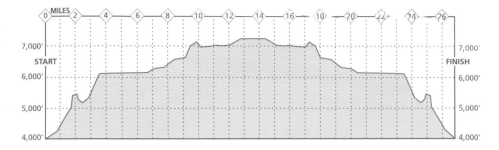

soon levels out and passes from sunlight into shade, and the Merced changes from a rushing, raging torrent to become quiet, dark, and deep.

At 4.3 miles your trail parts company with the John Muir Trail, which heads off to the left (northeast) toward Half Dome while you continue straight. After slogging through heavy sand for a half mile, another lateral trail at 4.8 miles takes off to the left to join the John Muir and Half Dome trails. Ahead is Little Yosemite Valley, your first camping opportunity. *Note:* Camping is prohibited for the next 2 miles beyond Little Yosemite Valley.

It's a busy and popular place, especially for bears. There are plenty of bear-proof boxes for food storage, but you should be carrying a canister anyway. There is also an architecturally elegant two-story solar composting toilet. The National Park Service has constructed two communal fire rings for campers to share. Please do not scar this already overused area by building another one.

Beyond Little Yosemite Valley the trail continues through level forest for a little more than a mile where steep granite walls close in, pinching shut Little Yosemite Valley, forcing the river to pick up speed and vigor. It cascades noisily for a short time before slowing and widening out once again through Lost Valley, severely burned in a recent fire. Climb out of the valley, passing below the enormous dome of Bunnell Point across the river, where the water pours over the long slippery slide of Bunnell Cascade and is finally crossed on a footbridge to the south side. Climb switchbacks blasted out of the smooth granite, then pause to wipe away the sweat and enjoy the sight and sound of the river roaring through its spectacular rocky gorge.

▶ Watch for brilliant red snow plants and the taller, drabber, brownish pinedrops on the forest floor where little sunlight comes through. These live on decaying material in the soil, so they have no need of green leaves and can survive in deep shade.

Descend once again, cross back over the river, and soon enter Echo Valley, another badly burned-over flat where several creeks flow in to join the Merced. At 11.4 miles, where Echo Creek flows into the valley, a trail to Sunrise High Sierra Camp cuts off to the north. Soon the Merced begins to race beside the trail again as you climb the final mile to Merced Lake. There is a stock gate at the west end of the lake at 12.7 miles. Be sure to close it behind you. Skirt the lakeshore until you reach

Merced Lake High Sierra Camp

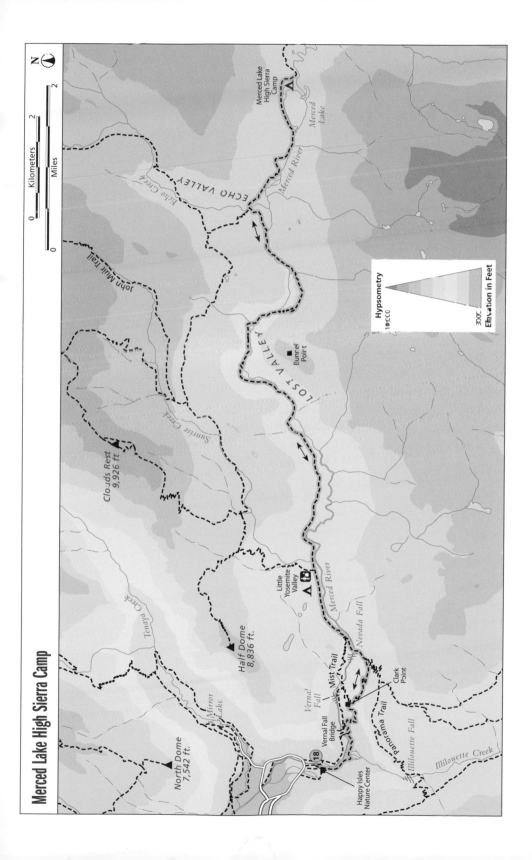

Merced Lake High Sierra Camp

Merced Lake

Merced River

ECHO VALLEY

Echo Creek

John Muir Trail

Sunrise Creek

LOST VALLEY

Bunrel Point

Clouds Rest
9,926 ft.

Half Dome
8,836 ft.

Tenaya Creek

Mirror Lake

North Dome
7,542 ft.

Little Yosemite Valley

Merced River

Vernal Fall

Mist Trail

Nevada Fall

Clark Point

Panorama Trail

Illilouette Fall

Illilouette Creek

Vernal Fall Bridge

Happy Isles Nature Center

18

Hypsometry

10000

3000

Elevation in Feet

N

Kilometers
0   2

Miles
0   2

the High Sierra Camp at 13.4 miles. The backpack camp is a short distance beyond. Campers may use the water tap at the campground, but are asked to use the toilets at the backpack campground. You can buy emergency items and snacks during posted hours at the High Sierra Camp. Less than a mile beyond the camp is a ranger station, open all summer. From here you can return to Yosemite Valley or continue north to Vogelsang High Sierra Camp to continue the loop.

Miles and Directions

0.0 Happy Isles Trailhead

0.8 Vernal Fall Bridge; cross the bridge, turn left

0.9 Mist Trail junction; keep right

2.3 Clark Point; continue straight ahead

3.3 Panorama Trail junction; keep left

3.5 Cross the footbridge over Nevada Fall

3.0 Upper end of the Mist Trail; keep right

4.3 John Muir Trail junction; continue straight ahead

4.8 Little Yosemite Valley

11.4 Echo Valley; keep right at Sunrise Trail junction

12.7 West end Merced Lake

13.4 Merced Lake High Sierra Camp

26.8 Return to Happy Isles Trailhead

19 Vogelsang High Sierra Camp

This overnight loop to the highest of the High Sierra Camps may be hiked in either direction, approaching Vogelsang from the west via Rafferty Creek or from the east via the Lyell Fork and Evelyn Lake. If you have only one night to spend, you can make an out-and-back hike of 13.4 miles via Rafferty Creek, but this area really deserves more time, at least 3 days. It will be described here in a clockwise direction, that is, via Lyell Fork, returning via Rafferty Creek, because the ascent is more gradual.

Start: John Muir Trailhead at the Dog Lake parking lot
Total distance: 19.1-mile loop
Hiking time: 2 to 4 days
Difficulty: Moderate
Elevation change: 2,000 feet
Seasons: Late June to Sept

Nearest facilities: Food and phones at Tuolumne Meadows; gas at Crane Flat and Lee Vining
Permits: Required; available in advance or at the Tuolumne Meadows Wilderness Center
Maps: USGS Vogelsang Peak and Tioga Pass quads

Finding the trailhead: From the west drive Tioga Road (CA 120) eastward past the Tuolumne Meadows Visitor Center, store, and campground, all on the right. Cross the bridge over the Tuolumne River. After about a mile turn right at the entrance to the wilderness center. Follow the road as it curves around to the left for about a half mile to the Dog Lake parking lot on the left. You might see broken glass on the asphalt where bears have broken into cars containing improperly stored food. Leave ice chests and all food in the bear-proof boxes provided. You can also ride the Tuolumne Meadows shuttle bus to the Dog Lake Trailhead (stop 2). Trailhead GPS: N37 52.39 / W119 20.20

The Hike

Cross the road south of the parking lot to the "John Muir Trailhead" sign. Follow the trail southeast to the footbridge over the Dana Fork at 0.2 mile. Ignore the cutoff back to the lodge and cross the bridge, then turn left and follow the river upstream. The route bends slightly to the right, crosses a low rise, and reaches the twin bridges over the Lyell Fork at 0.6 mile. This is surely one of the most sublime vistas in Yosemite, with the clear turquoise river winding toward you through the green meadow. The color of the water comes from glacial "flour," rock ground so fine by the Lyell Glacier upstream that it remains suspended in the water and reflects this lovely green light. In places, deep bowls have been carved into the granite by the scouring force of the silt carried by spring runoff. The massive gray hulk on the left is Mammoth Peak (not to be confused with Mammoth Mountain, the ski resort, which lies farther south).

Soon after you leave the twin bridges, another path leads back to the Tuolumne Meadows Campground at 0.7 mile. Continue left on the John Muir Trail through

Catch your breath at the rest stop on Rafferty Creek.

lodgepole pine forest and over open rock to 1.3 miles, where the Rafferty Creek Trail, the more direct route to Vogelsang, leads uphill to the right (south). You will be returning on this trail. Cross the bridge over the creek on your left and continue through forest and meadows, which in early season are a solid mass of pale lavender shooting stars (and mosquitoes). Soon the sound of the river becomes apparent—it's been hidden for a while behind a low ridge—and another glorious view of Lyell Canyon opens up before you.

Follow the path along the river to 5.6 miles, where the Vogelsang Trail leaves the John Muir Trail and angles off to the southwest, leaving the river behind. Near this junction are some good campsites to the right of the trail. This is a notorious bear hangout, and the bears here are intelligent and resourceful. Keep your bear canister locked.

Beyond the junction and the camping area, the trail begins to climb, switchbacking through lodgepole pine, sometimes through patches of wild strawberries and alpine prickly currant bushes. As the trail nears the creek on the left, a lovely little meadow appears. Be sure to pause for a moment and look up and ahead for the waterfall flowing from Ireland Lake, just out of sight in the bowl above. Beyond the meadow the trail leaves the stream, first heads southwest, then makes a dogleg to the north and reaches a junction with the Ireland Lake Trail at 8.0 miles. The trail sign here incorrectly gives the distance to Ireland Lake as 3.0 miles. It is actually only 1.5 miles (each way) and is well worth a detour if you have the time. The lake lies in a huge open glacial cirque above timberline beneath Parsons and Amelia Earhart Peaks.

Back on the Vogelsang Trail, cross a little creek, then climb a rocky slope that becomes steep toward the top, on tight switchbacks. Stay alert. It's easy to zig when you should have zagged and miss the route. Your goal is obvious, however—it is the low point on the ridge ahead. This is the highest point of your hike at 10,600 feet, and it offers sensational views. The vegetation has changed from upright lodgepole pine to whitebark pine forest that is less than knee-high on this windy ridgetop. Behind you to the northeast is the light-colored Kuna Crest, and beyond that, the Koip Crest, which marks the park boundary. To the south are black Amelia Earhart and Parsons Peaks, and beyond them, the group of tall peaks on the horizon includes Mount Lyell, highest point in Yosemite. To the west an unnamed lake occupies a broad green bowl, with your trail skirting its northwest shore before vanishing over the next ridge.

Descend from the saddle to the outlet of this little lake, noting that the whitebark pines, though still twisted and gnarled, are now growing upright. Hop the outlet stream, cross a low ridge, and enter a larger bowl containing Evelyn Lake. Off to the north beyond Tuolumne Meadows lie the high peaks of Yosemite's north boundary country, crowned by Mount Conness, third highest peak in the park. The trail now crosses the outlet of Evelyn Lake, tops another rise, then descends through a notch that often holds patches of snow well into summer, and as a result is usually filled with flowers. Downhill to the right are glimpses of Boothe Lake and of the Rafferty Creek Trail leading back to Tuolumne Meadows. A little farther along, Fletcher Lake, lying at the base of Fletcher Peak, comes into view on the left. A long meadow dotted with whitebark pine stretches out ahead.

Vogelsang High Sierra Camp (10,100 feet) lies at the far end of Fletcher Lake at 11.5 miles. There are plenty of campsites beneath the trees in the meadow away from the lakeshore. Be sure to camp only on pine duff and not on the fragile green meadow vegetation. There are a few especially fine sites toward the north side of the meadow near the cliff edge with views of Boothe Lake and Mount Conness. There is a distinctive, oddly shaped solar composting toilet for backpackers that has been out of order for years, but backpackers are discouraged from using the toilets at the High Sierra Camp. There is a tap with potable water just outside the camp office that you may use if you don't want to purify lake water, but the water from the free-standing tap several yards away from the building is not safe to drink. Emergency supplies and snacks are available during posted hours at the camp.

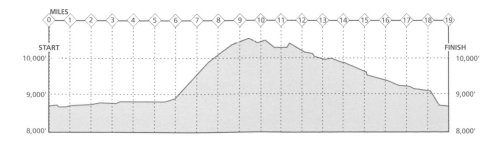

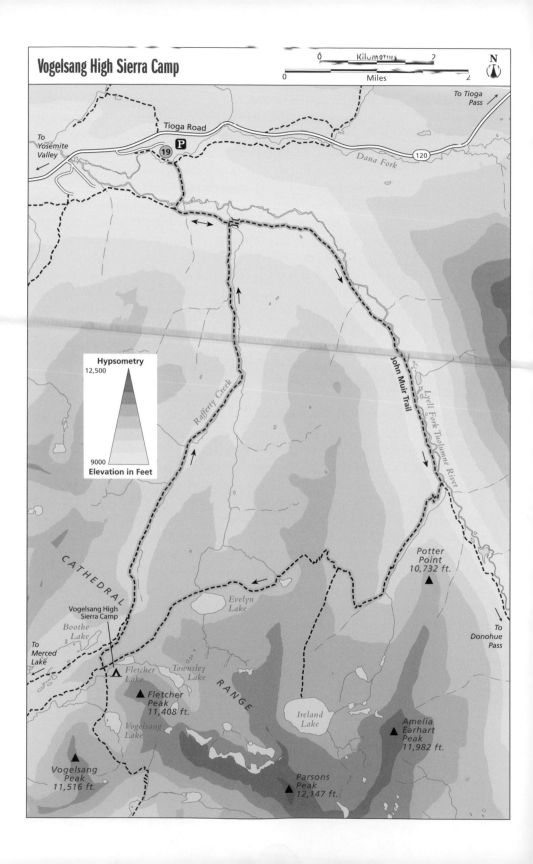

Vogelsang High Sierra Camp

0   Kilometers   2

0   Miles   2

N

To Tioga Pass

Tioga Road

P

19

To Yosemite Valley

Dana Fork

120

Hypsometry

12,500

9000

Elevation in Feet

Rafferty Creek

John Muir Trail

Lyell Fork Tuolumne River

CATHEDRAL

Potter Point 10,732 ft.

Vogelsang High Sierra Camp

Evelyn Lake

Boothe Lake

To Merced Lake

Fletcher Lake

Townsley Lake

RANGE

To Donohue Pass

Fletcher Peak 11,408 ft.

Ireland Lake

Amelia Earhart Peak 11,982 ft.

Vogelsang Lake

Vogelsang Peak 11,516 ft.

Parsons Peak 12,147 ft.

When you are ready to return to Tuolumne Meadows, find the signed junction in front of the High Sierra Camp and descend north, then northeast, gently down the ridge above Boothe Lake to Tuolumne Pass, where you will find another junction at 12.3 miles. You can make a detour of 0.4 mile for a look at Boothe Lake or continue gently downhill along Rafferty Creek for a long stretch, sometimes through forest, sometimes at the edge of the meadow. Toward the end the descent steepens and at last switchbacks down to the junction of the John Muir Trail at 17.8 miles, closing the loop. From here return the way you came to Tuolumne Meadows.

Miles and Directions

0.0   Dog Lake parking lot/John Muir Trailhead
0.2   Bridge over Dana Fork and junction with Tuolumne Meadows Lodge; keep right
0.3   Gaylor Lakes Trail; turn right
0.6   Cross the twin bridges over the Lyell Fork
0.7   Cutoff to Tuolumne Meadows Campground; turn left
1.3   Rafferty Creek Trail junction; keep left
5.6   John Muir Trail/Vogelsang Trail junction; turn right
8.0   Ireland Lake Trail; continue straight ahead
11.5   Vogelsang High Sierra Camp
12.3   Tuolumne Pass/Boothe Lake junction; turn right
17.8   John Muir Trail/Rafferty Creek Trail junction; turn left
19.1   Return to Dog Lake parking lot/John Muir Trailhead

Options: Vogelsang Lake and Vogelsang Pass—If you have time, do not pass up the opportunity to see this stunning lake and the wild expanse of alpine country beyond the pass. On the way you can look all the way down to Half Dome at the head of Yosemite Valley, and beyond the pass, southward to the colorful Clark Range. The trail starts at the big stone cairn in front of the High Sierra Camp, circles around to the back, then winds its way up to Vogelsang Lake through miniature wildflower gardens. It crosses the lake's outlet, then climbs the slope above the western shore along the base of Vogelsang Peak to reach the pass at almost 10,500 feet. You will encounter late-lying patches of snow well into the summer, and you must watch carefully for trail ducks to keep you on course. The round-trip distance from the High Sierra Camp is 2.4 miles.

20 May Lake High Sierra Camp

This is the High Sierra Camp most easily reached from the road (not counting Tuolumne Meadows Lodge), so you are bound to have plenty of company on the trail. The lake lies at the base of Mount Hoffman, which marks the geographic center of the park. There are great views back down Tenaya Canyon toward Yosemite Valley along the way.

Start: May Lake Trailhead at Snow Creek
Total distance: 2.4 miles out and back
Hiking time: 2 to 4 hours
Difficulty: Easy
Elevation change: 490 feet
Seasons: All summer, whenever the road is open and free of snow

Nearest facilities: Food and phones at Tuolumne Meadows; gas at Crane Flat
Permits: None required for a day hike; available for overnights in advance or at the Tuolumne Meadows Wilderness Center
Map: USGS Tenaya Lake quad

Finding the trailhead: From Tioga Road (CA 120), drive 27 miles east of Crane Flat or 20 miles west of Tioga Pass to the May Lake Road junction. Follow the narrow road north about 2 miles through a meadow known as Snow Flat to the trailhead. Drive carefully here—in many places the road is only wide enough for one vehicle at a time. Leave any food or ice chests in the bear-proof boxes at the trailhead. Trailhead GPS: N37 49.96 / W119 29.46

The Hike

Begin your walk in a shady glen with a variety of conifers—lodgepole pine, silver pine, mountain hemlock, and fir—then pass a discolored little pond teeming with fairy shrimp and other interesting creatures. The well-used trail climbs slowly at first, passing through a granite corridor where cracks in the rock bloom with ferns, mountain pride penstemon, shaggy hawkweed, and other wildflowers. Eventually the trail begins a steeper, winding climb with some switchbacks toward the top, revealing good views now and then down Tenaya Canyon past Clouds Rest and Half Dome. The dramatic pointy peak in the distance is Mount Clark. Back up the canyon in the other direction you can just barely see Tenaya Lake.

The trail flattens out in forest and in just a few yards reaches a fork. To the left, just beyond the substantial outhouse as well as a spigot dispensing potable water, is the backpack camping area; to the right is the

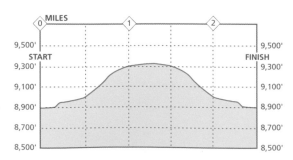

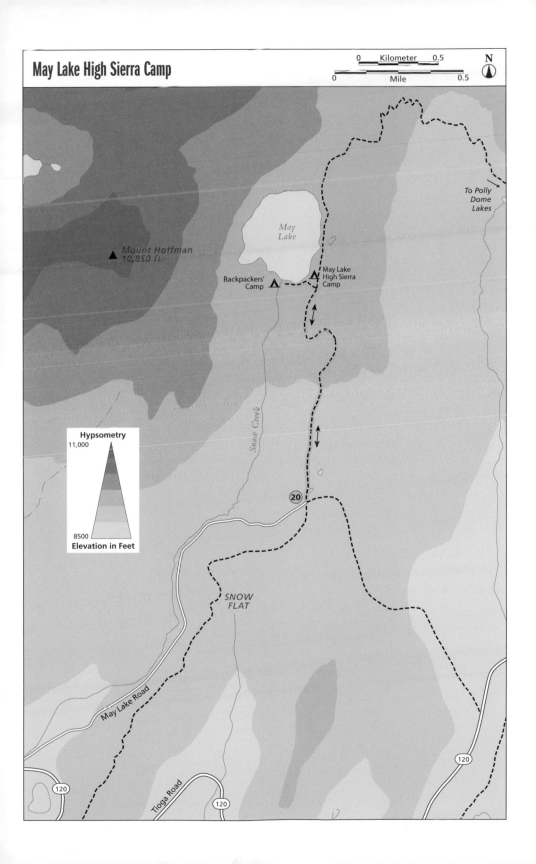

May Lake High Sierra Camp

0 Kilometer 0.5

0 Mile 0.5

N

To Polly Dome Lakes

May Lake

▲ *Mount Hoffman 10,850 ft.*

Backpackers' Camp

May Lake High Sierra Camp

Hypsometry

11,000

8500

Elevation in Feet

Snow Creek

20

SNOW FLAT

May Lake Road

Tioga Road

120

120

120

Mount Hoffman, the geographical center of Yosemite, frames May Lake.

High Sierra Camp near the lakeshore. Enjoy the lake from camp, but do not jump in. This is the local water supply, and swimming is prohibited. Mount Hoffman, at 10,850 feet, rises dramatically behind the lake. It is well worth a scramble to the top if you have the time because of its central location in the park and 360-degree views. Allow a minimum of 2 extra hours for the climb.

Miles and Directions

0.0 Trailhead

1.1 Junction: May Lake High Sierra Camp right, backpack campground left

1.2 May Lake

2.4 Return to trailhead

21 Glen Aulin High Sierra Camp

There are more scenic wonders along the Glen Aulin trail, mile for mile, than on any other route below the high alpine zone anywhere in Yosemite. For most of its length, it follows the course of the Tuolumne River as it wanders through broad meadows beneath the fabulous domes and spires of the Cathedral Range, then rushes and tumbles down in waterfall after waterfall as the canyon steepens and narrows. Your goal, the High Sierra Camp, lies in an idyllic setting beside a pool at the base of an exquisite cascade. Because the route is fairly short and easy, because it is part of the High Sierra Camp loop and the Pacific Crest Trail, and because it is so beautiful, the trail always has plenty of traffic and wilderness permits go quickly. Solitude? Not a chance, but worth the trip anyway.

Start: Glen Aulin Trailhead near Lembert Dome in Tuolumne Meadows
Total distance: 10.4 miles out and back
Hiking time: 6 to 10 hours
Difficulty: Easy as a backpack, moderate as a day hike
Elevation change: 800 feet to Glen Aulin
Seasons: All summer, whenever the Tioga Road is open
Nearest facilities: Tuolumne Meadows Store, Grill, and Mountain Shop are just west of the Tuolumne Meadows Campground. Gas at Crane Flat and Lee Vining

Permits: None required for a day hike; available for overnights in advance or at the Tuolumne Meadows Wilderness Center
Maps: USGS Falls Ridge and Tioga Pass quads
Special considerations: Because this is such a popular destination, Glen Aulin is notorious for troublesome bears. There are a couple of bear boxes at the backpack campground, but there are not enough for everybody. Hanging food is out of the question here. Carry your canister and keep it locked even if it's right beside you.

Finding the trailhead: From the west follow the Tioga Road (CA 120) past the Tuolumne Meadows Visitor Center, store, cafe, and campground, all on your right. Just after crossing the bridge over the Tuolumne River, turn left (north) into the Lembert Dome parking lot. From the east (Tioga Pass) follow the Tioga Road past the turnoff to the wilderness center on your left and continue about a hundred yards to the Lembert Dome parking area on your right. You can also ride the Tuolumne Meadows shuttle bus to Lembert Dome (stop 4). Overnight parking is prohibited in the parking lot, so if you are planning to backpack, park along the paved road parallel to Tioga Road. The road turns right at a closed gate, where your hike begins. Trailhead GPS: N37 52.44 / W119 21.30

The Hike

Go through the gate and follow the road (closed to vehicles) westward through the meadow, keeping right and climbing a small rise where the road splits. From the top of the rise, head toward the ramshackle log structure partially containing Soda Springs at mile 0.5, a naturally carbonated spring bubbling up rusty water. Just beyond

The White Cascade drops into a pool in front of Glen Aulin High Sierra Camp.

is Parsons Lodge, a stone building with historical exhibits, and beyond that, a log cabin used by park volunteers. There is a public restroom behind the cabin. The path splits in front of the cabin at mile 0.6. Turn right. The left fork goes to the sewage treatment plant.

The trail to Glen Aulin, marked by a big sign, meets the road a few yards beyond. Turn left this time. Walk through flowery meadows and lodgepole pine forest on footing that is heavy and dusty since pack trains going to and from the High Sierra Camp use the path too. Ford Delaney Creek, at mile 1.2, is usually shallow enough to wade, though you can keep your boots dry by crossing on a big log just upstream.

At 1.6 miles meet a junction with one of the trails that heads north to Young Lakes. Continue northwest, descending very gradually. In less than a mile, you emerge from behind a low ridge to behold the spectacular Cathedral Range with the Tuolumne River in the foreground. The next couple of miles along the trail offers one incredible photo op after another. Sometimes the trail passes over highly polished granite, buffed by glacial ice to a blinding sheen. Follow the ducks across these open spaces to stay on the trail. Climb around a low shoulder of rock and keep watch on your left for the Little Devil's Postpile, an unusual volcanic feature much younger than the surrounding rock.

The trail turns sharply right and drops down a short, steep notch and very soon reaches a pair of footbridges across the Tuolumne River at 3.5 miles. From this point on the river picks up speed and cascades over a series of falls, one after another, all the way to Glen Aulin. One of these, Tuolumne Falls, is close enough to the trail for hikers to feel the spray. Continue descending, enjoying views up Cold Canyon to

Glen Aulin High Sierra Camp

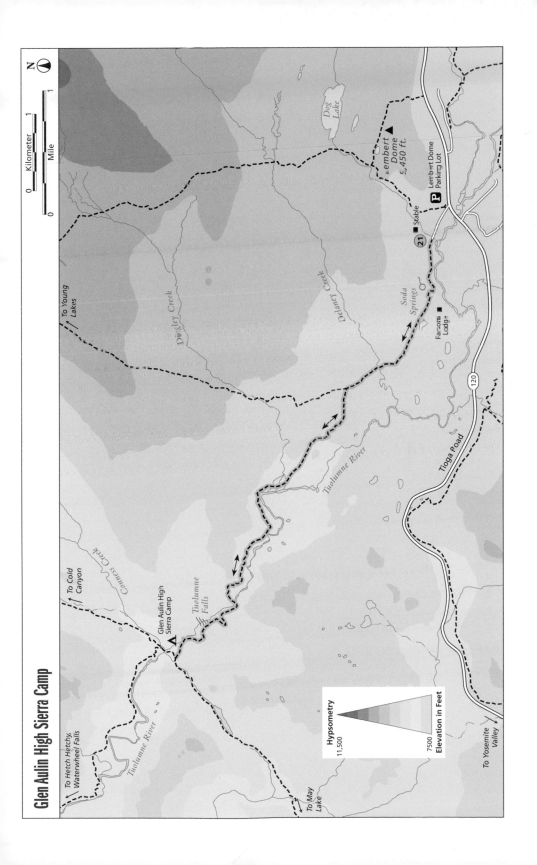

N

0   Kilometer   1

0   Mile   1

To Young
Lakes

Dingley Creek

Delaney Creek

Soda
Springs

Parsons
Lodge

Dog
Lake

Lembert
Dome
9,450 ft.

21 ■ Stable

P Lembert Dome
Parking Lot

120

Tioga Road

To Cold
Canyon

Conness Creek

Tuolumne River

Glen Aulin High
Sierra Camp

Tuolumne Falls

Tuolumne River

To Hetch Hetchy
Waterwheel Falls

To May
Lake

To Yosemite
Valley

Hypsometry

11,500

7500

Elevation in Feet

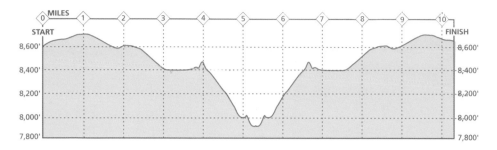

Matterhorn Peak and Mount Conness on the northern boundary of the park. The trail dives into and out of deep forest lined with Labrador tea and corn lily twice, then emerges again into sunlight on cobblestones or smooth granite marked with ducks. Finally it meets a junction with the May Lake Trail at 5.0 miles. A few more steep, slippery switchbacks lead down to a bridge and back to the other side of the river. Few hikers can resist the urge to stop on the bridge and snap a photo, or simply gape at the frothy White Cascade splashing into a pool in front of Glen Aulin High Sierra Camp. You have come 5.2 miles.

To reach the camp, cross a second bridge to the right over Cold Creek. Northward, behind the High Sierra Camp, is a backpack campground with bear-proof boxes and a solar composting toilet. The campground is much bigger than it looks, as it is divided into three separate sections on terraces one above another following the ridge above Cold Creek. Each section has a group fire ring to be shared with other campers. Do not build a new one. If you are not going on to Waterwheel Falls, retrace your steps to the trailhead.

Miles and Directions

0.0 Glen Aulin/Soda Springs Trailhead
0.3 Road splits; keep right, uphill
0.5 Soda Springs
0.6 Parsons Lodge; turn right, then left at the trail sign
1.2 Delaney Creek
1.6 Junction with Young Lakes Trail; keep left
3.5 Twin Bridges
5.0 May Lake Trail junction; turn sharp right, downhill
5.2 Glen Aulin High Sierra Camp; turn right, cross the bridge over the Tuolumne, right again over Cold Creek
10.4 Return to the Glen Aulin/Soda Springs Trailhead

Option: Waterwheel Falls—If you plan a hike to Glen Aulin early in the season, at least before the end of July, do not miss seeing the famous Waterwheel Falls, 2.7 miles and 1,400 feet down the river gorge from the High Sierra Camp. Most hikers spend two nights at Glen Aulin and make the steep Waterwheel Falls trip as a day hike.

The roaring Tuolumne River rushes down a smooth slope until it hits a series of grooves in the rocks that sometimes fling the water more than 20 feet into the air in series of huge arcs. To get there from the camp, cross the bridge over Cold Creek to the west side, climb over a ridge, and wander through a waist-high field of lupines that have flourished since the Glen was burned years ago. Some people still do camp in the Glen to avoid the crowds at the High Sierra Camp, but the only really desirable sites are too near the river and the trail to be strictly kosher. In another mile both trail and river drop over a long series of stairsteps down past California Falls and LeConte Falls to the Waterwheels. Watch for a little unmarked spur trail leading toward the bottom of the falls for a better view, but do not walk out onto the slippery rock beside the water, especially if it is wet. Slimy algae on polished rock is slick as glass, and a slip could be fatal.

22 Sunrise High Sierra Camp

This out-and-back route leads you from Tenaya Lake steadily upward past all three Sunrise Lakes, skirts the north end of Sunrise Mountain, then descends to a terrace above a long and lovely meadow laced with meandering streams. You can do it as a day hike, visit the High Sierra Camp, or spend the night. The John Muir and Pacific Crest Trails meet this route in the meadow.

Start: Sunrise Lakes Trailhead at Tenaya Lake
Total distance: 10.4 miles out and back
Hiking time: 5 to 8 hours
Difficulty: Moderate
Elevation change: 1,500 feet
Seasons: All summer, when Tioga Road is open

Nearest facilities: Food and phones at Tuolumne Meadows; gas at Crane Flat and Lee Vining
Permits: None required for a day hike; available for overnights in advance or at the Tuolumne Meadows Wilderness Center
Map: USGS Tenaya Lake quad

Finding the trailhead: Drive to the southwest end of Tenaya Lake on Tioga Road (CA 120). The trailhead is across the street from the lake on the south side. You can also ride the Tuolumne Meadows shuttle to Sunrise Lakes Trailhead. Be sure to leave food and ice chests in the bear-proof boxes provided. Trailhead GPS: N37 49.52 / W119 28.18

The Hike

The trail begins on a boardwalk behind and to the left (east) of the parking area and heads toward the shore of Tenaya Lake, where you will find a little beach and a spectacular photo op. Beyond the lakeshore you cross a sandy-bottomed creek draining the lake that you will probably have to wade early in the year. Just beyond is a trail junction and a sign that says "Sunrise: 4.9 Miles," where you turn right (south). At 0.2 mile a trail leading back to Tuolumne Meadows Lodge goes off to the left. Your trail dips and rises now, and then as it crosses several little streams it begins to climb the east slope above Tenaya Canyon. The switchbacking climb is relieved by views of Mount Hoffman and Tioga Road across the canyon.

At the crest of the ridge you have been climbing (2.5 miles), the trail splits. The right (south) fork leads back to Clouds Rest and Half Dome, and the left (east) leads to Sunrise Lakes. For a spectacular view of Half Dome and Clouds Rest, climb the little knoll to the right of the junction just a few dozen feet off the trail.

From the junction follow a ridgeline for a short time, then drop into the bowl containing the first of the Sunrise Lakes. Its depth makes it a rich, improbable royal blue. Camping is not recommended here because the sides of the bowl slope too steeply and the immediate lakeside is much too fragile (not to mention illegal) for camping. The trail now climbs up out of the bowl and follows its south rim. The

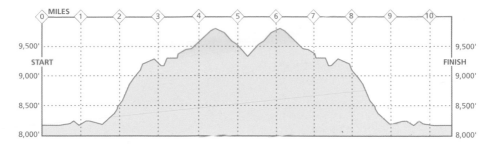

second Sunrise Lake, only occasionally visible, lies somewhat below the trail to the north and offers better camping than the first one.

The route crosses a smooth, round lump of classic exfoliating Yosemite granite to reach the uppermost, and largest, of the lakes. Camping is no longer allowed along the north shore, and the formerly overused and abused site is recovering well. Continue up a moderate hill alongside a wildflower-lined creek until reaching a wide, sandy saddle with scattered mountain hemlock and pine. The jagged Clark Range defines the horizon to the south. The trail eases gently down to the backpack camping area

Enjoy sunflowers like this Rudbeckia *near Sunrise High Sierra Camp.*

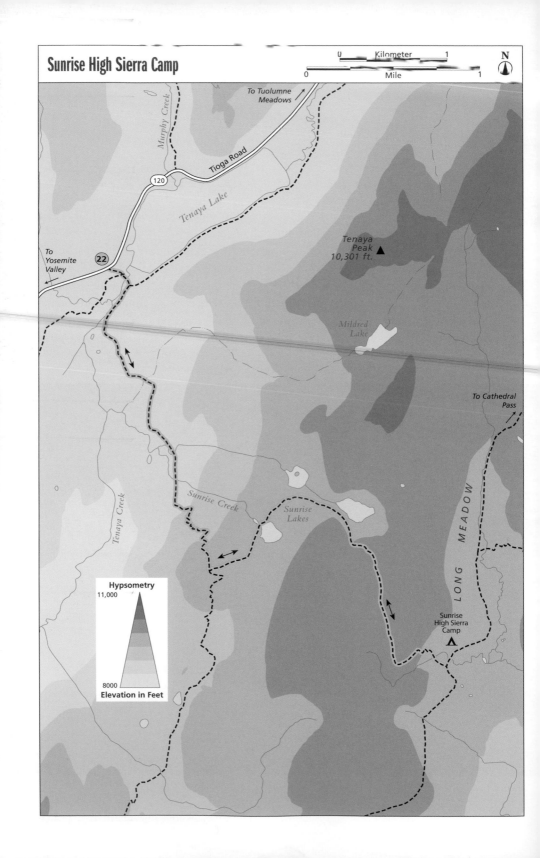

Sunrise High Sierra Camp

Kilometer

0   1
Mile

N

Hypsometry

11,000

8000

Elevation in Feet

Murphy Creek

To Tuolumne
Meadows

Tioga Road

120

Tenaya Lake

To
Yosemite
Valley

22

Tenaya
Peak
10,301 ft.

Mildred
Lake

To Cathedral
Pass

Tenaya Creek

Sunrise Creek

Sunrise
Lakes

LONG MEADOW

Sunrise
High Sierra
Camp

0

0

Yellow-bellied marmots are common in the high country.

above and behind the Sunrise High Sierra Camp, where there is a toilet, piped water, and bear boxes.

Just beyond and downhill at 5.1 miles, the trail meets a junction with the John Muir/Pacific Crest Trail. Turn left and follow the deeply worn ruts along the edge of the meadow to the High Sierra Camp. From the camp's front door, the view of an emerald green meadow backed by Merced Peak to the southeast and Mount Clark to the southwest invites contemplation and rest. The High Sierra Camp sells snacks and emergency supplies for a limited number of hours during the day. Return the way you came.

Miles and Directions

0.0 Sunrise Lakes Trailhead
0.2 Tuolumne Meadows Lodge cutoff
2.5 Clouds Rest/Half Dome trail junction
5.1 John Muir Trail junction
5.2 Sunrise High Sierra Camp
10.4 Return to Sunrise Lakes Trailhead

23 The High Sierra Camp Loop

You can visit all of the High Sierra Camps in one multiday backpack on this classic Yosemite route over some of the finest and most varied scenery in the park. Each of the camps has an adjoining camping area for backpackers with pit toilets and piped water. It is a heavily traveled route—backpackers, guests of the camps, horses, and packers carrying personal gear and supplies all travel these same trails; campgrounds are usually very busy; and permits are at a premium. You cannot expect a deep wilderness experience, but the camaraderie that comes from sharing the day's adventures with other hikers almost makes up for it. There are frequently bears hanging out around the camps. You can begin this loop from any of the trailheads to any of the camps, but beginning at Tuolumne Meadows, making Glen Aulin your first stop, gives you an easy first day on the trail and extra time to adjust to the high elevation.

Start: Glen Aulin Trailhead near Lembert Dome in Tuolumne Meadows
Total distance: 47.6-mile loop
Hiking time: About 6 days
Difficulty: Moderate
Elevation change: 6,000 feet
Seasons: All summer, whenever Tioga Road is open

Nearest facilities: Food, water, and phones in Tuolumne Meadows; gas at Crane Flat and Lee Vining
Permits: Required; available in advance or at the Tuolumne Meadows Wilderness Center
Maps: USGS Falls Ridge, Tioga Pass, Tenaya Lake, Merced Peak, Vogelsang Peak, and Mount Lyell quads

Finding the trailhead: From the west follow Tioga Road (CA 120) past the Tuolumne Meadows Visitor Center, store, cafe, and campground, all on your right. Just after crossing the bridge over the Tuolumne River, turn left (north) into the Lembert Dome parking area. From the east (Tioga Pass), follow Tioga Road past the turnoff to the wilderness center on your left and continue about a hundred yards to the Lembert Dome parking area on your right. You can also ride the Tuolumne Meadows shuttle bus to Lembert Dome (stop 4). Overnight parking is prohibited in the parking lot, so park along the road that runs parallel to the Tioga Road toward the stables. Where the road makes a sharp right turn, you will find a closed gate with the trailhead sign. Trailhead GPS: N37 52.44 / W119 21.30

The Hike

Go through the gate and follow the road (closed to vehicles) westward through the meadow, keeping right and climbing a small rise where the road splits. From the top of the rise, head toward the ramshackle log structure partially containing Soda Springs at mile 0.5, a naturally carbonated spring bubbling up rusty water. Just beyond is Parsons Lodge, a stone building with historical exhibits. The path splits at mile 0.6, where you turn right to a big "Glen Aulin Trail" sign. The trail meets the road a few yards beyond; turn left. Walk through flowery meadows and lodgepole pine forest on footing that is heavy and dusty from lots of horse and foot traffic. Ford Delaney Creek at mile 1.2. A trail heads north to Young Lakes, but your route stays left (northwest). In less than a mile of gradual descent, you emerge from behind a low ridge to behold the spectacular Cathedral Range with the Tuolumne River in the foreground. The next couple of miles along the trail offers one incredible photo op after another. Sometimes the trail passes over highly polished granite, buffed by glacial ice to a blinding sheen, and you will need to watch for ducks across these open spaces to stay on track. After passing through another short stretch of forest, climb around a low shoulder of rock and keep watch on your left for the Little Devil's Postpile, an unusual volcanic feature much younger than the surrounding rock.

The trail turns sharply right, drops down a short steep notch, and very soon reaches a pair of footbridges across the Tuolumne River at 3.5 miles. From this point on the river picks up speed and cascades over a series of falls, one after another, all the way to Glen Aulin. One of these, Tuolumne Falls, is close enough to the trail for hikers to feel the spray. Continue descending, enjoying views up Cold Canyon to Matterhorn Peak and Mount Conness on the northern boundary of the park. The trail twice dives into and out of deep forest lined with Labrador tea and corn lily, then emerges again into sunlight on cobblestones or smooth granite marked with ducks. Finally it meets a junction with the McGee Lake/May Lake Trail at 5.0 miles, where you turn right. A few more steep, slippery switchbacks lead down to a bridge and back to the other side of the river. Few hikers can resist the urge to stop on the bridge and snap a photo or simply gape at the frothy White Cascade splashing into a pool in front of the Glen Aulin High Sierra Camp. You have come 5.2 miles.

To reach the camp, cross a second bridge to the right over Cold Creek. Northward, behind the High Sierra Camp, is a backpack campground with potable water and a solar composting toilet. The campground is much bigger than it looks, as it is divided into three separate sections on terraces one above another following the ridge above Cold Creek. Each section has a group fire ring to be shared with other campers. Do not build a new one.

To continue on to May Lake Camp, retrace your steps across the bridge over Cold Creek, turn left and cross the next bridge to the south side of the Tuolumne River, then climb the short slope to meet the McGee Lake junction at 5.4 miles; turn right. McGee Lake is oddly situated at the top of a narrow saddle, each side of which is topped by a dome. Skirt the north shore of the lake, looking straight down the canyon to Tuolumne Peak. There are a few campsites at the lakeside. Now descend mostly through forest to cross Cathedral Creek, then climb again to meet a trail at 9.6 miles that runs down to Tenaya Lake via Murphy Creek. Take the right fork here, and soon meet the May Lake junction at 10.0 miles. Turn left (south).

The trail begins a fairly steep, beautiful climb up an open slope, down which little creeks trickle, each watering a miniature garden. Enjoy the views across the canyon to Mount Conness, then drop briefly down the west side of the rocky ridge. When you reenter the forest and swing west, keep an eye out for Raisin Lake through gaps in the rocks. This warm lake is a great place for a swim after your long, hot climb. May Lake is not far away, but swimming there is prohibited. Beyond Raisin Lake another short set of switchbacks takes you up past a meadow with an ephemeral pond, then meets the northeast end of May Lake and skirts its shore to the May Lake High Sierra Camp at 13.3 miles. The backpack camping area is beyond the camp at the lake's southern end. Mount Hoffman makes a great day hike if you have time because it is at the center of the park and offers a 360-degree sweep.

From May Lake follow the heavily traveled trail down to the May Lake Trailhead at the end of a road at 14.5 miles. Turn left when you reach the parking lot and walk a few yards to a sign directing you toward Sunrise High Sierra Camp. From here descend through forest to cross Tioga Road at 15.9 miles. There is a complicated set of junctions here, but it's easy to see where to go. Just head north toward Tenaya Lake to the Sunrise Lakes Trailhead at 16.0 miles. (The topographic map shows a campground here, but it was dismantled years ago.)

A paved trail begins behind the Sunrise parking area, on which you turn left (east). After the pavement ends you cross a sandy-bottomed creek draining Tenaya Lake that you'll probably have to wade early in the year. The trail swings right (south) just across the creek at 16.1 miles. A bit later, a trail leading back to Tuolumne Meadows Lodge goes off to the left. Your trail dips and rises now and then as it crosses several little streams; then it begins to climb the east slope above Tenaya Canyon. The switchbacking climb is relieved by views of Mount Hoffman and Tioga Road across the canyon.

At the crest of the ridge (18.5 miles), the trail splits. The right (south) fork leads back to Clouds Rest and Half Dome, and the left (east) leads to Sunrise Lakes. For a spectacular view of Half Dome and Clouds Rest, climb the little knoll to the right of the junction just a few dozen feet off the trail. From the junction follow the ridgeline for a short time, then drop into the bowl containing the first of the Sunrise Lakes, whose depth gives it a rich royal blue color. Climb out of the bowl and follow along its south rim. The second Sunrise Lake, only occasionally visible, lies below the trail to the north and offers better camping than the first one. The route crosses a smooth, round lump of classic exfoliating Yosemite granite to reach the uppermost, and largest, of the lakes. There are plenty of camping spaces along the north shore, but the area is showing signs of overuse. Continue up a moderate hill alongside a wildflower-lined creek until reaching a wide, sandy saddle with scattered mountain hemlock and pine where the jagged Clark Range defines the horizon to the south. The trail eases gently down to the backpack camp above and behind the High Sierra Camp. There is a toilet, piped water, and a few bear boxes.

Just downhill at 21.1 miles, the trail meets a junction with the John Muir/Pacific Crest Trail. Turn left and follow the deeply worn ruts along the edge of the meadow to Sunrise High Sierra Camp. From the High Sierra Camp, head north on the John Muir Trail to a junction at 22.0 miles with Cathedral Pass Trail. Turn right (east), cross the stream and the meadow, and climb to the Cathedral Fork of Echo Creek. The trail swings south and descends, crossing a couple of tributaries of the Cathedral Fork,

You'll find Fletcher Lake and whitebark pine at Vogelsang High Sierra Camp.

to meet the main branch, which you cross on a bridge to the south side, then back to the northeast side again on a second bridge. There are great views up the Merced River Canyon from here.

In about a half mile, meet a cutoff back to the John Muir Trail to the west at 28.1 miles. Continue ahead (south) to reach the Merced Lake Trail in Echo Valley at 28.9 miles. There is space for camping here, but the area has been burned over more than once and is not very attractive. Turn right (east). Just past the junction cross several little branches of Echo Creek yet again and follow the Merced River upstream along its north shore. Pass through a gate to arrive at Merced Lake, whose edge you skirt very closely, pass the marshy meadow at the lake's upper end, then meet the spur to the Merced Lake High Sierra camp at 31.0 miles. The backpack camp is just beyond.

Now on your way to Vogelsang, walk east through lodgepole pine and fir forest, crossing several little creeks on footbridges. At 31.3 miles the Merced Lake Ranger Station and corral appear on the right. Turn left (north) at the junction here and switchback steeply up above Lewis Creek to meet the Fletcher Creek Trail at 32.3 miles. There are good views up the Fletcher Creek drainage and back down to Merced Lake.

You have two choices of routes to Vogelsang from this point. The Fletcher Creek Trail passes to the west of Vogelsang Peak and is shorter by about a mile. The Lewis Creek Trail passes to the east and is the one described here because, though it is longer, it is much more scenic and less frequently used. Following the right fork, you pass the cutoff to the Isberg Pass Trail at 33.3 miles. Continue northeast past the

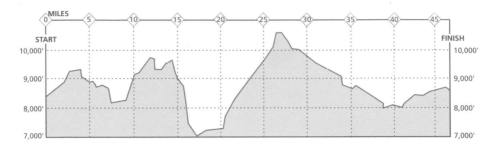

confluence with Florence Creek with its beautiful little waterfall, past the cutoff to Bernice Lake at 36.3 miles, and toil up the open rocky grade to Vogelsang Pass, the highest point on the loop at almost 11,000 feet (37.7 miles). The view back down Lewis Creek is spectacular, with the entire Clark Range spread out to the south. Across the drainage lonely Gallison and Bernice Lakes nestle in their barren cirques. Round a corner at the top of the pass, skirt some tiny ponds, then descend the boulder-y slope to Vogelsang Lake at the base of Vogelsang Peak, where fat marmot sentries watch and whistle alarm calls from nearby rocks. Cross the lake's outlet on logs and wind down the partly rocky, partly muddy slope toward the huddle of white tents of the High Sierra Camp below. The outlet stream just behind the camp comes from unseen Fletcher Lake around the corner; cross it on a log and make your way around to the front of the Vogelsang High Sierra Camp at a junction at 39.0 miles. The backpack camping area, with toilets and a few bear boxes, is on the north side of Fletcher Lake, east of the High Sierra Camp.

When you are ready to return to Tuolumne Meadows, find the signed junction in front of the High Sierra Camp and descend north, then northeast, gently down the ridge above Boothe Lake to Tuolumne Pass, where you will find another junction at 39.8 miles. Turn right and continue gently downhill along Rafferty Creek for a long stretch, sometimes through forest, sometimes along the edge of the meadow. Toward the end the descent steepens and at last switchbacks down to a junction with the John Muir Trail at 45.3 miles. Keep left to mile 45.9, where your trail turns right. The other fork goes into the back of the Tuolumne Meadows Campground. In a few dozen yards, cross the twin bridges over Lyell Fork of the Tuolumne River and enjoy one of the most sublime vistas in all of Yosemite southward up the canyon. Now just follow the signs through the forest to the Tuolumne Meadows Lodge/High Sierra Camp at mile 46.6. From here you can walk the spur road back to the Tioga Road and follow that westward back to your car near Lembert Dome.

Miles and Directions

0.0 Glen Aulin Trailhead
0.5 Soda Springs
0.6 Parsons Lodge; turn right, then left
1.2 Ford Delaney Creek

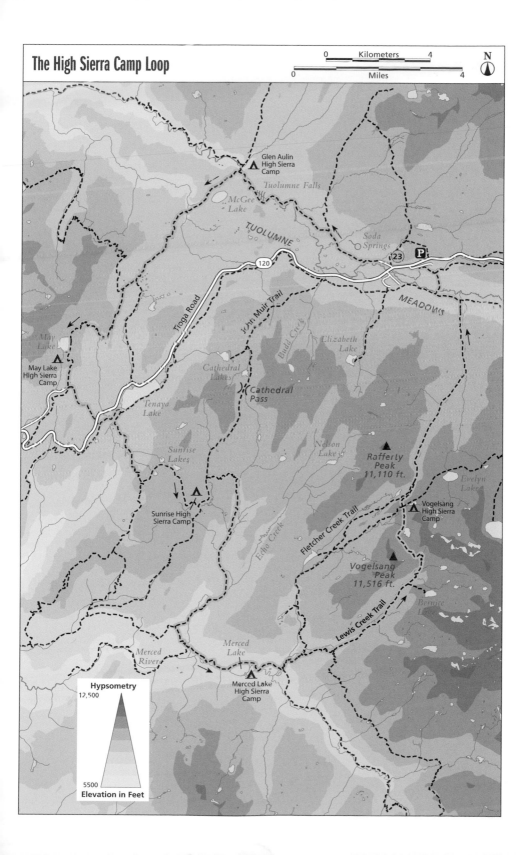

The High Sierra Camp Loop

Kilometers
0   4

Miles
0   4

N

Glen Aulin
High Sierra
Camp

Tuolumne Falls

McGee
Lake

TUOLUMNE

Soda
Springs

120

23

P

MEADOWS

May
Lake

May Lake
High Sierra
Camp

Tioga Road

John Muir Trail

Budd Creek

Elizabeth
Lake

Cathedral
Lakes

Cathedral
Pass

Tenaya
Lake

Sunrise
Lakes

Nelson
Lake

Rafferty
Peak
11,110 ft.

Evelyn
Lake

Sunrise High
Sierra Camp

Echo Creek

Fletcher Creek Trail

Vogelsang
High Sierra
Camp

Vogelsang
Peak
11,516 ft.

Bernice
Lake

Lewis Creek Trail

Merced
River

Merced
Lake

Merced Lake
High Sierra
Camp

Hypsometry
12,500

5500
Elevation in Feet

1.6   Young Lakes cutoff; keep left

3.5   Cross bridges over the Tuolumne River

5.0   May Lake and McGee Lake Trail junction; turn right

5.2   Glen Aulin High Sierra Camp

5.4   Return to May Lake Trail junction; turn right

9.6   Murphy Creek Trail; keep right

10.0   May Lake Trail junction; turn left

13.3   May Lake High Sierra Camp

14.5   Cross May Lake Trailhead road

15.9   Cross Tioga Road; turn left

16.0   Sunrise Trailhead

18.5   Clouds Rest/Sunrise Lakes Trail junction; turn left

21.1   Sunrise High Sierra Camp and John Muir Trail junction

22.0   Cathedral Pass Trail junction; turn right, leaving John Muir Trail

28.1   Cutoff back to the John Muir Trail

28.9   Echo Valley; turn right

31.0   Merced Lake High Sierra Camp

31.3   Merced Lake Ranger Station; turn left

32.3   Fletcher Creek Trail junction; turn right

33.3   Isberg Pass Trail cutoff

36.3   Bernice Lake cutoff

37.7   Vogelsang Pass

39.0   Vogelsang High Sierra Camp

39.8   Boothe Lake junction; turn right

45.3   Rejoin John Muir Trail; keep left

45.9   Tuolumne Meadows High Sierra Camp cutoff; turn right

46.6   Tuolumne Meadows Lodge/High Sierra Camp

47.6   Return to Glen Aulin Trailhead

The Southern Park

The trails into the southern park begin from Wawona, Glacier Point Road, or the short spur road off CA 41 to the Mariposa Grove of Big Trees. Most trailheads start at around 4,000 feet and offer hiking opportunities earlier in the season than in other parts of Yosemite. You'll find more solitude in this part of the park, too, because there is less water in high summer, the time when most people come to Yosemite. The crown of the southern park is Mount Clark, whose distinctive, narrow summit can be seen from many miles away.

Many of the southern trails begin near Wawona, the site of a historical overnight stage stop on the way to Yosemite Valley. The beautiful old Wawona Hotel, built in the 1870s, is still in operation. You can visit the Pioneer Yosemite History Center to learn about the early days of Yosemite, or even play a round of golf. There is a campground, gas station, gift shop, grocery store, and stables. Wawona is about 4 miles inside the park from the CA 41 entrance to Yosemite. Just past "town" a new bridge crosses the Merced River, and just past that is Chilnualna Fall Road on the right. Many of the trailheads out of Wawona are off this road, all are clearly marked, and all have parking areas and bear boxes. The road ends just past North Wawona, a little settlement with a store and a few cottages for rent. It is part of an inholding (private property surrounded by a national park). You can get information and wilderness permits at the wilderness center located in Hill's Studio, right next door to the Wawona Hotel.

Another approach to the southern park is by way of Chiquito Pass in the Ansel Adams Wilderness, part of the Sierra National Forest at the southeast corner of Yosemite. The drive to the trailhead is a long one, but the rewards are great. This is some of the finest hiking in Yosemite: classic glacial scenery, abundant water well into fall, and fewer people. You can get into this area from Wawona on a 2- or 3-day, pleasant but unspectacular trip, but the Chiquito Pass trailhead puts you into prime high country in only 2 miles.

Since the trailhead is outside of Yosemite, wilderness permits are issued by the Sierra National Forest. You can reserve a permit by mail or pick one up on a first-come, first-served basis from the Wilderness Office in Oakhurst. They can also give you information about road conditions. Call them at (559) 877-2218. You can get gas and supplies, restaurants, and accommodations at the resort town of Bass Lake, 20 miles from the trailhead. There is camping nearby at both Upper and Lower Chiquito Campgrounds.

24 Mariposa Grove of Big Trees

The giant sequoias are the largest living things on earth and are among the oldest, living up to 3,000 years. The bristlecone pines in the White Mountains to the east are older, and the coast redwoods are taller, but these are certainly the most massive and arguably the most awe-inspiring. The Mariposa Grove, the largest of three in Yosemite, is divided into upper and lower groves. A veritable maze of trails, all well marked, runs through both, so you can easily design your own hike to be longer or shorter than the one described here. This hike takes you past all the highlights of both groves with a minimum amount of backtracking. Trails are marked by a series of interpretive panels with fascinating bits of information about the trees and their habitat.

Start: Mariposa Grove shuttle bus station at Wawona

Total distance: 5.9-mile double loop

Hiking time: 2 hours to all day

Difficulty: Moderate, but only because there are some relatively steep ups and downs

Elevation change: 1,000 feet

Seasons: Spring, summer, and fall, whenever the road is open

Permits: None

Nearest facilities: Store and gas at Wawona; restrooms and water at the trailhead and the museum

Map: USGS Mariposa Grove quad

Finding the trailhead: From the entrance station to Yosemite on Wawona Road (CA 41), head left (west) for 4 miles to Wawona, where you can board a free shuttle bus to the trailhead at the Mariposa Grove. There is no parking at the trailhead, so park at the lot across the street from the entrance station or in front of the store at Wawona and take the free shuttle bus to the grove. The buses run every 20 minutes. Trailhead GPS: N37 30.09 / W119 36.35

The Hike

From the trailhead follow the signed trail eastward to the Fallen Monarch at mile 0.1, a sequoia made famous by old photos of a group of US Cavalry—on their horses—lined up on top of it. In 2008 a small fire blackened a section of the grove near the beginning of the trail, creating an opportunity for you to observe how the forest regenerates itself over time. Follow the trail on past a beautiful grouping of trees called the Bachelor and the Three Graces at 0.3 mile, then climb to the massive, beheaded Grizzly Giant at 0.8 mile, said to be the largest tree in the grove. Walk around to the far side of the Grizzly Giant and follow the path 0.1 mile downhill to the California Tunnel Tree. The tunnel was cut in 1895 for stagecoaches full of tourists to pass through. Some things never change. Go through the Tunnel Tree and continue uphill northwest to the Faithful Couple at 1.6 miles: two trees that have grown so closely together that they appear to be one at the base. Cross the tram road to reach the aptly named Clothespin Tree, and at 2.0 miles reach a somewhat confusing four-way

▶ Between 2015 and 2017 the Mariposa Grove has undergone a dramatic restoration. The grove had been losing its tranquil, cathedral-like atmosphere over the years to the chatter of tour buses and the noise and bustle of the gift shop and parking lot. Worse, the giant sequoias themselves were being threatened by the stamping of innumerable feet that compacted the soil over their shallow roots and disrupted the normal flow of water through the grove. The National Park Service and the Yosemite Conservancy together, in an effort to "preserve the grove and sequoias while enhancing the visitor experience," have removed the parking lot, gift shop, and tram tours, replacing pavement with boardwalks and trails and reestablishing sequoia habitat.

trail junction. Just follow the signs there to the museum at 2.2 miles, in a lovely little meadow with a nature trail through it. The museum has exhibits and books about the trees, a knowledgeable volunteer to answer questions, a water fountain, and restrooms nearby.

From the museum head north. You are in the upper grove now; the crowds will have thinned, and the still, solemn dignity of the forest begins to settle over you . . . unless you are joined by a chattering, scolding chickaree, or Douglas squirrel (not to be confused with the chickadee, a small bird that also resides here). Chickarees are among the most entertaining creatures of sequoia and fir forests, lively and quick and very vocal. Their backs are gray-brown, their undersides buffy white. A black racing stripe running horizontally along the body separates top from bottom. They play an important role in giant sequoia reproduction.

At 2.7 miles look downhill to the right to spot the Fallen Wawona Tunnel Tree. This is the highest point on the hike at 6,600 feet. There's not much to see now, but from 1881, when the tunnel was cut through the standing Big Tree, this was one of the most popular tourist attractions in California. In 1969 a heavy snowfall finally toppled it. Continue toward the south, following the signs to the Telescope Tree at 3.1 miles. It's off the trail a few yards to the left. Don't miss the experience of standing inside and gazing up and out the top of a still living tree.

Continue on downhill back to the four-way junction at 3.6 miles, then follow the signs back to the trailhead.

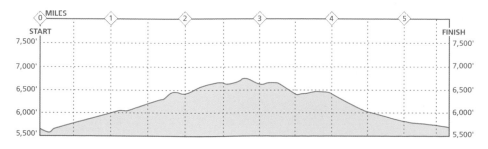

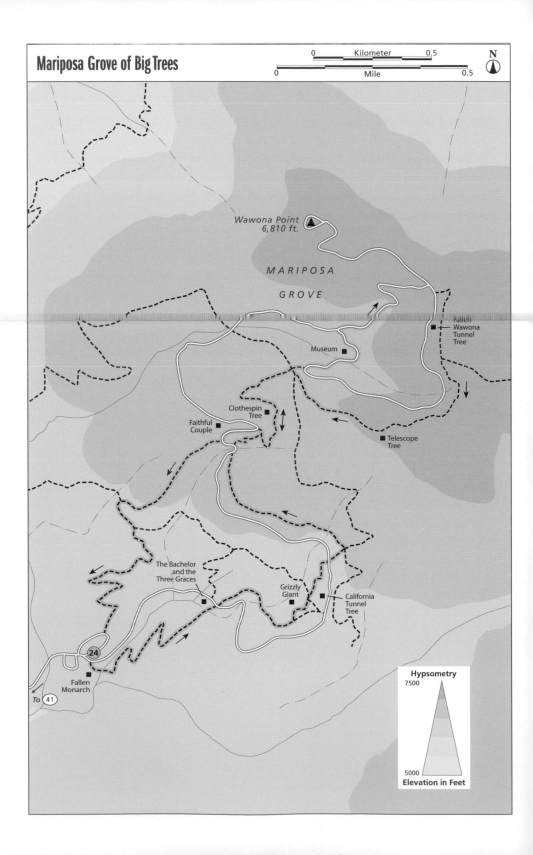

Mariposa Grove of Big Trees

Kilometer
0   0.5

Mile
0   0.5

N

Wawona Point
6,810 ft.

MARIPOSA

GROVE

Fallen
Wawona
Tunnel
Tree

Museum

Clothespin
Tree

Faithful
Couple

Telescope
Tree

The Bachelor
and the
Three Graces

Grizzly
Giant

California
Tunnel
Tree

24

Fallen
Monarch

To 41

Hypsometry
7500

5000
Elevation in Feet

Miles and Directions

0.0 Trailhead

0.3 Bachelor and the Three Graces

0.8 Grizzly Giant

1.6 Faithful Couple

2.0 Clothespin Tree

2.2 Museum

2.7 Fallen Wawona Tunnel Tree

3.1 Telescope Tree

3.6 Return to four-way trail junction; take path to the left (southwest) back to the Clothespin Tree

5.9 Return to trailhead

Options: Wawona Point and Wawona–Mariposa Grove Trail—From either the museum or the Fallen Wawona Tunnel Tree, Wawona Point is only 1 mile more (round-trip) and 200 feet of climbing to the top of the ridge at 6,810 feet for a bird's-eye view of the whole Wawona area with the Merced River snaking through the middle.

The Wawona–Mariposa Grove Trail takes you to (or from) the Mariposa Grove on foot. The distance from the Grizzly Giant back to the Wawona Hotel is 6.5 miles, with an elevation change of about 1,700 feet. It can be a long, hot, dusty, and smelly hike round-trip because the elevation is low and the lower section of the trail is used regularly by horses, but many hikers take the shuttle bus from Wawona up to the Mariposa Grove and walk this route back down.

Douglas squirrels, also known as chickarees, play an important role in sequoia reproduction.

In Addition

Making Baby Sequoias

You don't have to know anything at all about giant sequoia ecology to enjoy the sense of wonder that a stroll through one of these enchanted groves brings. Still, even a superficial study of the trees reveals one surprise after another, each one deepening your respect and admiration.

Despite their immense size and great age, they are dependent for their very existence on the unlikely aid of a beetle, a squirrel, and fire.

The average Big Tree might have as many as 11,000 cones on it at any one time, dispersing up to 400,000 seeds. That ought to be enough to produce dozens of seedlings, but getting these seeds planted and germinated isn't easy and the trees can't do it without help. The cones and the seeds within them are very small. Unlike many other conifers, sequoias do not drop their cones from the tree when they are ripe, nor do the cones open while still on the tree, dropping their seeds to the ground. The seeds must get planted some other way.

Fortunately, Douglas squirrels, also called chickarees, love to eat the young green scales of Big Tree cones. They are territorial creatures whose loud, scolding chatter warns neighboring chickarees to "stay away from *my* tree." They may begin gnawing into the cone scales right on the branch where they are found, opening the cones and allowing the seeds to fall. (Sequoia seeds are so tiny that most animals do not seek them for food.) At other times, the chickarees cut down enormous numbers of cones, gather the pile from beneath the tree, and cache them away to eat later. They usually pick dark, damp storage places to keep the cones moist and fresh, but some do dry out and release the seeds into the soil.

A much less conspicuous animal, a small wood-boring beetle, does her bit for the giant sequoia by depositing her eggs in the seams where the bracts or scales of the cone fit together. When the babies hatch, they chew their way inside, frequently cutting the vessels that supply the cones with water and minerals. The scales dry out, shrink, and separate, and the seeds fall out.

Fire plays several roles in sequoia health and reproduction. Intense heat helps to dry the cones so that the seeds can be released, clears the ground beneath the trees of litter, and keeps the soil soft and light so the tiny seeds can germinate. The groves have obviously coexisted with fire for millennia. Almost every mature tree in the grove shows the scars of repeated burns. Their bark is extremely thick, lacks much flammable pitch, and is impregnated with fire-resistant tannins. Our misdirected efforts to protect the groves from fires over the past few decades have almost been their undoing. Until recently, when more information about the ecology of the giant sequoias became available, we had been carrying out an unintended program of Big Tree birth control.

25 Chilnualna Fall

Chilnualna Creek seldom flows slowly, but instead tumbles in cascades and waterfalls almost constantly for most of its length. The most spectacular sections and highest waterfalls are found at the beginning and end of the hike, and the trail has been built so that it comes closest to the river at the beginning and end. It's a steady, uphill pull, but the grade is comfortable. This route would be much more heavily used if it were not tucked away in a little corner of Yosemite. The waterfall is as exciting as any in Yosemite Valley, but few tourists know about it.

Start: Chilnualna Fall Trailhead off Chilnualna Fall Road

Total distance: 8.2 miles out and back

Hiking time: 6 to 8 hours

Difficulty: Moderate; it's short, but all uphill

Elevation change: 2,100 feet

Seasons: Spring, early summer, and fall; midsummer is hot, fall is pleasant but disappointing

Nearest facilities: Food, gas, and phones in North Wawona

Permits: None required for a day hike; available for overnights in advance or at Wawona

Maps: USGS Wawona and Mariposa Grove quads

Special considerations: Watch for rattlesnakes in this low-elevation area, especially in the morning and evening hours. They're not aggressive, but they do not like to be handled or stepped on.

Finding the trailhead: Follow Chilnualna Fall Road from Wawona through the little village of North Wawona for 2 miles to a signed parking lot on the right. Trailhead GPS: N37 32.53/W119 38.09

The Hike

Follow the trail signs from the parking lot and cross the paved road. Another sign there routes horse traffic to the left and foot traffic to the right. The footpath, much too rugged for horses, heads steeply up, sometimes on big granite stairsteps right beside the roaring water, then cuts away from the stream where the horse and foot trails rejoin in 0.2 mile at a big trail sign. Long, wide switchbacks make the northward climb almost painless. The forest floor is covered with a solid carpet of the white shrub called kit-kit-dizze under oak, pine, and incense cedar. At about a mile the trail switchbacks to a point near the creek, then climbs out of reach of water until very near the end of the hike, except for little tributary streams that are reliable only in early season. Views of the sensuous, rounded curve of Wawona Dome come and go. As you gain height, more of Chilnualna's upper fall comes into view behind clouds of rising mist. When the trail approaches the elevation of the falls, it rounds a ridge blasted out of the rock by dynamite and deposits the hiker right beside the

Chilnualna Fall, though relatively unknown, is one of Yosemite's most dramatic in springtime.

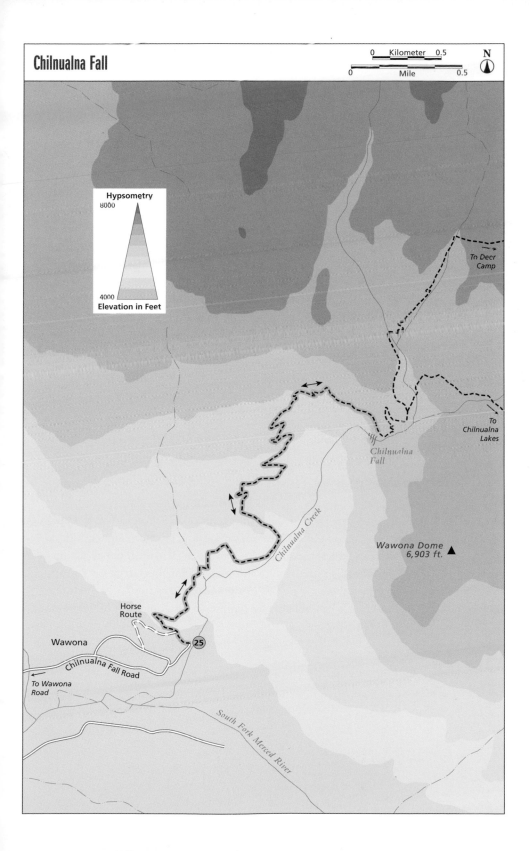

Chilnualna Fall

Hypsometry

8000

4000
Elevation in Feet

0 Kilometer 0.5
0 Mile 0.5

N

To Deer Camp

To Chilnualna Lakes

Chilnualna Fall

Chilnualna Creek

Wawona Dome
6,903 ft. ▲

Horse Route

Wawona

Chilnualna Fall Road

25

To Wawona Road

South Fork Merced River

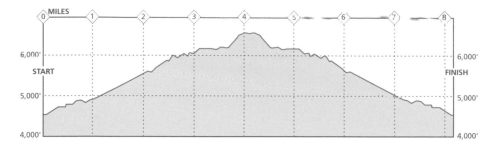

thundering cataract. Brilliant magenta mountain pride penstemon line cracks in the streamside rocks. From here you can see all the way back down to Wawona Meadow.

Climb a few more hot and brushy switchbacks until the trail emerges onto slabs of classic, scoured, exfoliating Yosemite granite, to an even more dramatic section of the falls. The smooth rock near the water invites exploration, but move carefully—the rocks are slippery and it's a long way down. A sign at a trail junction tells you that it is 5.6 miles back to Wawona, but that is the distance to the ranger station where the trailhead used to be, not to the one where you began. This is the end point of your day hike. Return the way you came.

Miles and Directions

0.0 Chilnualna Fall Trailhead; keep right at horse/foot trail split

0.2 Horse and foot trail rejoin; continue uphill

1.0 Trail is nearest the creek

4.1 Chilnualna Fall

8.2 Return to Chilnualna Fall Trailhead

Options: Bridalveil Creek Campground and Chilnualna Lakes—You can make Chilnualna Fall just the first leg of a multiday, early season outing. From the signed fork of the trail at the falls, you can go left for another 8.9 miles to Bridalveil Creek Campground on Glacier Point Road, or turn right, following Chilnualna Creek for 7 miles, to Chilnualna Lakes on the Buena Vista Crest Loop. There are campsites in the forest above Chilnualna Fall within a half mile of the trail junction along both routes.

26 Buena Vista Crest

This area returns lots of rewards for little effort. Elevations are low, so it is accessible when the higher country is still under snow, yet there is plenty of glacially sculpted scenery and lots of lakes, including Royal Arch Lake, one of the prettiest in the park. You can hike this lollipop-shaped loop in either direction, but the elevation gain is more gradual if you travel clockwise.

Start: Bridalveil Creek Campground Trailhead
Total distance: 28.2-mile lollipop
Hiking time: 3 to 6 days
Difficulty: Moderate in 3 days, easy in 4 to 6 days
Elevation change: 2,600 feet
Seasons: Early summer through fall, though many streams are dry by Aug
Nearest facilities: North Wawona, snacks and phones at Glacier Point
Permits: Required; available at the wilderness center in Wawona

Maps: USGS Half Dome and Mariposa Grove quads
Special considerations: This low-elevation country is at its finest before mid-July, when water sources become fewer and farther apart and wildflowers are past their prime. To experience this region of Yosemite at its best, you need to be prepared for swampy meadows and dicey stream crossings. The trail is sometimes flooded in the Chilnualna Lakes basin, making route-finding tricky. Carry a map, extra dry socks, and insect repellent. The scenery is worth the wet feet.

Finding the trailhead: Drive up Glacier Point Road 9 miles to the Bridalveil Creek Campground turnoff on the right. Turn in and drive straight through the campground to its south end. Just as the road begins to curve left, signs on the right say "Campfire Circle" and "Horse Camp 0.2 Mile." The trailhead is just beyond the signs. Because parking space is somewhat cramped, the trailhead sign will probably be hidden behind parked cars. Trailhead GPS: N37 39.42/W119 37.13

The Hike

Begin walking in a southeasterly direction along Bridalveil Creek. Yellow metal signs high up in the lodgepole pines mark cross-country ski trails. The trail rambles through forests and meadows filled with wildflowers. At 1.4 miles a side trail cuts back toward Glacier Point Road to connect with the Ostrander Lake Trail. This junction lies in a ghost forest of lodgepole pines that was burned in 1987, leaving ideal conditions for a spectacular wildflower display. Pass a campsite (arguably illegal; too near the stream and the trail), hop a branch of the creek, and at 2.2 miles meet a second trail that angles back to the northwest to meet the Ostrander Lake Trail again. Your path crosses a couple of small streams that may be dry by midsummer, then climbs moderately up a slope under both white and red fir glowing with chartreuse lichens.

The way becomes steeper and warmer as the forest cover thins to brush, then opens up in a sunny ridgetop clearing carpeted in pastels: yellow sulfur flower buckwheat, pink pussypaws, and blue Brewer's lupine. Top out at 7,650 feet, drop back down into forest, then slosh through a boggy meadow to reach another trail junction at 4.7 miles where the Deer Camp Trail takes off to the right (west). Continue south past Turner Meadow, waist-deep in corn lilies, to yet another trail junction at 6.0 miles, beyond which there is a good campsite. Continue along the left (southeast) fork until, at 6.7 miles, you reach the junction that marks the beginning of the loop part of the hike. Follow the trail sign left (east) toward Chilnualna and Buena Vista Lakes and climb along Chilnualna Creek until you reach the first of the lakes at 10.2 miles. There is plenty of good camping here. The lake is shallow, small, tranquil, and lovely in early season, but is rapidly silting-in on its way to becoming a meadow. It loses much of its appeal by August, though by that time the blueberry bushes surrounding the lake are loaded with fruit.

Leaving the first lake, pass over a low rise, hop over the outlet of the second Chilnualna Lake, about a half mile off the trail to the east, then skirt the third lake, which offers some camping that may be swampy and mosquito-ridden early in the year. Sometimes sections of the trail become completely inundated, so you

Graceful arches of granite crown Royal Arch Lake.

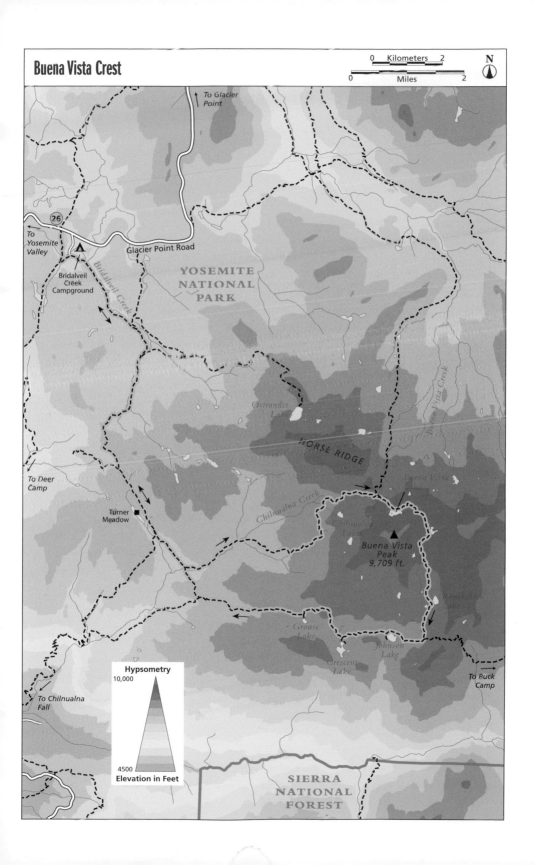

Buena Vista Crest

0   Kilometers   2
0   Miles   2

N

To Glacier
Point

26

To
Yosemite
Valley

Glacier Point Road

Bridalveil
Creek
Campground

Bridalveil Creek

YOSEMITE
NATIONAL
PARK

Ostrander
Lake

HORSE RIDGE

Buena Vista Creek

Buena Vista
Lake

To Deer
Camp

Turner
Meadow

Chilnualna Creek

Chilnualna
Lake

Buena Vista
Peak
9,709 ft.

Royal Arch
Lake

Grouse
Lake

Johnson
Lake

Crescent
Lake

To Buck
Camp

Hypsometry
10,000

To Chilnualna
Fall

4500
Elevation in Feet

SIERRA
NATIONAL
FOREST

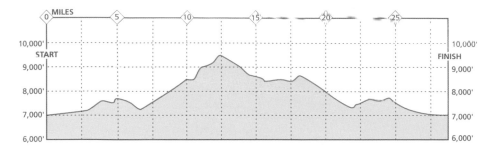

will have to consult your map and watch for tree blazes to stay on course. Climb up out of the lake basin along a rubbly granite slope where the foliage parts at the top to unveil a fabulous vista all the way to the Cathedral Range to the north. To the east dramatic Mount Clark pulls the colorful Clark Range—Red Peak, Gray Peak, Merced Peak—behind it on a collision course with Half Dome and Mount Starr King. Here, at 11.9 miles, a trail heads northward toward Mono Meadow on Glacier Point Road, but your route continues straight ahead to Buena Vista Lake, sparkling in its glacial cirque at 12.2 miles. The highest point on the ridge above the lake is Buena Vista Peak (9,709 feet), an easy scramble. There is plenty of good camping here.

Climb out of this lake basin, then to Buena Vista Pass—the highest point on this loop at 9,300 feet—at 12.8 miles, then descend, first through flowery meadows, then over exfoliating granite slabs, and finally through forest. You'll emerge at the small but stunning Royal Arch Lake at 15.0 miles. Hugh granite slabs have popped free and peeled away from the underlying rock like layers of onion, leaving graceful arches that frame the lake. There is limited camping at the south end of the lake. Be sure to camp at least 100 feet from the fragile lakeshore.

As you proceed downhill, the Buck Creek Trail cuts off to the left (east) at 15.7 miles. Your route turns right (west) and descends past grassy Johnson Lake, then ascends to Crescent Lake, about a half mile farther where there are better campsites—and blueberries! Rock-hop your way across Crescent Lake's inlet stream, cross a moraine dotted with red fir, and pass Grouse Lake (hidden in the trees to your left; watch for a cairn and a faint trail on the left). Continue down, down, down to a junction at 20.7 miles, where you turn right (north). The left fork leads back to Wawona via Chilnualna Fall. Very soon, at 21.5 miles, you rock-hop Chilnualna Creek to meet the junction closing the loop section of your hike. From here retrace the "stick" portion of the lollipop to the trailhead at Bridalveil Creek Campground.

Miles and Directions

0.9 Trailhead at Bridalveil Creek Campground

1.4 Connector trail to Ostrander Lake Trail; continue straight ahead

2.2 Second connector trail to Ostrander Lake Trail; continue straight ahead (south)

4.7   Deer Camp Trail junction; go left

6.0   Chilnualna Fall Trail junction; keep left

6.7   Chilnualna Lakes junction; keep left. The loop part of the hike begins here.

10.2 First Chilnualna Lake

11.9 Mono Meadow Trail junction; continue slightly right

12.2 Buena Vista Lake

12.8 Buena Vista Pass

15.0 Royal Arch Lake

15.7 Buck Creek Trail junction; keep right

20.7 Wawona via Chilnualna Fall junction; keep right

21.5 Chilnualna Lakes Trail junction; keep left. This closes the loop part of the hike.

28.2 Return to trailhead at Bridalveil Creek Campground

27 Wawona Meadow

This is one of Yosemite's often-overlooked gems, especially for wildflower lovers, who will find some rare and unusual species blooming in early season. Except for an occasional group of equestrians, you'll have this little piece of the park mostly to yourself. The going is easy along a dirt road no longer used by vehicles, with almost no elevation change. The route is a loop, described in a counterclockwise direction, but you can go either way.

Start: Wawona Meadow Trailhead at a big signboard with photos and information about the area
Total distance: 3.5-mile loop
Hiking time: 1 hour if you jog, most of a day if you botanize
Difficulty: Easy

Elevation change: 200 feet
Seasons: May and June for wildflowers, though the trail is open all year
Nearest facilities: Wawona
Permits: None
Map: USGS Wawona quad

Finding the trailhead: Drive to the little village of Wawona on the Wawona Road (CA 41). The Wawona Hotel is on the north side of the road; the golf course is on the south. Just across from the hotel, a road cuts through the middle of the golf course to a parking area and trailhead marked with a big sign. Trailhead GPS: N37 32.11 / W119 39.23

The Hike

Begin by skirting the south side of the golf course under a cover of incense cedar and ponderosa pine. Very soon the manicured lawn of the golf course is left behind and the real meadow begins. The trail runs between forest and meadow for most of the way, and this border zone, known as the ecotone, is usually the richest in living organisms. You are almost guaranteed a cluster of mule deer. They are very tame, but do not attempt to pet or feed them. Deer account for more serious injuries in Yosemite than bears.

Now and then a little spur trail leads out into the meadow. It can be boggy and muddy toward the center and the vegetation is fragile, so step with care. Down among the grasses and sedges, look for little three-petaled white star tulips in May. The tall, cabbage-like stalks growing in clumps are poisonous corn lily, sometimes confused with skunk cabbage. There are islands of willow and chokecherry, usually broadcasting birdsong selections from warblers and blackbirds.

On the shady forest floor, watch for leafless, fleshy plants that live on decaying material in the soil like the scarlet snow plant; the knobby, brown spikes of pinedrops; and the odd little orchids, like coral root. You can even find lady's slipper orchids in

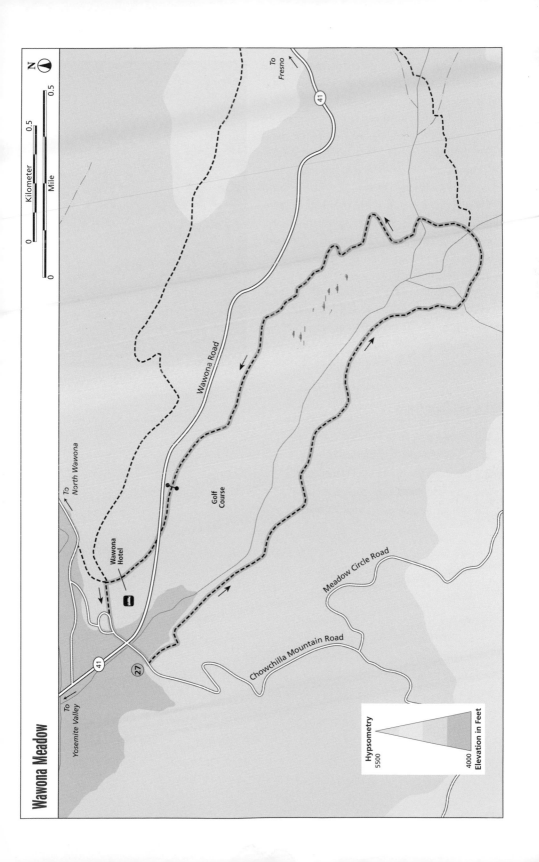

damp patches. In June great fragrant clumps of western azalea burst into bloom, along with several kinds of lilies.

At 1.7 miles another trail coming down from the Mariposa Grove joins the road from the right alongside a little creek. Stay on the road and step across another little chokecherry-lined rivulet flowing around rock islands crowded with monkey flowers. The road becomes partly eroded asphalt and runs through a section of forest in which the bases of the trees are slightly blackened from a management fire.

At 3.2 miles reach a closed gate, and just beyond it cross Wawona Road. The trail continues on to the Wawona Hotel, where, at 3.4 miles, it crosses the road to the south side again and cuts back through the golf course to the trailhead.

Damp and shady forest floor is home to this lady's slipper orchid.

Miles and Directions

0.0 Wawona Meadow Trailhead

1.7 Creek crossing and trail junction; stay on the road

3.2 Wawona Road; cross to the north side

3.4 Wawona Road; cross back to the south side

3.5 Return to Wawona Meadow Trailhead

28 Ostrander Lake

The stone hut at Ostrander Lake is a favorite winter destination for skiers. In summer there is good camping near the lakeside and lots of flowers along the way. The out-and-back trail is relatively flat at the beginning, undulates a bit in the middle, and leaves most of the serious elevation gain for the end.

Start: Ostrander Lake Trailhead off Glacier Point Road

Total distance: 12.4 miles out and back

Hiking time: 5 to 10 hours

Difficulty: Strenuous as a day hike, moderate as a backpack

Elevation change: 1,600 feet

Seasons: All summer, whenever the Glacier Point Road is open

Nearest facilities: Wawona; snacks and phones at Glacier Point

Permits: None for a day hike; available for overnights at Wawona or Yosemite Valley

Maps: USGS Half Dome and Mariposa Grove quads

Finding the trailhead: Drive up the Glacier Point Road about 9 miles from the Chinquapin turnoff on the Wawona Road (CA 41) to a marked parking area on the right, about a mile past (east of) the turnoff to the Bridalveil Creek Campground. (Glacier Point shuttle bus does not stop here.) Trailhead GPS: N37 40.02 / W119 36.13

The Hike

The trail begins in a dense growth of young lodgepole pines jostling one another for sun and space. The forest was burned in 1987, opening the ground to sunshine and flowers and vigorous new trees. The tall dead snags still standing are good habitat for woodpeckers, and those still decomposing host brown creepers, mountain chickadees, and northern flickers harvesting insects in the decaying wood. In the more open places, yarrow, paintbrush, lupine, goldenrod, and tall, purple fireweed grow in a riot of color; in the marshier areas are willow, lilies, yampah, and Bigelow's sneezeweed— nature renewing itself in a flamboyant explosion of new life. At 1.7 miles find a junction with a trail that cuts back to the right to join the Bridalveil Creek Campground Trail; keep left and continue on through alternating sun and shade to a second fork, where in a little clearing another connector trail turns right to join Bridalveil Creek in another place. You keep left again.

You'll probably notice that the mileage figures on the trail signs at this junction do not agree. Don't let it confuse you. The difference is slight and the route is the same. Past this point there is only an occasional burned snag among the flourishing white fir and ponderosa pine. This is fortunate for the hiker, because now the trail begins to climb. Traces of old asphalt appear underfoot, evidence that this used to be a road. The trail leaves the forest and passes over open rock slabs skirting the base of domelike

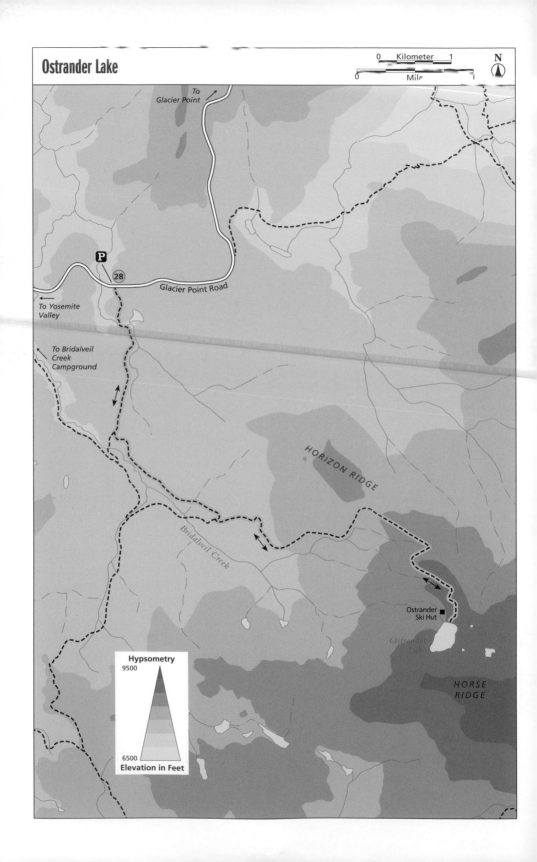

Ostrander Lake

0   Kilometer   1

0   Mile   1

N

To
Glacier Point

P

(28)

Glacier Point Road

← To Yosemite
Valley

← To Bridalveil
Creek
Campground

HORIZON RIDGE

Bridalveil Creek

Ostrander
Ski Hut

*Ostrander
Lake*

HORSE
RIDGE

Hypsometry

9500

6500

Elevation in Feet

The stone ski hut sits next to Ostrander Lake.

Horizon Ridge among patches of low-growing manzanita and silvery sagebrush. Now it swings northward to a saddle, abruptly turns southeast to climb straight up a smooth, rounded hill, then makes one broad switchback before reaching the summit. A worn path on the left leads to a view of Half Dome and Mount Starr King, and behind the trees to the right, the Clark Range.

The main trail now descends through a pure stand of red fir and drops into the rocky basin containing Ostrander Lake at 6.2 miles. Horse Ridge, a wonderful example of exfoliating granite, bounds the lake on the south. Its overhanging brow makes it distinguishable from many miles away, even though it is not very high. The ski hut overlooks the lake on the north; campsites are found to the west. A sign on the hut warns winter visitors not to attempt to cross Horse Ridge due to avalanche danger. Enjoy lunch or set up camp, then return the way you came.

Miles and Directions

0.0   Ostrander Lake Trailhead
1.7   First connector trail to Bridalveil Creek Campground; keep left
2.3   Second connector trail to Bridalveil Creek Trail; keep left again
6.2   Ostrander Hut
12.4 Return to Ostrander Lake Trailhead

29 Ottoway Lakes

This is the shortest route into the rugged and remote Clark Range. The first part of the hike is through a recent burn, but the dramatic setting of the colorful Ottoway Lakes basin more than makes up for the less interesting beginning. There's a good deal of climbing involved, but nothing extremely steep, unless you decide to make the optional side trip to Red Peak Pass.

Start: Mono Meadow Trailhead off the Glacier Point Road
Total distance: 30.4 miles out and back
Hiking time: 2 to 4 days
Difficulty: Strenuous if you do it in 2 days, moderate if you take more time
Elevation change: 3,200 feet
Seasons: July through Sept

Nearest facilities: Wawona for most needs; snacks and phones at Glacier Point
Permits: Required; available in advance or from the wilderness centers in Wawona or Yosemite Valley
Maps: USGS Half Dome and Merced Peak quads

Finding the trailhead: From Wawona Road (CA 41), drive 10 miles up the Glacier Point Road from Chinquapin. (Glacier Point shuttle bus does not stop here.) The trailhead, with ample parking, is on the right. (The trailhead sign is behind the parking area. It is not visible from the road.) Trailhead GPS: N37 40.17 / W119 35.07

The Hike

From the trailhead sign drop down from the Glacier Point Road on a much-trampled soft dirt path into soggy Mono Meadow at 0.6 mile. The numerous creeklets through the meadow support a dense growth of tall wildflowers of all kinds and colors, sometimes thick enough to obscure the trail. Back in dense lodgepole pine forest, the trail crosses a tributary of Illilouette Creek. A log, slightly hidden in willows to the left, is the easiest way to the other side. A little later, after negotiating some fairly steep downhill switchbacks, arrive at a junction at 2.9 miles. The placement of the signs is confusing because there are two sets of them. Go straight past the first sign (toward Nevada Fall), and in just a few yards you'll see the second, where you turn right (east) toward Ottoway Lakes and Merced Pass.

Plod through heavy sand over open ground beneath a series of bare, rounded domes, the largest of which is Mount Starr King. Reenter what used to be Jeffrey pine forest, bleak and fire-blackened now. The trail draws nearer and nearer to the south bank of Illilouette Creek. When you are near enough to the stream to spot the trampled barren dirt below the trail where people have camped too near the water, stay alert for a line of small boulders/big rocks across the trail that indicate the ford. Pause to pick out the place where the trail resumes on the other side, between cut logs, before you start across.

Evening alpenglow illuminates Lower Ottoway Lake.

It's hard to find if you cross at a different place. The creek is wide and deep enough to go over your boot tops for most of the year, though sometimes you can find a log or rock crossing upstream by late summer. On the north side of the creek is a sandy flat and another junction at 3.1 miles. Turn right (east) toward Merced Pass. Head gradually upward, passing yet a third cutoff to the left back toward Nevada Fall at mile 4.5.

The grade through the charred remains of forest is gradual and a bit tedious until you reach the Clark Fork of Illilouette Creek at mile 5.5, above a pretty waterfall. Nearby there are a couple of campsites among trees that escaped the fire. It may not be apparent from the ground, but a glance at your map shows how many streams draining the Clark Range flow together to swell the main branch of Illilouette Creek. One of these feeder streams is Red Creek, which you cross just a few hundred yards beyond the Clark Fork. Now climb steadily alongside the northern bank of Illilouette Creek, hopping or wading several more tributary streams. None are deep enough to pose any problem in crossing, but they do inundate the trail in early season.

At 12.1 miles reach the Merced Pass junction. The right fork leads to timbered Merced Pass and on to Fernandez Pass on the eastern boundary of the park. Follow the left fork toward Ottoway Lakes. This junction lies between Upper and Lower Merced Pass Lakes, neither of which is visible from the trail. The lower lake is down in a bowl to the west of the junction. The upper one is more scenic and has some camping. Follow an unmarked trail to the east about midway between the Merced Pass and Ottoway Lake trails for a few hundred yards to find it.

As you draw nearer to Ottoway Lakes, more of the red metamorphic rock of parts of the Clark Range comes into view. Finally, at 15.2 miles, Lower Ottoway Lake appears right at the contact between the younger gray granite and the ancient red slate.

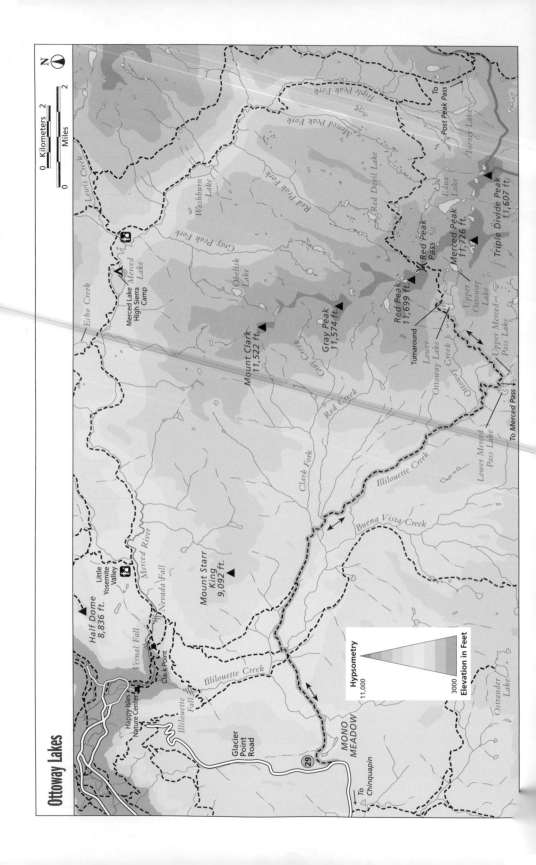

Ottoway Lakes

N

0 Kilometers 2
0 Miles 2

Hypsometry

11,000
3000
Elevation in Feet

Half Dome
8,836 ft.

Little
Yosemite
Valley

Merced River

Nevada Fall

Clark Point

Vernal Fall

Happy Isles
Nature Center

Illilouette Fall

Glacier
Point
Road

29

MONO
MEADOW

To Chinquapin

Mount Starr
King
9,092 ft.

Illilouette Creek

Clark Fork

Buena Vista Creek

Illilouette Creek

Lower Merced
Pass Lake

To Merced Pass

Ottoway Creek

Lower
Ottoway Lake

Upper
Ottoway
Lake

Upper Merced
Pass Lake

Red Creek

Red Peak
11,699 ft.

Turnaround

Gray Peak
11,574 ft.

Gray Creek

Red Peak
Pass

Merced Peak
11,726 ft.

Triple Divide Peak
11,607 ft.

Edna
Lake

Red Devil Lake

Mount Clark
11,522 ft.

Obelisk
Lake

Gray Peak Fork

Washburn
Lake

Red Peak Fork

Merced Peak Fork

Triple Peak Fork

Merced Lake
High Sierra
Camp

Merced
Lake

Echo Creek

Lewis Creek

Post Peak Pass

Auniq Lake

To
Post Peak Pass

Ostrander
Lake

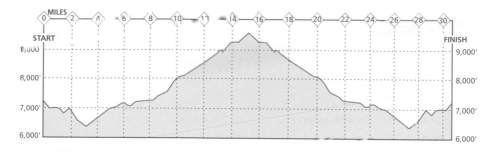

The setting of this lake is stunning, with the sharp point of Merced Peak behind the cascading creek connecting the upper and lower lakes. The irregular rocky shoreline of the lake has dozens of little bays and inlets trimmed with white Labrador tea and red mountain heather that invite many hours of exploration. There are several small campsites among the rocks and whitebark pines at the west side of the lake near the outlet.

If you plan to continue on up to or over Red Peak Pass, Lower Ottoway Lake is the last timber for many miles. If a thunderstorm is brewing, wait it out here. If this is your final destination, return the way you came.

Miles and Directions

0.0 Muño Meadow Trailhead

0.6 Mono Meadow

2.9 Double junction; at the first sign go straight toward Nevada Fall, and at the second sign turn right toward Ottoway Lakes

4.5 Another Nevada Fall Junction; keep right

5.5 Clark Fork crossing

12.1 Merced Pass Trail junction; turn left

15.2 Lower Ottoway Lake

30.4 Turn around and return to Mono Meadow Trailhead

Option: Red Peak Pass—For an additional 2.9 miles (one way) and 1,600 feet of elevation gain, you earn one of the most superb sights in Yosemite: Red Peak Pass. From Red Peak Pass at 11,200 feet, you can look out over a vast bowl of multicolored rock dotted with lakes in blues ranging from turquoise to lapis lazuli, beyond which lie the park's biggest mountains, including 13,114-foot Mount Lyell. To get there from Lower Ottoway Lake, follow the path that skirts the northwestern shore, then works its way up the north side of the cirque to a point above bleak and beautiful Upper Ottoway Lake and another unnamed tarn. The route then swings left and heads up a notch on switchbacks that become shorter and steeper as you reach the top. The pass is tucked into a narrow slot in the ridgeline that limits what you can see, so hike down the far side for just a few minutes more for the best views. The worn spot on the left at the top of the pass is the place where climbers leave the trail to bag Red Peak.

30 The Clark Range and Red Peak Pass

The distinctive, finlike shape of Mount Clark dominates southern Yosemite and is recognizable from high points all over the park. This multiday backpack circumnavigates the mountain, crossing the Clark Range at Red Peak Pass. The scenery is unrivaled in beauty and variety, a treat for the eye and the mind—colorful metamorphic rocks, dozens of lakes and waterfalls, broad vistas of neighboring ranges, and wildflowers galore. It's also less crowded, at least after the first day of hiking, than most other parts of Yosemite. The route described here begins and ends at Happy Isles in Yosemite Valley, but you can begin and end at any one of several points, including Glacier Point and Mono Meadow. If wilderness permits are not available for one trailhead, you can try another.

Start: John Muir Trailhead at Happy Isles
Total distance: 50.6-mile loop
Hiking time: 4 to 8 days
Difficulty: Strenuous
Elevation change: 7,200 feet
Seasons: July through Sept
Nearest facilities: Almost anything you need (except gas) in Yosemite Valley

Permits: Required; available in advance or from the wilderness center in Yosemite Valley
Maps: USGS Half Dome, Merced Peak, and Mount Lyell quads
Special considerations: Check with the park service about trail conditions before starting out since Red Peak Pass is frequently buried under snow until late in the season, and stream crossings are dangerous at high runoff times.

Finding the trailhead: Park in the backpack parking lot next to Curry Village and follow the well-marked path to Happy Isles, or ride the Yosemite Valley shuttle bus from anyplace in the valley and get off at Happy Isles (stop 16). Trailhead GPS: N37 43.51 / W119 33.33

The Hike

From the big sign marking the beginning of the John Muir Trail, join the throngs of tourists ascending the asphalt path through black oak and ponderosa pine forest among enormous lichen-draped boulders. In about a half mile, across the thundering Merced to your right, watch for 370-foot Illilouette Fall tucked back into a deep cut in the Panorama Cliff. The trail steepens briefly, then suddenly descends to the Vernal Fall Bridge at mile 0.8. Upstream, Vernal Fall drops 317 feet over the lowest step of the Giant Staircase.

Cross the bridge to the south side of the river and turn left, upstream. Just beyond, at mile 0.9, meet the Mist Trail, an alternate route to the top of Nevada Fall, not recommended for backpacking since it is steep, slippery, and wet. Shortly beyond this junction ignore a lateral trail on the right for horses only that leads back to the stables. Stay on the John Muir Trail, which switchbacks relentlessly uphill. There are plenty of excuses to stop and rest on the way. Across the valley to the northwest is Upper Yosemite Fall. To the northeast across the river gorge, the rounded back side of Half Dome comes into view, along with Mount Broderick, Liberty Cap, and finally, 594-foot Nevada Fall. This heart-stopping view is finest at Clark Point (2.3 miles), where a lateral trail cuts over to the Mist Trail nearer to the river. Continue climbing, passing beneath a dripping rock overhang decorated with delicate hanging gardens of ferns, columbines, and monkey flowers.

At 3.3 miles the Panorama Trail, leading back to Glacier Point, joins this one from the right (south). The trail drops a bit, hops a couple of little rivulets, then emerges into a wide, sunny expanse of smooth granite at the top of Nevada Fall. Here, at 3.5 miles, a footbridge crosses the river. Stay behind the protective railings; hikers ignore the warning signs and are washed over the falls with depressing regularity. This is a perfect place for lunch or a snack, but please do not share your food with the pan-handling squirrels and jays.

Cross the footbridge back over the river and follow its north shore to a junction at 3.8 miles with the upper end of the Mist Trail, just beyond an outhouse. Continue upstream, climbing the heavily used trail over inlaid cobbles. The path soon levels out and passes from sunlight into shade, and the Merced changes from a rushing, raging torrent to become quiet, dark, and deep.

At 4.3 miles your trail parts company with the John Muir Trail, which heads off to the left (east) toward Half Dome. Keep right. After slogging through heavy sand for a half mile, another lateral trail at 4.8 miles takes off to the left to join the John Muir and Half Dome Trails. Just ahead is Little Yosemite Valley, your first camping oppor-tunity (and your last for the next 2 miles where camping is prohibited). It's a busy and popular place, especially for bears. You should be carrying a bear canister, but there are also lots of bear-proof boxes at the campground, along with an elegant, two-story solar composting toilet. The park service has constructed two communal fire rings for campers to share. Do not scar this already overused area by building another one.

Beyond Little Yosemite Valley the trail continues through level forest. In a little more than a mile, beneath Moraine Dome, the steep granite walls close in, pinching the valley shut, forcing the river to pick up speed and vigor. It cascades noisily for a short time before slowing and widening out once again through Lost Valley, black-ened by a recent fire. Climb out of the valley, passing under the enormous dome of Bunnell Point on the right, where the river pours down the long slippery slide of Bunnell Cascade and is finally crossed on a bridge to the south side. Climb switch-backs blasted out of the granite, then pause to wipe away the sweat and enjoy the view of the river roaring through the spectacular gorge ahead.

Descend again to recross the river and enter Echo Valley, another repeatedly burned-over flat where several creeks flow in to join the Merced. At 11.4 miles, where Echo Creek comes in, a trail to Sunrise High Sierra Camp cuts off to the north. Keep right. Soon the Merced begins to race beside the trail again as you climb the final mile to Merced Lake. There is a stock gate at the west end of the lake at

12.6 miles. Be sure to close it behind you along the lakeshore to reach the Merced Lake High Sierra Camp at the far end of the lake at 13.3 miles. The backpack camp is beyond the High Sierra Camp, where you can buy emergency items and snacks during posted hours. There are bear boxes and toilets at the campground. Campers may use the water tap at the High Sierra Camp to avoid purifying water, but are asked to use the toilets at the backpack campground.

The route continues east through lodgepole pine and fir forest, crossing several little creeks on footbridges. At 14.1 miles the Merced Lake Ranger Station, manned all summer, appears on the right. There is also a junction with the Lewis Creek Trail here. You keep right (southeast), climbing gradually at first, then more steeply until you reach the west end of pretty Washburn Lake at 15.8 miles. Wade three tributary streams flowing into the lake from the north; the third of these is deep enough to go over your boot tops in early season. Past the lake the trail rambles along the ever-changing river, now cascading from one pool to another, now sliding slowly through sensuous curves. Just beyond a packer campsite, complete with stump table and chairs, cross the river again on a pair of footbridges. The trail begins to climb in earnest now, passing perfect viewpoints for watching first the Lyell Fork and later the Triple Peak Fork tumble over the cliffs in spectacular waterfalls. Cross the Merced Peak Fork on yet another footbridge and climb over steep, open rock to join the Triple Peak Fork

View of Upper Ottoway Lake from Red Peak Pass

above the falls. The climb tops out at about 8,800 feet before leveling off to wander through flowery meadows for several miles. Camping is marginal on your side of the river; there is not much level ground and it's often marshy. If the river is low enough to wade, however, there are plenty of good dry sites on the other side.

At 24.2 miles meet the Isberg/Red Peak Pass Trail junction. Turn right (west), climbing at first moderately and then more steeply as you cross a ridge coming down from Triple Divide Peak. The timber becomes more scattered and stunted, and the trail becomes less distinct as you ascend. After a mile or so, you lose 200 feet of hard-won elevation gain as you drop into a lakelet-dotted bowl where it is possible to find a few small, sheltered campsites. As you climb out of the basin, you can see Red Devil Lake off the trail to the north. It's more heavily timbered than the topographic map indicates, and is the last place to camp before the pass. The skyline to the east becomes more spectacular with every step. In the center are the fairly regular twin peaks of Mount Maclure (left) and Mount Lyell (right), the highest peaks in the park. To the left of these, beyond Mounts Florence and Rogers, are Mounts Ritter, Banner, and the Minarets. On a different scale, dozens of snowmelt rivulets at your feet nourish miniature gardens of alpine flowers.

At last, at mile 28.5, the trail makes a dogleg to the left, the switchbacks shorten and steepen, and you top Red Peak Pass, tucked between two blocky rock towers at 11,200 feet. Pause long enough to catch your breath and marvel at the panorama of red-and-white rock, splattered with blue lakes, backed by the high peaks.

Descend steeply down the far side of the pass on sandy switchbacks, heading straight for Upper Ottoway Lake and its neighboring tarns, then swing right (west) on rougher, rockier footing to reach the north shore of Lower Ottoway Lake. There is little opportunity for camping until you reach the western edge of the lake near its outlet at mile 31.4. The elevation here is 9,700 feet, so fires are not allowed. Campsites are small and bouldery, but the setting is stunning. Merced Peak presides over the lake at the head of its sheltering cirque. The shoreline is dotted with graceful mountain hemlocks and whitebark pines, white Labrador tea, and carpets of red mountain heather, and has lots of interesting bays and inlets that invite exploration and swimming.

From the lake the trail descends along the north side of the outlet stream, crossing it at mile 32.0. The route drops through mostly mixed forest, but at times crosses slabs of granite, crisscrossed with white dikes and blotched with chunks of darker material. The forest floor between the rocks is often soggy since snow lingers late in the year in this shady notch. At mile 34.5 meet the Merced Pass Trail junction; keep right. The left fork leads to timbered Merced Pass and on to Fernandez Pass on the eastern boundary of the park. The junction lies between Upper and Lower Merced Pass Lakes, though neither is visible from the trail. The lower lake is down in a bowl to the west of the junction. The upper one is more scenic and has some camping. To find it, follow an unmarked trail to the east about midway between the Merced Pass and Ottoway Lake Trails for a few hundred yards.

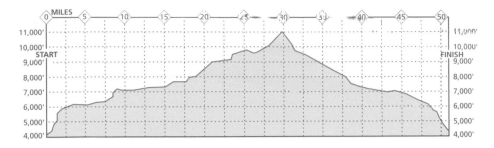

From here descend to the right (northwest). The trail drops to pick up Illilouette Creek at mile 35.5, where the first of a number of tributaries join the main stream. None are deep enough to pose any problem in crossing, but they do inundate the trail in early season. Keep an eye on tree blazes to stay on track. Soon the trail crosses to the north side of Illilouette Creek and descends through forest that changes from lodgepole pine, silver pine, and red fir to Jeffrey pine, white fir, and incense cedar. The open rocky spots host gnarled junipers.

Illilouette Creek continues to splash down through a flower-lined gulch to your left, but in a couple of miles the hillside loses most of its former charm. A recent fire has denuded the valley for several miles, leaving nothing but black stumps. At mile 40.1 the trail crosses Red Creek, then the Clark Fork of Illilouette Creek, where there is a campsite sheltered by unburned trees just before the crossing. The trail then climbs a rise toward the base of Mount Starr King to meet a signed junction at mile 42.0 with the Nevada Falls Trail. Turn right here and continue around the ridge above Illilouette Creek, through brush, over open rock, and through burned forest, to meet the Panorama Trail at 45.6 miles. Keep right and follow switchbacks down to meet the John Muir Trail at mile 46.7. Turn left and retrace your steps back to Happy Isles at 50.6 miles.

Miles and Directions

0.0 Happy Isles/John Muir Trailhead

0.8 Vernal Fall Bridge; turn left, upstream

0.9 Mist Trail

2.3 Clark Point

3.3 Panorama Trail junction

3.5 Footbridge at Nevada Fall; turn left and cross bridge

3.8 Upper end Mist Trail; keep right

4.3 John Muir/Half Dome Trail junction; keep right, leaving the John Muir Trail

4.8 Second John Muir Trail junction at Little Yosemite Valley

11.4 Echo Valley; keep right at the Sunrise Trail junction

12.6 Stock gate; close behind you

13.3 Merced Lake High Sierra Camp

14.1 Merced Lake Ranger Station

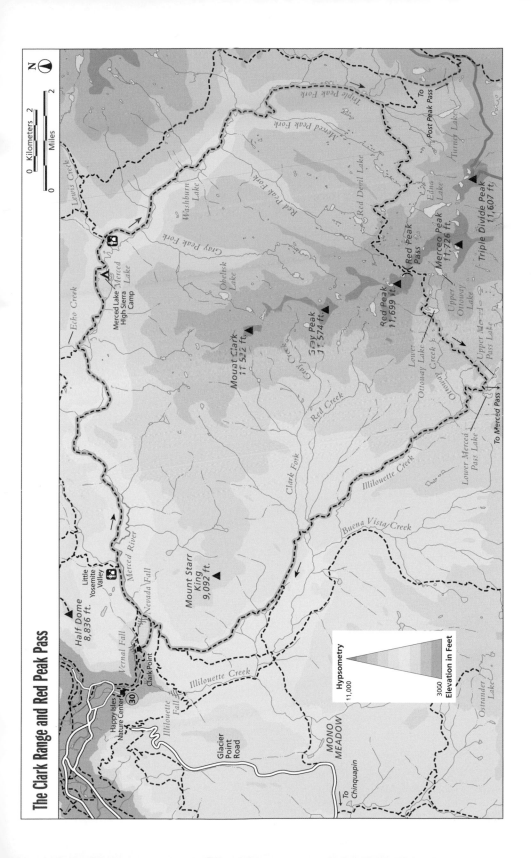

The Clark Range and Red Peak Pass

Hypsometry
11,000
3000
Elevation in Feet

N

0 Kilometers 2
0 Miles 2

Half Dome
8,836 ft.

Little Yosemite Valley

Merced River

Nevada Fall

Vernal Fall

Clark Point

Happy Isles Nature Center

30

Illilouette Fall

Glacier Point Road

Illilouette Creek

MONO MEADOW

To Chinquapin

Ostrander Lake

Mount Starr King
9,092 ft.

Buena Vista Creek

Illilouette Creek

Clark Fork

Red Creek

Gray Creek

Mount Clark
11,522 ft.

Gray Peak
11,574 ft.

Red Peak
11,699 ft.

Lower Ottoway Creek

Lower Ottoway Lake

Upper Ottoway Lake

Red Peak Pass

Merced Peak
11,726 ft.

Triple Divide Peak
11,607 ft.

Edna Lake

Turner Lake

To Post Peak Pass

Red Devil Lake

Obelisk Lake

Washburn Lake

Gray Peak Fork

Red Peak Fork

Merced Peak Fork

Triple Peak Fork

Echo Creek

Lewis Creek

Merced Lake

Merced Lake High Sierra Camp

Upper Merced Pass Lake

Lower Merced Pass Lake

To Merced Pass

15.8	Washburn Lake
24.2	Isberg/Red Peak Pass Trail junction; turn right
28.5	Red Peak Pass
31.4	Lower Ottoway Lake outlet
32.0	Cross stream
34.5	Merced Pass Trail junction; keep right
35.5	Meet Illilouette Creek
40.1	Cross Clark Fork
42.0	Nevada Falls Trail; turn right
45.6	Panorama Trail; turn right
46.7	John Muir Trail; turn left
50.6	Return to Happy Isles/John Muir Trailhead

31 Merced River High Trail

This extended backpack route is one of Yosemite's best-kept secrets. There is lots of trail traffic between Yosemite Valley and Merced Lake, but not much beyond. A few hikers go on to Red Peak Fork, then head south over Red Peak Pass, but very few turn north. Those who do are rewarded with mountain scenery of indescribable beauty, as well as an experience of the Merced River from a perspective you can't get anywhere else. You can trace the river's course from the snowfields of the Clark Range and the lake-dotted country at its base where countless tributary streams originate, then watch the smaller streams merge to become bigger ones that fling themselves over the cliffs of the Merced River gorge in dozens of waterfalls. From here the river rushes toward the Giant Staircase, where it plunges over Vernal and Nevada Falls into Yosemite Valley. Another advantage to this loop is that because it is lower in elevation than the route south over Red Peak Pass, you can get into the backcountry earlier in the season while the higher passes are still under snow.

Start: Happy Isles Trailhead
Total distance: 51.5-mile lollipop
Hiking time: 4 to 8 days
Difficulty: Moderate if you take your time, strenuous if you hurry
Elevation change: 6,700 feet
Seasons: July through Sept

Nearest facilities: Everything you need (except gas) in Yosemite Valley
Permits: Required; available in advance or from the wilderness center in Yosemite Valley
Maps: USGS Half Dome, Merced Peak, and Mount Lyell quads

Finding the trailhead: Park in the backpack parking lot next to Curry Village and follow the well-marked path to Happy Isles, or ride the Yosemite Valley shuttle bus from anyplace in the valley to Happy Isles (stop 16). Trailhead GPS: N37 43.51 / W119 33.33

The Hike

From the big sign marking the beginning of the John Muir Trail, join the throngs of tourists ascending the asphalt path through black oak and ponderosa pine forest among enormous lichen-draped boulders. In about a half mile, across the thundering Merced to your right, watch for 370-foot Illilouette Fall tucked back into a deep cut in the Panorama Cliff. The trail steepens briefly, then suddenly descends to the Vernal Fall Bridge at mile 0.8. Upstream, Vernal Fall drops 317 feet over the lowest step of the Giant Staircase.

Cross the bridge to the south side of the river and turn left, upstream. Just beyond, at mile 0.9, meet the Mist Trail, an alternate route to the top of Nevada Fall, not recommended for backpacking since it is steep, slippery, and wet. Shortly beyond this junction ignore a lateral trail on the right that leads back to the stables. Stay on the

John Muir Trail, which switchbacks relentlessly uphill. There are plenty of excuses to stop and rest on the way. Across the valley to the northwest is Upper Yosemite Fall. To the northeast across the river gorge, the rounded back side of Half Dome comes into view, along with Mount Broderick, Liberty Cap, and finally, 594-foot Nevada Fall. This heart-stopping view is finest at Clark Point (2.3 miles), where a lateral trail cuts over to the Mist Trail nearer to the river. Continue climbing, passing beneath a dripping rock overhang decorated with delicate hanging gardens of ferns, columbines, and monkey flowers. At 3.3 miles the Panorama Trail, leading back to Glacier Point, joins this one from the right (south). The trail drops a bit, hops a couple of little rivulets, then emerges into a wide, sunny expanse of smooth granite at the top of Nevada Fall. Here, at 3.5 miles, a footbridge crosses the river. Stay behind the protective railings; hikers ignore the warning signs and are washed over the falls with depressing regularity. This is a perfect place for lunch or a snack, but please do not share your food with the panhandling squirrels and jays.

Cross the footbridge back over the river and follow its north shore to a junction at 3.8 miles with the upper end of the Mist Trail, just beyond an outhouse. Continue upstream, climbing the heavily used trail over inlaid cobbles. The path soon levels out and passes from sunlight into shade, and the Merced changes from a rushing, raging torrent to become quiet, dark, and deep.

At 4.3 miles your trail parts company with the John Muir Trail, which heads off to the left (east) toward Half Dome. After slogging through heavy sand for a half mile, another lateral trail at 4.8 miles takes off to the left to join the John Muir and Half Dome Trails. Just ahead is Little Yosemite Valley, your first camping opportunity (and your last for the next 2 miles where camping is prohibited). It's a busy and popular place, especially for bears. You should be carrying a bear canister, but there are also lots of bear-proof boxes at the campground, along with an elegant, two-story solar composting toilet. The park service has constructed two communal fire rings for campers to share. Do not scar this already overused area by building another one.

Beyond Little Yosemite Valley the trail continues through level forest. In a little more than a mile, beneath Moraine Dome, the steep granite walls close in, pinching the valley shut, forcing the river to pick up speed and vigor. It cascades noisily for a short time before slowing and widening out once again through Lost Valley, blackened by a recent fire. Climb out of the valley, passing under the enormous dome of Bunnell Point on the right, where the river pours down the long slippery slide of Bunnell Cascade and is finally crossed on a bridge to the south side. Climb switchbacks blasted out of the granite, then pause to wipe away the sweat and enjoy the view of the river roaring through the spectacular gorge ahead.

Descend again to recross the river and enter Echo Valley, another repeatedly burned-over flat where several creeks flow in to join the Merced. At 11.4 miles, where Echo Creek comes in, a trail to Sunrise High Sierra Camp cuts off to the north. Soon the Merced begins to race beside the trail again as you climb the final mile to Merced Lake. There is a stock gate at the west end of the lake at 12.6 miles. Be

Polished granite forms the dramatic gorge of the Merced River.

sure to close it behind you. Skirt the lakeshore to reach the Merced Lake High Sierra Camp at the far end of the lake at 13.3 miles. The backpack camp is beyond the High Sierra Camp, where you can buy emergency items and snacks during posted hours. There are bear boxes and toilets at the campground. Campers may use the water tap at the High Sierra Camp to avoid purifying water, but are asked to use the toilets at the backpack campground.

The route continues east through lodgepole pine and fir forest, crossing several little creeks on footbridges. At 14.1 miles the Merced Lake Ranger Station, manned all summer, appears on the right. There is also a junction with the Lewis Creek Trail here. You keep right (southeast), climbing gradually at first, then more steeply until you reach the west end of pretty Washburn Lake at 15.8 miles. Wade three tributary streams flowing into the lake from the north; the third of these is deep enough to go over your boot tops in early season. Past the lake the trail rambles along the ever-changing river, now cascading from one pool to another, now sliding slowly through sensuous curves. Just beyond a backpack campsite, complete with stump table and chairs, cross the river again on a pair of footbridges. The trail begins to climb in earnest now, passing perfect viewpoints for watching first the Lyell Fork and later the Triple Peak Fork tumble over the cliffs in spectacular waterfalls. Cross the Merced Peak Fork on yet another footbridge and climb over steep, open rock to join the Triple Peak Fork above the falls. The climb tops out at about 8,800 feet before leveling off to wander through flowery meadows for several miles. Camping is marginal

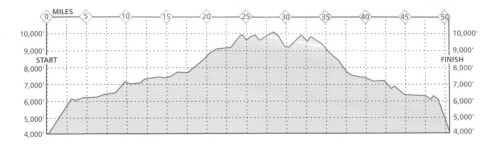

on your side of the river; there is not much level ground and it's often marshy. If the river is low enough to wade, however, there are plenty of good dry sites on the other side. At 24.2 miles meet the Isberg/Red Peak Pass Trail junction. The right fork takes you into the Clark Range.

Your route follows the left fork. Immediately rock-hop or wade the river, then plod steadily upward, first toward the south, then northeast, following a giant switchback. At 25.4 miles reach another trail junction, where you turn left (north). The right fork leads to Isberg Pass at the border of the park. You are now on the High Trail. At first it dips and climbs along the east side of the ridge with only a few frustrating glimpses of the open, lake-filled country to the east, but hold on to your hat! In about a mile the vegetation thins and you cross to the west side of the crest, where a stupendous panorama of the multicolored Clark Range unfolds, stretching from Triple Divide Peak to Mount Clark. Far below, the Merced River flows through the canyon, fed by dozens of cascades and waterfalls rushing down the slickrock on the opposite side. Your trail drops about 400 feet to cross Foerster Creek, climbs again, then passes a small pond and proceeds over fairly level ground. There are many excellent campsites between Foerster Creek and the pond with flat sitting-rocks for comfortable sunset viewing. Shortly thereafter the trail tops out at 10,000 feet. Just beyond the crest another stunning view of the Merced River Canyon and Washburn Lake opens out. Beyond lie the highest peaks in Yosemite, including Mount Lyell, highest in the park at 13,114 feet.

Now the trail plunges downward for almost 1,000 feet on steep switchbacks to meet and cross the Lyell Fork. This crossing can be dangerous in early season. The safest way across is on a big fallen log about 200 yards downstream. The climb back out of this canyon is fortunately more gradual than the trail into it.

The trail continues to follow the ridge, at one point passing through a broad crack in the cliff, occasionally affording more stunning views of the Clark Range. It dips to ford two forks of the stream that feeds Washburn Lake, climbs, then contours around the base of Cony Crags, a distinctively rugged rock outcrop, and at last drops steeply down into the gorge cut by Lewis Creek. Here, at 35.4 miles, is where another trail heads back northeast to Vogelsang Trail before continuing to descend to a second Vogelsang junction at 36.4 miles. Here your solitude ends. Just ahead lies Merced Lake High Sierra Camp. If you want one more night away from the crowds,

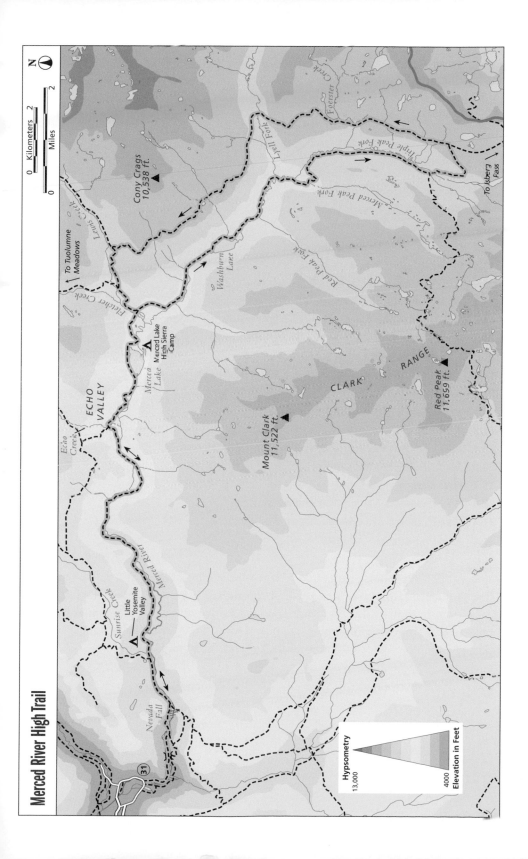

Merced River High Trail

N

0 Kilometers 2

0 Miles 2

Hypsometry
13,000
4000
Elevation in Feet

To Tuolumne Meadows

Fletcher Creek

Lewis Creek

Cony Crags
10,538 ft.

Lyell Fork

Foerster Creek

Triple Peak Fork

Merced Peak Fork

To Isberg Pass

Washburn Lake

Red Peak Fork

ECHO VALLEY

Echo Creek

Merced Lake High Sierra Camp

Merced Lake

CLARK RANGE

Mount Clark
11,522 ft.

Red Peak
11,659 ft.

Little Yosemite Valley

Merced River

Sunrise Creek

Nevada Fall

31

detour about a quarter mile up the Fletcher Creek Trail to a well-developed campsite. Upon returning to the main trail, continue to descend on steep switchbacks until you reach the Merced Lake Ranger Station at a junction with the Merced Lake Trail at 37.4 miles, closing the loop. Return to Merced Lake and back to Happy Isles the same way you came.

Miles and Directions

- **0.0** Happy Isles
- **0.8** Vernal Fall Bridge; turn left, upstream
- **0.9** Mist Trail
- **2.3** Clark Point
- **3.3** Panorama Trail junction
- **3.5** Footbridge at Nevada Fall; turn left and cross the bridge
- **3.8** Upper end of Mist Trail; keep right
- **4.3** John Muir/Half Dome Trail junction; keep right, leaving John Muir Trail
- **4.8** Second John Muir Trail junction at Little Yosemite Valley
- **11.4** Echo Valley; keep right at the Sunrise Trail junction
- **12.6** Stock gate; close gate behind you
- **13.3** Merced Lake High Sierra Camp
- **14.1** Merced Lake Ranger Station
- **15.8** Washburn Lake
- **24.2** Isberg/Red Peak Pass Trail junction; turn left, crossing the river
- **25.4** Second Isberg Pass Trail junction; turn left
- **35.4** Lewis Creek Trail to Vogelsang Trail; keep left
- **36.4** Second Vogelsang Trail junction; keep left
- **37.4** Merced Lake Trail at the Ranger Station, closing the loop; turn right
- **51.5** Return to Happy Isles Trailhead

Option: High Trail back to the Valley—If you have a lot of time, you can take the High Trail back to the valley that heads up, north out of Echo Valley to the Sunrise Trail, then west to meet the John Muir Trail, and follow it back to the valley. You are only retracing your steps for a short distance between the Merced Lake Ranger Station and Echo Valley, and again from Little Yosemite Valley to Happy Isles.

32 Chain Lakes

This is a perfect weekend hike into the classic glacial scenery that is the hallmark of Yosemite. The route takes you up a glacial moraine, then along a series of lakes gouged out by the flow of ice, over rock that displays fine examples of glacial polish and striations. There are wildflowers in profusion and trout in the lakes. This corner of the park is less well known because it's off the beaten path, and the drive to the trailhead is longer than most, but it's well worth your time. A possible bonus is that you might have better luck getting a permit to enter the park here than at some of the more familiar trailheads.

Start: Chiquito Pass Trailhead in the Sierra National Forest south of the park boundary
Total distance: 16.0 miles out and back
Hiking time: 8 to 12 hours
Difficulty: Strenuous as a day hike, moderate as an overnight
Elevation change: 2,200 feet
Seasons: Mid-June through Sept, whenever Beasore Road is open
Nearest facilities: Bass Lake
Permits: None required for a day hike; available for overnights in person from the Visitor Information Center on CA 41 in Oakhurst or in advance by mail from the North Fork Ranger Station; permits are free, but a per-person fee is charged for reservations; there are quotas in place and reservations are recommended
Map: USGS Sing Peak
Trail contacts: Bass Lake Ranger District, Attn: Wilderness Permits, 57003 Road 225, North Fork, CA 93643, (559) 877-2218
Special considerations: Since you are entering the park from forest service territory, get your permit from the forest service in Oakhurst, not in Yosemite. This is bear country, too, so carry a canister. There are no bear boxes at the trailhead. Dispose of all your garbage before you get there and hide ice chests.

Finding the trailhead: From CA 41 just north of Oakhurst, turn right (southeast) on Road 222 toward Bass Lake. In 4 miles the road forks. Take the left (southeast) fork, Road 274, and drive 2 miles to another fork, where you make a sharp turn to the left (north) on Road 7, Beasore Road. Continue on Beasore Road for 20 miles up and over Cold Springs Saddle and back down again to FS Road 5S04, where you turn left (north). It's hard to miss this junction. Globe Rock, an enormous granite orb balancing on an alarmingly puny pedestal, perches just above the road on the right. Road 5S04 is unpaved but well maintained. Follow it for 2.5 miles to a clearing at the top of a ridge to the signed Chiquito Pass Trailhead and its parking area. There is no water at the trailhead. Trailhead GPS: N37 30.57 / W119 25.08

The Hike

The sign at the trailhead tells you Chiquito Pass is 2.0 miles ahead, the Yosemite boundary 3.0 miles. (The USDA Forest Service rounds off mileage to whole numbers.) From the sign head northwest through Jeffrey and lodgepole pines and white firs, climbing easily. At about 1.0 mile the path crosses a tributary of Chiquito Creek and becomes steeper and rockier as it follows the main branch of the creek upstream. At mile 2.1 the way levels out and officially enters the Ansel Adams Wilderness, then resumes its ascent and levels out again through a section of boggy—and buggy—forest. Cross Chiquito Creek just below the outlet of the lake at a wide and muddy ford (or cross on big boulders upstream) and soon reach the south end of Chiquito Lake at mile 2.6. The lake is shallow and surrounded by sedges and reeds, and is obviously on its way to becoming a meadow. Camping is possible nearby, but is not especially attractive because the lakeside is hard to reach through the vegetation and mud. Besides, you're not in Yosemite yet and may have to share the lakeshore with some smelly cattle.

The trail veers away from the lakeside and at mile 2.7 meets a signed junction with the Quartz Mountain Trail heading off to the left. Keep right. The Quartz Mountain Trail leads to another trailhead that cuts off a mile of hiking to the pass, but the road to reach it is sometimes rocky and deeply rutted. Continue straight ahead on the Chiquito Pass Trail through dense wildflower gardens, and at mile 3.1 top the pass, enter Yosemite, and ignore another cutoff to the Quartz Mountain Trailhead. Pass through a gate, making sure to close it behind you to keep the cows out of Yosemite. On the other side of the fence is another junction with a trail whose

Grassy Chiquito Lake is the first stop on the Chain Lakes Trail.

left fork connects with trails to the Wawona area. Turn right (northeast) here toward Chain Lakes. Pass a little pond on your left and plod upward on deep heavy footing to the top of a glacial moraine, a ridge of unsorted dirt and boulders deposited by a glacier long since melted. Both red firs and silver pines join the white firs and lodge-pole pines as you gain elevation. The trail winds its way through a series of soupy but riotously blooming open bits of forest, and wades a tributary of the south fork of the Merced River at mile 4.5. The grade you ascend now is moderate, but the sandy trail makes it seem steeper. At mile 6.0 you reach a high point of 8,700 feet before rounding the shoulder of a ridge and dipping to cross a creek drain-ing Chain Lakes at mile 6.5. This creek is deep and swift and potentially dangerous to cross early in the season.

> **Chain Lakes are good examples of what geologists call glacial chain lakes, glacial step lakes, or, most colorfully, paternoster lakes, because from above they look like a string of rosary beads. Paternoster lakes are fairly common features of mountain valleys that have been cut into stairsteps by glaciers.**

On the far side of the creek is another trail junc-tion. The left fork heads downhill toward Moraine Meadow and Fernandez Pass. The trail sign says you will find the Chain Lakes 0.9 mile away to the right (east), but you reach the shore of the first lake in a shorter distance than this at mile 7.0. A sign gives the lake's elevation as 9,050 feet. The lake's setting is charming and there are campsites nearby, but check out the higher lakes first before pitching your tent. The trail arcs around the upper, eastern end of this first lake, now almost completely silted in, then follows the creek connecting the first lake with the next one. Notice the beautifully ice-polished and incised granite on the way.

The second lake, at mile 7.4, has an irregular, aesthetically pleasing shoreline and several little islands in the middle decorated with groupings of mountain hemlock that seem too perfectly arranged to be accidental. As you draw near the shore, how-ever, you'll note that the lakeside is rather trampled. There are some good campsites on the other side of the trail from the lake you should use if you plan to stay here.

To reach the highest lake, climb the rocky ridge north of the second lake, tak-ing care not to lose the trail in the jumble of boulders. The terrace above the ridge is enchanting, dotted with lovely little tarns connected by tinkling creeks that drop over mossy rocks in miniature waterfalls. Their shorelines bloom with red mountain heather and azalea-like bushes of Labrador tea, and the cracks in every rock out-cropping are bursting with hot pink mountain pride penstemon. Unfortunately, the hordes of voracious mosquitoes that breed in the pools can spoil your appreciation of this little paradise early in the season, but most are gone by August. The last, and larg-est, of the Chain Lakes, at mile 8.0, is snuggled deep into a cirque at the base of Gale Peak at about 9,300 feet. It's definitely worth a visit, but camping nearby is difficult because there is so much water and so few flat, dry sites. The second lake is the most popular camping spot. Return the way you came.

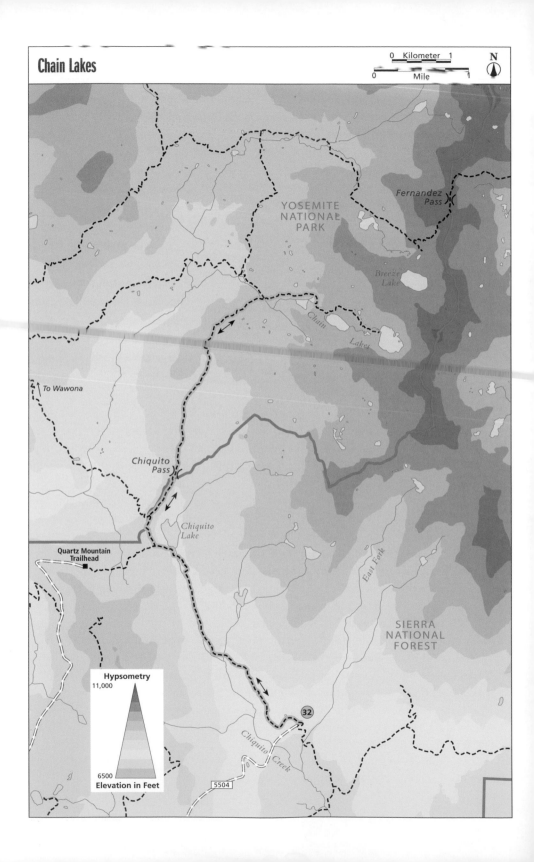

Miles and Directions

0.0   Chiquito Pass Trailhead

2.1   Ansel Adams Wilderness entrance

2.6   Chiquito Lake

2.7   Quartz Mountain Trail junction; keep right

3.1   Chiquito Pass; go through a gate, close it behind you, and keep right at junction

4.5   South Fork Merced River crossing

6.0   High point of the hike

6.5   Fernandez Pass Trail junction; turn right

7.0   Lowest Chain Lake

7.4   Middle Chain Lake

8.0   Upper Chain Lake

16.0   Return to Chiquito Pass Trailhead

Options: If you are planning a trip to Chain Lakes and have more than just one night to spend, Breeze Lake–Fernandez Pass (10,175 feet) is a great, if fairly vigorous (11 miles round-trip), destination for a day hike on a layover day. From the Chain Lakes/Fernandez Pass junction, head north to Moraine Meadows, then southeast through flowery forest, and finally climb steeply northeastward up a rocky notch to meet the Ansel Adams/Yosemite border again at the pass. The views to the south are thrilling, with Mounts Ritter and Banner and the Minarets on the skyline and the peaks of the Clark Range marching away toward the north. About 0.7 mile before you reach the pass, a short spur trail heads south to Breeze Lake, lying in a deep cirque beneath Gale Peak. There are campsites not far from the shore.

Honorable Mention

Alder Creek Falls

This is a good early or late season hike for wildflower lovers in a quiet and infrequently traveled section of the park. There are no high peaks or grand vistas, but the route passes through a variety of habitats from oak woodland to pine and fir forest and culminates at the spot where Alder Creek pours over a cliff in a 60-foot year-round waterfall. The walk begins with a short climb through a prescribed burn, proceeds gently up and down for about a mile, then follows a perfectly flat former roadway for another mile. The round-trip distance from the trailhead is 7.8 miles, with about 1,500 feet of elevation gain. If you want a longer hike or an overnight backpack, continue on beyond the waterfall to a junction where you can take any one of several routes connecting with trails to other parts of the park. If you do plan to spend the night, pick up a wilderness permit at Wawona before you start. The trailhead is about 4 miles north of Wawona on the right side of CA 41, the Wawona Road, beside a sign that says "Mosquito Creek." Parking with a bear box is on the left. (**Note:** About a mile beyond Mosquito Creek, you'll notice another sign, also on the right, marked "Alder Creek." This is *not* the trailhead.)

South of Tuolumne Meadows

C A 120, the Tioga Road, is the only automobile route that runs all the way across Yosemite. It leaves the park on its northeastern border at Tioga Pass at 9,945 feet, the highest automobile pass in California. Tuolumne Meadows is the only developed area on this side of Yosemite, with a visitor center, store, cafe, mountaineering shop, campground, lodge, and gas. This is the largest high-elevation meadow in the Sierra Nevada, and its beauty is stunning. The land to the south contains some of the most sensational peaks and passes in the park, especially the Cathedral Range, with its crowning glory, Cathedral Peak, and Mount Lyell with its associated glacier. Dozens of day hikes and backpacks begin from Tioga Road between Tenaya Lake and Tioga Pass, as well as a number of trails connecting Tuolumne Meadows with Yosemite Valley, including the John Muir and Pacific Crest Trails.

A free shuttle bus runs between Tuolumne Lodge and Olmstead Point every hour, and from Tuolumne Lodge to Tioga Pass four times each day. The Tuolumne Meadows Hikers' Bus leaves Yosemite Valley and stops at Crane Flat and White Wolf on the way to Tuolumne Meadows Lodge every day. There is a charge for this one, the amount depending upon where you want to be dropped off. A schedule and map of shuttle stops are available at the visitor center.

The only camping is at the Tuolumne Meadows Campground (part reservation; part first-come, first-served), and there is a walk-in camping area for backpackers limited to a one-night stay. Tuolumne Lodge has tent cabins and meals, available by reservation far in advance, or sometimes by last-minute good luck.

You can get wilderness permits for overnight stays in the backcountry at the Tuolumne Meadows Wilderness Center if you have not applied in advance. The wilderness center is just off Tioga Road on the way to the Tuolumne Lodge east of the campground. This region is very popular for backpackers, so get there early and be flexible in your trip planning.

33 Tenaya Lake

By Yosemite standards, Tenaya is a very big lake, and a very popular one, too, because of its wide sandy beach and proximity to the Tioga Road. You can stroll along the eastern shore for as long as you like on relatively flat trail, then return the way you came, or you can begin at one end and hike to the other, using the free shuttle bus to return to the start. It is also possible to circumnavigate the entire lake on foot, but that involves about a mile alongside the busy Tioga Road.

Start: Picnic area at the northeast end of the lake
Total distance: 1.7 miles as a shuttle, 3.4 miles out and back
Hiking time: From half an hour to half a day
Difficulty: Easy
Elevation change: Less than 100 feet

Seasons: All summer, whenever the Tioga Road is open
Nearest facilities: Food and lodging at Tuolumne Meadows; gas at Crane Flat and Lee Vining
Permits: None
Map: USGS Tenaya Lake quad

Finding the trailhead: Ride the free shuttle bus from Tuolumne Meadows to stop 9 at the northeast end of Tenaya Lake, or drive to the same spot on the Tioga Road (CA 120). Turn into the picnic area parking lot, where you will find toilets, bear boxes, and a sign directing you to the trail. Trailhead GPS: N37 50.26 / W119 27.12

The Hike

Follow the trail sign in the parking lot to the picnic tables on the beach and head south along the shore. Unless it is quite late in the summer, you will probably have to wade the inlet creek or look for a log crossing upstream. The beach is a good vantage point from which to watch climbers clinging to the bare rock faces of the surrounding domes, polished to a sheen by the glacier that gouged out the lake. Pick up the obvious trail that runs alongside the lake's south shore and stroll through a garden beside several trickling brooks. This spot is open and sunny because winter avalanches slide down the steep slopes of Tenaya Peak almost every year, keeping the forest open. Notice how some of the substantial tree trunks above you have been snapped like matchsticks, and how a few young pines have sprung up here and there between slides until the next big one comes and snaps them off, too. Beyond the avalanche chute, pass through a forest of silver pine, lodgepole pine, white fir, and mountain hemlock with associated shade-loving plants beneath them.

As you approach the southwest end of Tenaya Lake, look directly across the water to knobby-topped Mount Hoffman, which is the geographic center of

▶ Tenaya Lake was named for Chief Tenaya, who, with all his people, was driven from his home in Yosemite by the US Cavalry in 1852.

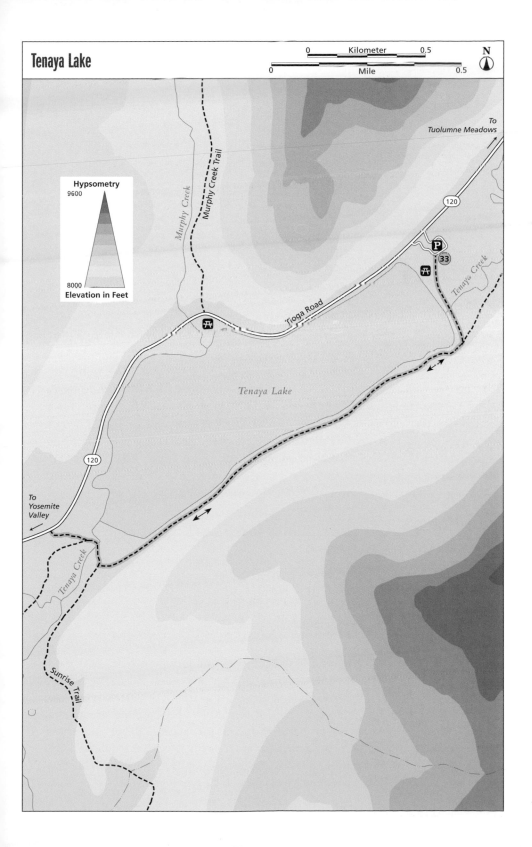

Tenaya Lake

N

Kayakers paddle Tenaya Lake beneath Mount Hoffman.

Yosemite. At mile 1.5 meet a trail coming from the Tioga Road heading north toward Sunrise High Sierra Camp, where you turn right (south). When you reach a sign marking the wilderness boundary, turn left to cross the shallow, if not dry, creek on stepping stones. Pick up the path that takes you to the Sunrise Lakes Trailhead and shuttle bus stop 10 (mile 1.7). Ride the shuttle back to the Tenaya Lake Trailhead at stop 9, or walk back the way you came. The topographic map shows a campground here, but it has been dismantled.

Miles and Directions

0.0 Tenaya Lake picnic area trailhead

0.2 Stream crossing, first Sunrise trail junction; turn right

1.5 Second Sunrise Trail junction; turn right again

1.7 Sunrise Lakes Trailhead (shuttle stop 10)

3.4 Return to Tenaya Lake picnic area trailhead

Option: If you plan to circumnavigate the entire lake on foot, turn right (northeast) from the Sunrise Lakes Trailhead onto the Tioga Road and follow it back to the East Tenaya trailhead. Some of this route is on trail, a short section is on sidewalk, but part of the way hugs the edge of the road where drivers may be paying more attention to the scenery than to pedestrians. Stay alert! You will pass another picnic area across the street from the Murphy Creek Trailhead at mile 2.7 (there is no shuttle stop here), then continue on to your starting point at the east end of Tenaya Lake to close the loop at mile 3.4. The distance is about the same as hiking out and back.

34 Clouds Rest

The narrow summit of Clouds Rest is the best seat in the house for enjoying the drama of Yosemite Valley and the country around it. From this vantage point the star of the show, Half Dome, appears impossibly enormous as it thrusts its way up from the flat valley floor. The Sunrise Lakes Trailhead at Tenaya Lake is the nearest and most direct route to Clouds Rest, but is still a hard workout as a day hike. Fortunately, you can spend the night near a tributary of Tenaya Creek about 4.5 miles from the start.

Start: Sunrise Lakes Trailhead at Tenaya Lake
Total distance: 14.4 miles out and back
Hiking time: 8 to 10 hours
Difficulty: Strenuous
Elevation change: 1,970 feet
Seasons: All summer, whenever Tioga Road is open
Nearest facilities: Food, phones, and lodging at Tuolumne Meadows; gas at Crane Flat and Lee Vining
Permits: None for a day hike; available for overnight in advance or from the wilderness center in Tuolumne Meadows or Yosemite Valley

Map: USGS Tenaya Lake quad
Special considerations: The actual summit is not advised for those who have no head for heights. It's a long and narrow knife-edged ridge, not at all dangerous if you watch your step, but very high and exposed. Fortunately, it is possible to bypass the scary part on a parallel horse trail near the top where you can still get good views. Don't even think about this hike if there is the slightest chance of a thunderstorm.

Finding the trailhead: Drive to the southwest end of Tenaya Lake on Tioga Road (CA 120). The trailhead is across the street from the lake on the south side. You can also ride the Tuolumne Meadows shuttle to stop 10, Sunrise Lakes Trailhead. Be sure to leave food and ice chests in the bear-proof boxes provided. Trailhead GPS: N37 49.52 / W119 28.18

The Hike

The trail begins on a boardwalk behind the parking area and heads left (east) toward the shore of Tenaya Lake, where you will find a little beach and a spectacular photo op. Leave the lakeshore to cross a sandy-bottom creek draining Tenaya Lake that you'll probably have to wade early in the year. The trail swings right (south) just across the creek at 0.1 mile to a sign reads "Sunrise: 5 Miles." At 0.2 mile another trail leading back to Tuolumne Meadows Lodge goes off to the left. The trail dips and rises as it crosses several little streams, then begins to climb the east slope above Tenaya Canyon. The switchback ascent is relieved by views of Mount Hoffman and Tioga Road across the canyon.

At the crest of the ridge (2.5 miles), the trail splits. The left (east) fork leads to Sunrise Lakes. Continue due south, following the sign to Clouds Rest, and descend to the base of Sunrise Peak, whose slickrock slabs swoop gracefully down to a little meadow. The trail skirts the meadow, then climbs a ridge of boulders shed from the

Grab a view of Half Dome from Clouds Rest.

peak on which some scraggly aspens are fighting for a foothold. As you drop into deeper forest, you get one teasing glimpse partway down into Yosemite Valley before the trail levels out. Pass a small pond, then cross several little tributaries of Tenaya Creek. There are some small campsites nearby at mile 4.5, and these are your last sources of water. Now climb easily to the Merced Lake junction at 4.7 miles and continue straight ahead (southwest), climbing more steeply through an open forest of western white pine. The thin slice of granite that is the summit gradually appears as you gain elevation. Follow the ridgetop as it swings around toward the peak and watch for Mount Clark protruding from the crest across Merced Canyon like a giant shark tooth. As the trail climbs, it crosses to the west side of the ridge and gives you a taste of the view up Tenaya Canyon from the top.

At 7.0 miles you reach the base of the summit itself. To the right, slightly above you, watch for the sign that says "Footpath to Clouds Rest." It isn't conspicuous, but if you should miss it, you can continue around the eastern flank of the peak on a horse trail to meet a more obvious signed junction, then double back up to the summit. On the footpath scramble steeply over rocks weathered to the shapes of gigantic stacks of pancakes, with little bunches of purple rockfringe and pale buckwheat lining their edges. From here it becomes clear why the Sierra Nevada has been called the "Range of Light." The dazzling white granite rises in wave after wave of ridges to the horizon, with Tenaya Lake glowing like a jewel in the center and Matterhorn Peak and the Sawtooth Ridge crowning it all. Down-canyon you can look over the bulbous tops of North Dome and Basket Dome, and beyond them the long arm of Yosemite Valley stretching all the way to El Capitan. Directly ahead of you is Half Dome, seen from its most dramatic angle. If you have binoculars or very sharp eyes, you may be able to spot climbers struggling up

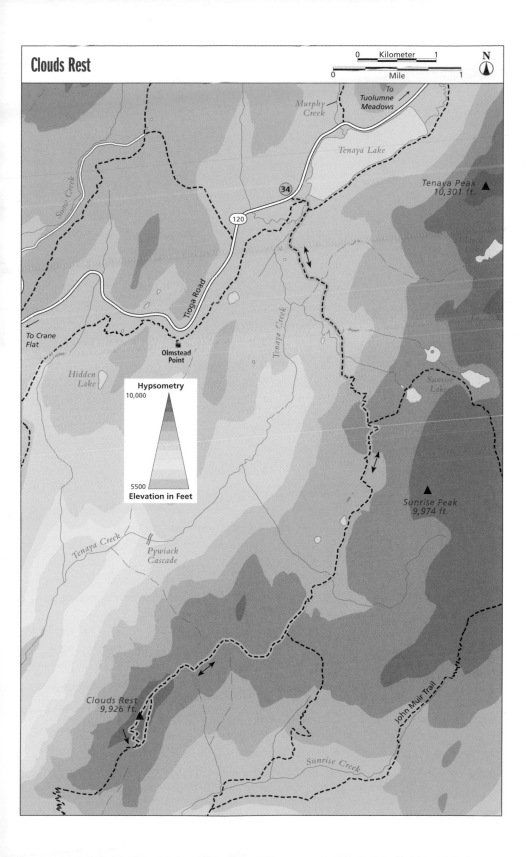

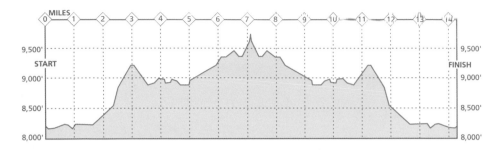

the steel cables to the summit. To the east the Merced River Canyon winds off into the distance below the park's highest peaks—Mounts Lyell, Maclure, and Florence. When you can tear yourself away, retrace your steps to your camp or the trailhead. Or to continue on to Half Dome from Clouds Rest (see Option below).

Miles and Directions

0.0   Sunrise Lakes Trailhead
0.2   Cutoff to Tuolumne Meadows Lodge
2.5   Sunrise Lakes junction
4.5   Campsites
4.7   Merced Lake junction
7.0   Clouds Rest footpath
7.2   Clouds Rest summit
14.4 Retrace the route to trailhead

Option: Half Dome—The route up Half Dome from Yosemite Valley is more direct, but this is a great way to bag two of Yosemite's premiere peaks on one trip. It's an exhilarating hike, though strenuous and somewhat exposed, with lots of ups and downs. It's too long for a day hike; the distance from the trailhead at Tenaya Lake and back is 25 miles, with more than 6,000 feet elevation gain, but there are campsites and water between Clouds Rest and Half Dome. You could also do this as a 20-mile shuttle, beginning at Tenaya Lake, going over Clouds Rest and Half Dome, ending in Yosemite Valley, and riding the bus back up to Tenaya Lake.

From Clouds Rest the trail drops steeply down along the west side of the ridge over big boulders and giant stairsteps toward the pointed teeth called the Pinnacles, then crosses back to the east side and switchbacks down to a junction where the horse trail rejoins the summit footpath. It then swings west beneath the pinnacles and drops on more steep switchbacks to meet the John Muir Trail. A short detour to the left (east) down the John Muir Trail leads to a few campsites and the only water between Half Dome and Clouds Rest. Return to the Half Dome Trail and begin climbing easily through forest, then laboring up the huge, sparsely timbered shoulder of Half Dome to the base of the summit. Steel cables help you negotiate the final 400 feet to the top. Do not proceed beyond the forest if bad weather threatens.

35 Cathedral Lakes

The hike to the two Cathedral Lakes is probably the most popular of any in the Tuolumne area (not counting the High Sierra Camp Loop), so wilderness permits are hard to come by, and the trail and lakeside show signs of overuse. Still, the setting of the lakes in the heart of the Cathedral Range is almost too picturesque to be real, and the distance from the Tioga Road is short. Cathedral Pass, above the upper lake, is a convenient route between Yosemite Valley and Tuolumne Meadows and is part of the John Muir Trail. The bears consider these lakes their local supermarket, so keep your canister locked.

Start: Cathedral Lakes Trailhead
Total distance: 8.0 miles out and back
Hiking time: 4 to 8 hours
Difficulty: Moderate as a day hike, easy as a backpack
Elevation change: 1,500 feet
Seasons: July through Sept

Permits: None for a day hike; available for overnights in advance or from the Tuolumne Meadows Wilderness Center
Nearest facilities: Food and supplies at Tuolumne Meadows; gas at Crane Flat and Lee Vining; nothing at the trailhead
Map: USGS Tenaya Lake quad

Finding the trailhead: Just west of the Tuolumne Meadows Visitor Center is the signed trailhead on the south side of the street. Parking is along both sides of the Tioga Road. You can also ride the Tuolumne Meadows shuttle to stop 7. Be sure to leave all food and ice chests in the bear-proof boxes. Trailhead GPS: N37 52.24 / W119 22.58

The Hike

Start hiking southwest on a wide, flat path 0.1 mile to a junction marked by a big sign with maps and trail information. Your route lies straight ahead, climbing easily through lodgepole pine forest and gaining about 500 feet in elevation before it levels out, skirting the base of what appears to be another standard issue Yosemite dome but is, in fact, the back half of Cathedral Peak. The trail passes alongside a flowery meadow, crosses several branches of Cathedral Creek, and resumes its climb, steeper now than it was in the beginning. When it levels out again, you can see that the rocky bulge on your left narrows toward the top, culminating in the graceful profile of Cathedral Peak. The wide, sandy trail descends a little, presenting a view to the south of another striking formation, the square, raggedy ridge of Tresidder Peak. Continue trending left through a lovely but often buggy dell to find the junction to Lower Cathedral Lake at 3.0 miles. To visit this one first, turn right (southwest) and descend through more exquisite flower gardens to the lower lake at 3.5 miles. The lake lies at the end of a meadow enclosed by a classic glacial cirque. You must traverse this meadow to reach the lakeshore, and it is muddy and laced with dozens of invisible little waterways

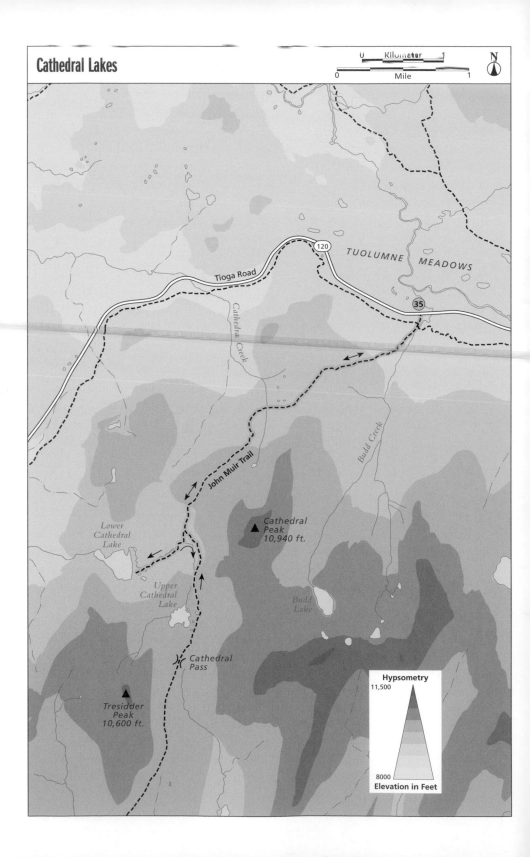

Cathedral Lakes

Kilometer

0   1
Mile
0   1

N

120

Tioga Road

TUOLUMNE   MEADOWS

35

Cathedral Creek

Budd Creek

John Muir Trail

Lower
Cathedral
Lake

Cathedral
Peak
10,940 ft.

Upper
Cathedral
Lake

Budd
Lake

Cathedral
Pass

Tresidder
Peak
10,600 ft.

Hypsometry

11,500

8000
Elevation in Feet

you will have to leap or wade until well into summer. Cathedral Peak seen head-on from here looks like a single, needle-like spire piercing the heavens. In the other direction, across the lake, rises Mount Hoffman at the center of the park. The lake is surrounded by warm, flat rock slabs that invite sun-bathing. There is plenty of overused camping toward the northwest shore. Wood fires are prohibited.

To reach the higher lake, return to the trail junction at 4 miles, then turn right and ascend a rocky path to the beautiful subalpine bowl containing Upper Cathedral Lake, surrounded by Cathedral, Echo, and Tresidder Peaks. The low saddle to the south is Cathedral Pass. It takes only minutes to reach the pass for the best view of the lake basin. There are plenty of campsites in the area.

The needlelike spire of Cathedral Peak is a prominent landmark.

A short climb to the top of the pass before returning to the trailhead is worth the effort. The view of the upper lake flanked by Cathedral Peak in craggy profile is stunning.

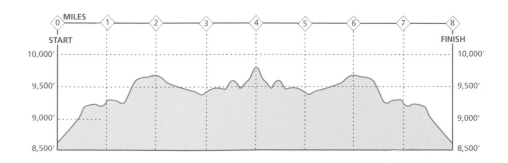

Miles and Directions

0.0 Cathedral Lakes Trailhead

0.1 Tuolumne Meadows High Sierra Camp/Tenaya Lake Trail junction

3.0 Cutoff to Lower Cathedral Lake; turn right

3.5 Lower Cathedral Lake

4.0 Return to cutoff; turn right

4.5 Upper Cathedral Lake; turn around and head north, back to the main trail

5.0 Reach the cutoff to the lower lake and retrace your steps back toward the trailhead

8.0 Return to Cathedral Lakes Trailhead

36 Elizabeth Lake

Elizabeth Lake lies in a picture postcard setting at the foot of Unicorn Peak, a walk of only an hour or two from the Tuolumne Meadows Campground, so it is very popular; start early in the morning to avoid the crowds. If you have less than a full day to spend in the high country, but would like a true taste of subalpine backcountry travel in a small dose, this hike is a good choice. It's also a perfect warm-up hike if you have just arrived in Tuolumne Meadows and need to acclimatize before tackling a longer or more demanding trip.

Start: Elizabeth Lake Trailhead in the Tuolumne Meadows Campground
Total distance: 4.6 miles out and back
Hiking time: 2 to 4 hours
Difficulty: Moderate, only because of steady climbing
Elevation change: 900 feet

Seasons: All summer, whenever Tioga Road is open
Nearest facilities: Food and phones at Tuolumne Meadows; gas at Crane Flat and Lee Vining; toilets and water at the trailhead
Permits: None
Map: USGS Vogelsang Peak quad

Finding the trailhead: Drive to the Tuolumne Meadows Campground, about 9.0 miles west of the Tioga Pass Entrance Station on Tioga Road (CA 120). At the kiosk at the campground entrance, pick up a map of the campground and a parking permit. Follow the map through the campground, turning left between Loops B and C, and pass the group campsites to where the road is barred by a locked gate. Park here and look for the clearly marked trailhead. Store all food and ice chests in the bear-proof boxes. Trailhead GPS: N37 52.13 / W119 21.18

The Hike

The trail climbs steadily uphill through forest, going straight ahead (south) at a junction with the John Muir Trail at 0.1 mile. As the path ascends, it draws nearer and nearer to Unicorn Creek, which drains Elizabeth Lake. A little beyond the halfway point, the slope becomes gentler and finally levels out at the end of a meadow dotted with young lodgepole pines that have been forced into contorted shapes by the weight of winter snows. The trail curves to the right and crosses Unicorn Creek, and

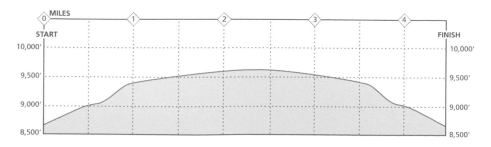

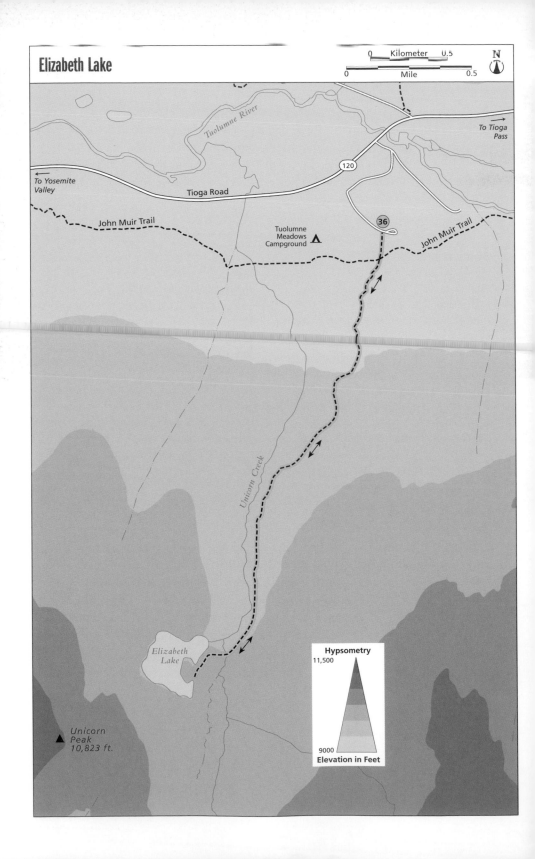

Elizabeth Lake

0　　　　Kilometer　　0.5
0　　　　Mile　　　　0.5

N

Tuolumne River

To Tioga Pass

120

To Yosemite Valley

Tioga Road

John Muir Trail

Tuolumne Meadows Campground

36

John Muir Trail

Unicorn Creek

Elizabeth Lake

▲ *Unicorn Peak*
10,823 ft.

Hypsometry

11,500

9000

Elevation in Feet

Elizabeth Lake lies at the base of Unicorn Peak.

soon Elizabeth Lake appears, sparkling at the foot of Unicorn Peak. A number of trails have been worn around the lake, so you can wander its shores as long as you like before retracing your steps to the trailhead. Do try to stick to the main trails as you do so to avoid further damage to the meadow. Because of the fragility of the vegetation and the lake's proximity to the campground and the road, overnight camping is prohibited. Return to the trailhead the way you came.

Miles and Directions

0.0 Elizabeth Lake Trailhead

0.1 John Muir Trail junction

2.3 Elizabeth Lake

4.6 Return to Elizabeth Lake Trailhead

37 Lyell Fork of the Tuolumne River

The first part of this hike is a beautiful, easy ramble along the Lyell Fork of the Tuolumne River as far as the Vogelsang Pass junction. It's an 11.2-mile round-trip journey from Tuolumne Meadows and a favorite weekend family backpack. Hardier hikers can continue all the way to the headwaters of the Lyell Fork at Donohue Pass just below the Lyell Glacier, tucked beneath the shaded crest of Mount Lyell, the highest peak in Yosemite at 13,114 feet. Mount Maclure, only slightly lower and farther west along the same ridge, shelters its own glacier that also feeds the Tuolumne River. Since this route follows both the John Muir Trail and the Pacific Crest Trail, you're bound to encounter lots of through-hikers along the way at the height of the summer season.

Start: John Muir Trailhead across the road from the Dog Lake parking lot

Total distance: 11.2 miles out and back

Hiking time: 4 to 8 hours to the Lyell Fork junction and back

Difficulty: Easy to the Vogelsang junction

Elevation change: 300 feet to the junction

Seasons: July through Sept

Nearest facilities: Groceries, cafe, and phones at Tuolumne Meadows; gas at Crane Flat and Lee Vining

Permits: Required; available in advance or from the Tuolumne Meadows Wilderness Center

Maps: USGS Tioga Pass, Vogelsang Peak, and Koip Peak quads

Special considerations: This is a notorious bear hangout, and the bears here are intelligent and resourceful. Carry a canister and remember to keep it locked.

Finding the trailhead: From the west drive Tioga Road (CA 120) eastward past the Tuolumne Meadows Visitor Center, store, and campground, all on the right. Cross the bridge over the Tuolumne River. In about a mile turn right at the entrance to the wilderness center. Follow the road as it curves to the left for about 0.5 mile to the Dog Lake parking lot on the left. The trailhead is on the right (south) side of the road. Trailhead GPS: N37 52.39 / W119 20.20

The Hike

Cross the road south of the parking lot to the trailhead sign. Follow the trail southeast to a footbridge over the Dana Fork at 0.2 mile. Ignore the cutoff back to the Tuolumne Meadows Lodge and cross the bridge, then turn left and follow the river upstream, pausing to enjoy the wildflower gardens along the shore, where dozens of different species vie for attention. The route now bends slightly to the right, crosses a low rise alongside a marshy area, and reaches the twin bridges over the Lyell Fork at 0.6 mile. This is surely one of the most sublime vistas in Yosemite,

▶ The turquoise color of the water in the Lyell Fork comes from glacial "flour," rock ground so finely by the Lyell Glacier upstream that it remains suspended in the current and reflects green light.

with the clear turquoise river winding toward you through the green meadow. At your feet deep bowls have been worn into the granite by the scouring force of silt carried from the mountains by spring runoff, and the water swirls in beautiful patterns from one bowl to the next. The massive gray hulk on your left is Mammoth Peak (not to be confused with Mammoth Mountain, the ski resort, which lies farther south).

Soon after you leave the twin bridges, another path leads back (right) to the Tuolumne Meadows Campground, at 0.7 mile. Continue left on the John Muir Trail through lodgepole pine forest and over open rock to 1.3 miles, where the Rafferty Creek Trail heads uphill to the right, the more direct of two routes to Vogelsang. Cross the bridge over the creek on your left and continue through forest and meadows that, in early season, are a solid mass of pale lavender shooting stars (and mosquitoes). Soon the sound of the river becomes apparent—it's been hidden for a while behind a low ridge—and a glorious view of Lyell Canyon opens up before you. Sometimes the river flows deep and clear; sometimes it slides over slickrock into perfect bathing pools. Any one of a thousand spots along the bank invites lunch, a snack, a sunbath, or a nap.

At 5.6 miles the John Muir Trail and the Vogelsang/Ireland Lake Trails split. Good campsites are just uphill to the right of the trail sign. This junction is the end of your hike. Retrace your steps to Tuolumne Meadows.

The glacier on Mount Lyell is the largest in Yosemite.

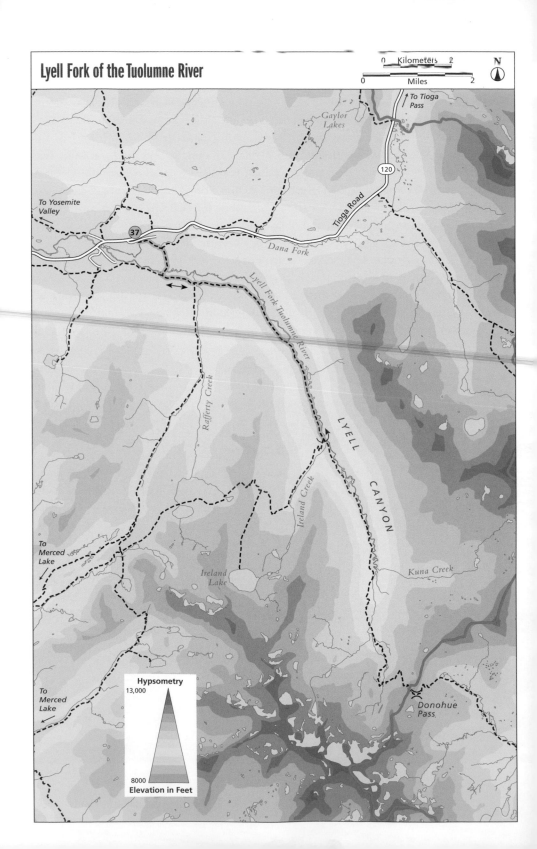

Lyell Fork of the Tuolumne River

0 Kilometers 2

0 Miles 2

N

To Tioga Pass

Gaylor Lakes

120

Tioga Road

To Yosemite Valley

37

Dana Fork

Lyell Fork Tuolumne River

Rafferty Creek

LYELL CANYON

Ireland Creek

Kuna Creek

To Merced Lake

Ireland Lake

To Merced Lake

Donohue Pass

Hypsometry

13,000

8000

Elevation in Feet

Miles and Directions

0.0 John Muir Trailhead at Dog Lake parking lot

0.2 Footbridge over Dana Fork; cross bridge and turn left

0.3 Cutoff to Gaylor Lakes; keep right

0.6 Twin Bridges

0.7 Tuolumne Meadows Campground cutoff; turn left

1.3 Rafferty Creek Trail junction; turn left, crossing the bridge

5.6 Vogelsang Trail junction; turn around for return to trailhead. (***Option:*** Keep left to continue on to Donohue Pass; see below.)

11.2 Return to the John Muir Trailhead at Dog Lake lot

Option: Donohue Pass—This option will add 13.6 round-trip miles and about 2,200 feet of elevation change to your trek, so pack for at least 3 days. To continue on to Donohue Pass, keep left at the trail split and accompany the meandering river upstream through the riotously blooming meadow. Just beyond the point where Kuna Creek drops down from the Kuna Crest to join the Lyell Fork from the east, the trail begins to climb, winding among avalanche debris. Views of the river snaking away to the north down the canyon get better and better as you gain elevation. Cross the river on a bridge to arrive at Lyell Base Camp (2.2 miles from the Ireland/Lyell Fork junction). It's a busy place, used by climbers preparing to tackle the mountain. There are plenty of good campsites here—and plenty of bears.

The trees begin to disappear as you climb beyond the camp, and from here on you get superb views up the canyon to the high peaks and glaciers. One of the finest of these is from the outlet of a little lake at the end of a meadow. This outlet can be tricky to cross at high water. It's safer to wade than to hop across on the slippery rocks, but the water is extremely cold. Just past this crossing is a low rocky rise sheltered by whitebark pines that could be used as a last, simply exquisite, campsite before the pass. Climb another little rise, turn left (east), and cross the outlet of another tarn, not as difficult as the last one. Now work your way up over open granite, negotiating snow patches that often remain until midsummer to Donohue Pass and the Yosemite park boundary at 11,000 feet. Beyond, the John Muir and Pacific Crest Trails descend through an open rocky basin toward Rush Creek in the Ansel Adams Wilderness. Retrace your steps to return to the John Muir Trailhead at Dog Lake lot.

In Addition

Lodgepole Pines

Lodgepole pines are by far the most common conifers in the Tuolumne region, and indeed throughout the entire Sierra Nevada at elevations between 7,000 and 10,000 feet. They're easy to identify: their trunks and branches have small irregular scales that look like gray cornflakes and they have small cones, less than 2 inches long. The surest way to know a lodgepole pine, however, is to examine the needles. The needles of all pine trees are attached to their twigs in bundles of one to five, held together at the base by a papery sheath. The number of needles in a bundle is a clue to the species. Several kinds of pines have three needles per bundle, several others have five, but only lodgepoles have two. To make it even easier, pluck a bundle of lodgepole needles and separate the two so that they are at right angles to one another. Now you have "L" for lodgepole.

These are a pioneering species, the first to move in around the edges of a meadow since they don't mind wet feet as much as other pines do, and may gradually transform the meadow to forest. They grow quickly, reproduce at an early age, and are adapted to periodic fires. (In fact, the subspecies that grows in the Rockies requires fire for reproduction, but Yosemite's do not.) They are also subject to periodic infestations of needle miners, moths whose larvae can destroy great swathes of forest in a season or two. You can see several of these "ghost forests" in the Tuolumne area, big patches of dead trees surrounded by healthy ones. It's part of the normal cycle of life and death; the forest will recover.

Their scientific name, *Pinus contorta*, reflects their growth habit when young. Young trees become twisted and bent into grotesque and interesting shapes by heavy winter snows and may retain their gnarled bumps and bends into maturity. Lodgepole pines in the Rockies reflect their common name better, growing straight, slender, and much closer together. Lodgepoles are sometimes erroneously called *tamaracks,* trees that do not grow in California.

38 Mono Pass

Mono Pass was a major trade route across the Sierra between the Miwok people on the west side and the Piutes on the east. It was also the site of the Golden Crown Mine, active in the early 1880s. Some of the structures built during that time are still standing. The setting is incomparable: a beautiful meadow at the eastern crest of the Sierra containing lakes of the most vivid blue ringed by the warm-red rocks of Mount Lewis and Mount Gibbs.

Start: Mono Pass Trailhead 1 mile south of the Tioga Pass Entrance Station on the Tioga Road
Total distance: 7.4 miles out and back
Hiking time: 4 to 6 hours
Difficulty: Moderate as a day hike, easy as a backpack
Elevation change: 910 feet
Seasons: Summer and fall, whenever Tioga Road is open
Nearest facilities: Food, lodging, water, and phones at Tuolumne Meadows; gas at Lee Vining

Permits: None for a day hike; available for overnights in advance or at the Tuolumne Meadows Wilderness Center
Maps: USGS Koip Peak, Mount Dana, and Tioga Pass quads
Special considerations: The entire watershed of the Dana Fork of the Tuolumne River is closed to camping, so you must go just a bit beyond Mono Pass itself to camp. Even the park service is a bit hazy about the precise location of the boundary line, but as long as you pitch your tent to the east of the old miners' cabins, you're legal.

Finding the trailhead: On the Tioga Road (CA 120), drive about 6.0 miles east of Tuolumne Meadows, or a little more than a mile south of the Tioga Pass Entrance Station. The marked trailhead and parking lot are on the southeast side of the road. Trailhead GPS: N37 53.27/W119 15.45

The Hike

From the parking area the trail winds its way generally southwestward through lodgepole pine forest alternating with little fingers of Dana Meadow. The Dana Fork of the Tuolumne River flows through one of these deeply enough to require wading early in the summer. Just beyond this creek the trail swings left (east), climbing through more forest and meadow. The bulky granite mass to the right is Mammoth Peak, the northern culmination of the Kuna Crest. (Don't confuse this with Mammoth Mountain, the ski area south of Yosemite.)

At mile 1.3 the remains of an old pioneer cabin slouch beside the trail, and at about the same time you pick up the gurgling of Parker Pass Creek on the right. Following the creek upstream, you cross a tributary stream feeding the main creek amid a dense exhalation of swamp onions, and just beyond, at mile 2.3, meet a junction with the Spillway Lake Trail that angles off to the south, taking Parker Pass Creek with it.

Parker Pass straddles the eastern boundary of Yosemite.

The Mono Pass Trail continues southeast and the grade steepens. As it climbs, you get glimpses across the valley of the light gray Kuna Crest to the right with a colorful strip of red, metamorphic rock at its base, a foretaste of things to come.

At 3.0 miles pass a rockslide where you're sure to see pikas scurrying around if you're willing to sit quietly for a few minutes. Another tributary of Parker Pass Creek burbles along on the other side of the trail. Pass a second tumbledown cabin. Just beyond it the forest opens to reveal red Mount Lewis at the head of the broad meadow. At mile 3.4 the signed Parker Pass Trail cuts off to the right (south) across the marshy meadow.

To the left an almost level stroll takes you to Mono Pass at mile 3.7 at the border between Yosemite and the Ansel Adams Wilderness. On the far side of Summit Lake, the largest of the two in the meadow, on a sandy bench among whitebark pines, are four more miners' cabins lined up in a neat row. An unmarked use trail cutting across the meadow takes you directly there. From Mono Pass you can explore the old mining prospects; climb Mount Gibbs just to the north; continue on down the main trail that drops steeply into Bloody Canyon to visit Sardine Lakes, notable for their startling turquoise color; or return the way you came.

Miles and Directions

0.0   Mono Pass Trailhead

1.3   Pioneer Cabin

2.3   Spillway Lake Trail junction

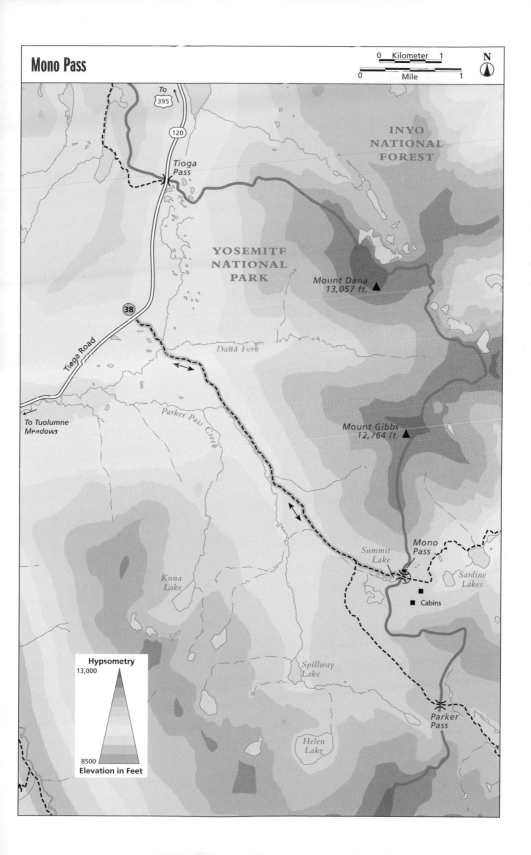

Mono Pass

0   Kilometer   1

0   Mile   1

N

To 395

120

Tioga Pass

INYO NATIONAL FOREST

YOSEMITE NATIONAL PARK

Mount Dana
13,057 ft.

38

Tioga Road

Dana Fork

Parker Pass Creek

To Tuolumne Meadows

Mount Gibbs
12,764 ft.

Kuna Lake

Summit Lake

Mono Pass

Sardine Lakes

Cabins

Spillway Lake

Parker Pass

Hypsometry
13,000

8500
Elevation in Feet

Helen Lake

Option: Parker Pass—At 11,000 feet, Parker Pass is the next gap south of Mono Pass on the Sierra Crest. It, too, marks the boundary of Yosemite and the Ansel Adams Wilderness, and camping is prohibited on the Yosemite side. It is very different from Mono Pass, wide and dry and windswept, flanked by weirdly shaped peaks, a landscape so like the Tibetan Plateau that a herd of yaks would not look out of place here. The trail crosses the meadow and climbs over a sandy ridge studded with whitebark pines, where you get a good view of Spillway Lake at the base of the Kuna Crest. The pass itself is marked by a veritable forest of signs. If you have the time and energy, the trail over the pass continues on down a beautiful valley past dozens of little ponds, then climbs again toward Koip Pass. Along the way, through gaps in the mountains, you can see all the way down to Mono Lake. The hike to Parker Pass will add about 2 miles to your Mono Pass journey.

Honorable Mention

Polly Dome Lakes

The Polly Dome Lakes are not spectacular in themselves, a collection of ponds tucked into lodgepole pine forest at the base of Polly Dome, and the source of Murphy Creek, a small stream that empties into Tenaya Lake. What makes this easy 5-mile hike worthwhile is the wealth of classic glacial features you'll see along the way. There are house-size erratics, boulders transported from their place of origin by ice and deposited wherever the ice could no longer carry them. There is shiny glacial polish and striations on the rocks showing the direction of the flow, sometimes interrupted by a series of crescent-shaped gouges called chatter marks, produced when the ice dragged big boulders, bounding and shuddering, across the surface.

The out-and-back route begins across the street from the picnic area on the south side of Tioga Lake, following Murphy Creek upstream on a moderate grade.

North of Tuolumne Meadows

The Grand Canyon of the Tuolumne River dominates this region and defines its northern boundary. The Lyell Fork of the Tuolumne originates at the Lyell Glacier and the Dana Fork rises from the snowfields of Mount Dana, both to the south. The forks meet in Tuolumne Meadows and wander languorously northwest for a few miles, then begin their headlong rush toward the Pacific Ocean in an almost continuous series of cascades and waterfalls. The canyon they carved was gouged even deeper by glaciers, which produced a narrow slot in the granite with vertical walls that are in some places higher than those of Yosemite Valley.

For general information about the Tuolumne Meadows area, including a discussion of facilities, services, permits, camping, and shuttle buses, see the South of Tuolumne Meadows section.

All the hikes described here explore the country between Tuolumne Meadows and this Grand Canyon. Since every trailhead in this section originates from or near Tioga Road, there will be other hikers in the backcountry, and there will be some competition for wilderness permits. Still, the trails in this region are not as heavily used as are those south of the road. There are high peaks, passes, waterfalls, and sensationally beautiful scenery, but overall the terrain is slightly less rugged and the average elevation is a little lower than the country to the south. Furthermore, there are no trails heading directly into Yosemite Valley.

Leafless flowers of the snow plant appear on the forest floor soon after snow melts.

39 Waterwheel Falls and the Grand Canyon of the Tuolumne

This is a rugged, multiday shuttle hike following the course of the Tuolumne River downstream from Tuolumne Meadows as it tumbles over waterfalls and cascades, including the famous Waterwheels, through the Grand Canyon of the Tuolumne almost as far as Hetch Hetchy Reservoir. The trail drops all the way to 4,200 feet before laboring back up 3,600 feet to White Wolf at the very end. It's a wild, exhilarating hike for those in good condition. You will need two cars, leaving one at White Wolf and the other at the Glen Aulin Trailhead, or take advantage of the Tuolumne Meadows shuttle.

Start: Glen Aulin Trailhead at Tuolumne Meadows

Total distance: 28.1-mile one-way shuttle

Hiking time: 3 to 5 days

Difficulty: Strenuous

Elevation change: 7,000 feet

Seasons: Early July is best for cooler temperatures and full-flowing waterfalls

Nearest facilities: Tuolumne Meadows; snacks and phones at White Wolf

Permits: Required; available in advance or from the Tuolumne Meadows Wilderness Center

Maps: USGS Falls Ridge, Hetch Hetchy Reservoir, Tamarack Flat, Ten Lakes, and Tioga Pass quads

Finding the trailhead: From the west follow Tioga Road (CA 120) past the Tuolumne Meadows Visitor Center, store, cafe, and campground, all on the right. Just after crossing the bridge over the Tuolumne River, turn left (north) into the Lembert Dome parking area. From the east (Tioga Pass), follow Tioga Road past the turnoff to the wilderness center on the left and continue about a hundred yards to the Lembert Dome parking area on the right. You can also ride the Tuolumne Meadows shuttle to Lembert Dome (stop 4). Overnight parking is prohibited in the parking lot, so park along the paved road parallel to Tioga Road. At a closed gate this road turns sharply right and heads toward the stables. The trail begins at the gate. Trailhead GPS: N37 52.44 / W119 21.30

The Hike

Go through the gate and follow the road (closed to vehicles) westward through the meadow, keeping right and climbing a small rise where the road splits. From the top of the rise, head toward the ramshackle log structure partially containing Soda Springs at mile 0.5, a naturally carbonated spring bubbling up rusty water. Just beyond is Parsons Lodge, a stone building with historical exhibits. There the path splits at mile 0.6, where you turn right to a big Glen Aulin Trail sign where the trail meets the road a few yards beyond. Turn left and walk through flowery meadows and lodgepole pine forest on footing that is heavy and dusty from lots of horse and foot traffic. Ford Delaney Creek at mile 1.2. A trail heading north to Young Lakes cuts off to the

Grooves in the rocks fling water into high arcs forming waterwheels.

right at mile 1.6, but your route stays left (northwest). In less than a mile of gradual descent, you emerge from behind a low ridge to behold the spectacular Cathedral Range with the Tuolumne River in the foreground. The next couple of miles along the trail offers one incredible photo op after another. Sometimes the trail passes over highly polished granite, buffed by glacial ice to a blinding sheen, and you will need to watch for ducks across these open spaces to stay on track. After passing through another short stretch of forest, climb around a low shoulder of rock and keep watch on your left for the Little Devil's Postpile, an unusual volcanic feature much younger than the surrounding rock.

The trail turns sharply right and drops down a short, steep notch, and very soon reaches a pair of footbridges across the Tuolumne River at 3.5 miles. From this point on the river picks up speed and cascades over a series of falls, one after another, mile after mile. As you descend, you can enjoy views up Cold Canyon to Matterhorn Peak and Mount Conness on the northern boundary of the park. The trail twice dives into and out of deep forest lined with Labrador tea and corn lily, then emerges again into sunlight on cobblestones or smooth granite marked with ducks. Finally it meets the May Lake/McGee Lake Trail at 5.0 miles. A few more steep, slippery switchbacks lead down to a bridge and back to the other side of the river. Few hikers can resist the urge to stop on the bridge and snap a photo or simply gape at the frothy White Cascade splashing into a pool in front of the Glen Aulin High Sierra Camp at 5.2 miles. If you plan to camp here, cross a second bridge over Cold Creek to the right and walk behind the High Sierra Camp to find the backpack campground.

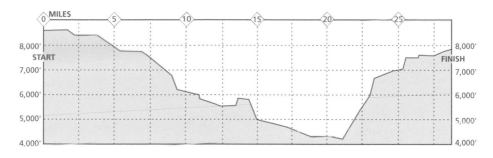

From the camp cross back over to the west side of Cold Creek, cross over a ridge, and descend into the burned-over glen. Wander for a mile through a waist-high sea of lupines that have taken advantage of the open ground newly created by a recent fire. The river flows quiet and deep beside you for a while; then both trail and river drop over the first of a long series of stairsteps down past California Falls, LeConte Falls, and finally the famous Waterwheels, at 7.8 miles. Here in early season the roaring Tuolumne rushes down a smooth slope until it hits a series of grooves in the rocks that sometimes fling the water more than 20 feet into the air. Watch for a little spur trail leading toward the riverside for a better view, but do not walk out onto the slippery rock beside the water, especially if the rock is wet. The combination of slimy algae on polished rock creates a surface as slick as glass, and a slip could be fatal.

Return to the main trail and continue to switchback down to a bridge over Return Creek at mile 9.6. Soon the canyon walls narrow and eventually become so precipitous at Muir Gorge that the trail must make a detour over the top of a smooth polished shoulder. It then drops steeply into the drainage of Register Creek, which you cross on rocks below a pretty cascade at mile 14.7. A little farther on, cross Rodgers Creek on a bridge. Now that you are well into the zone of black oak and chaparral, the canyon can be hot and the flies voracious. Stay alert for rattlesnakes as well. Fortunately, there are lots of inviting little pools alternating with lovely cascades for cooling off. As you approach Pate Valley, the ground becomes soggier and you wade through dense bracken fern and leopard lilies until you meet a junction at mile 19.5 with a trail that heads up Piute Creek to Pleasant Valley. Cross a couple of bridges over two branches of the river to its south side and enter Pate Valley proper. There are plenty of good campsites here along the river beneath shady oaks and ponderosa pines, where masses of white azaleas scent the air in June. This is a good place to spend the night no matter what time you arrive, because the climb up out of the canyon can be very hot and should be tackled early in the morning. Make sure you have plenty of water if it is past mid-July since Morrison Creek, the only stream you will meet on your way up, is sometimes dry by then.

Leave the river and begin the trudge up the switchbacks, eventually getting high enough to look back upon Hetch Hetchy Reservoir down the canyon. After the first set of switchbacks, cross Morrison Creek in a cool aspen grove, then climb another set of switchbacks alongside the creek. At 25.7 miles pass the first junction with a

Waterwheel Falls and the Grand Canyon of the Tuolumne

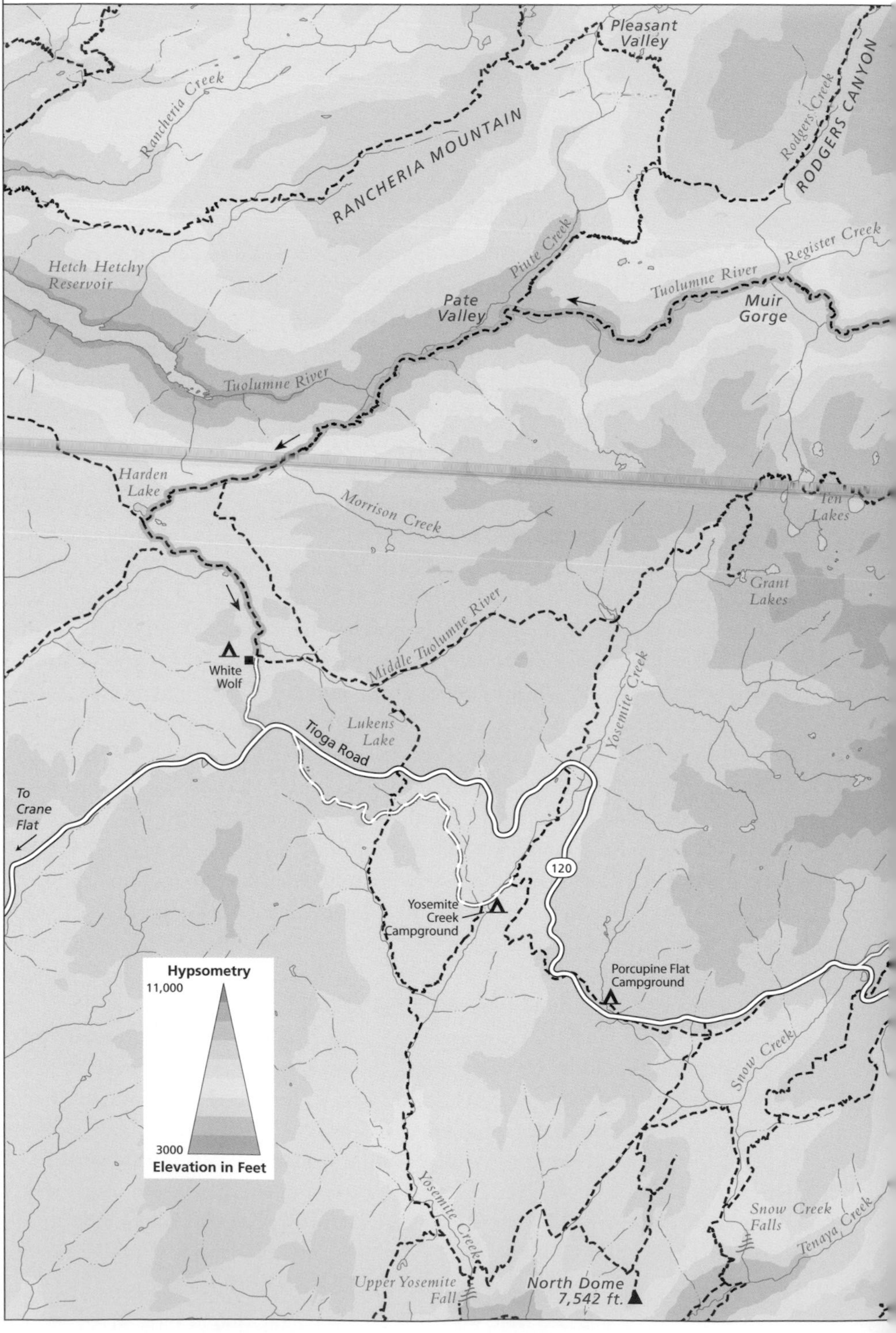

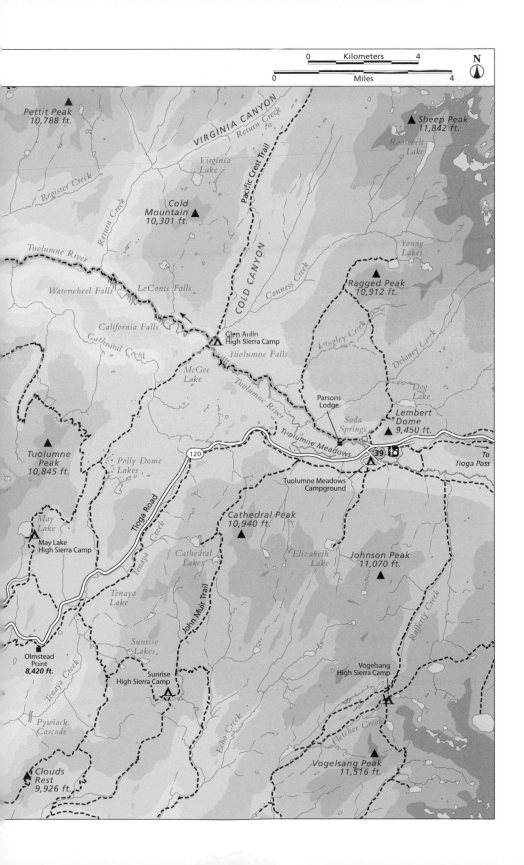

Kilometers 0 — 4

Miles 0 — 4

N

Pettit Peak
10,788 ft.

VIRGINIA CANYON

Return Creek

Sheep Peak
11,842 ft.

Roosevelt
Lake

Register Creek

Virginia
Lake

Pacific Crest Trail

Cold
Mountain
10,301 ft.

Return Creek

Young
Lakes

Tuolumne River

COLD CANYON

Conness Creek

Ragged Peak
10,912 ft.

Waterwheel Falls

LeConte Falls

California Falls

Cathedral Creek

Glen Aulin
High Sierra Camp

Tuolumne Falls

McGee
Lake

Tuolumne River

Lingley Creek

Delaney Creek

Dog
Lake

Parsons
Lodge

Soda
Springs

Lembert
Dome
9,450 ft.

Tuolumne Meadows

Tuolumne
Peak
10,845 ft.

Polly Dome
Lakes

120

Tenaya Creek

Tioga Road

39

To
Tioga Pass

Tuolumne Meadows
Campground

May
Lake

May Lake
High Sierra Camp

Cathedral
Lakes

Cathedral Peak
10,940 ft.

Elizabeth
Lake

Johnson Peak
11,070 ft.

John Muir Trail

Rafferty Creek

Tenaya
Lake

Olmstead
Point
8,420 ft.

Tenaya Creek

Sunrise
Lakes

Sunrise
High Sierra Camp

Echo Creek

Vogelsang
High Sierra Camp

Fletcher Creek

Pywiack
Cascade

Clouds
Rest
9,926 ft.

Vogelsang Peak
11,516 ft.

shortcut trail to Harden Lake and continue straight ahead (west), climbing less steeply at first, then mounting a last set of switchbacks to Harden Lake (no camping allowed) at 27.2 miles. From the lake follow the fire road back up to White Wolf at 28.1 miles.

Miles and Directions

0.0 Glen Aulin Trailhead

0.5 Soda Springs

0.6 Parsons Lodge; turn right, then left at the sign

1.2 Ford Delaney Creek

1.6 Young Lakes Trail junction; keep left

3.5 Cross Twin Bridges over the Tuolumne River

5.0 Junction with May Lake/McGee Lake Trail; turn right

5.2 Glen Aulin High Sierra Camp

7.8 Waterwheel Falls

9.6 Cross Return Creek

14.7 Cross Register Creek, then Rodgers Creek

19.5 Piute Creek junction; go straight into Pate Valley

25.7 First Harden Lake junction

27.2 Harden Lake

28.1 End at White Wolf

40 Lukens Lake

This easy and popular out-and-back day hike through forest and meadow to a quiet lake is a favorite with wildflower lovers.

Start: Lukens Lake Trailhead
Total distance: 2.4 miles out and back
Hiking time: 1 to 3 hours
Difficulty: Easy
Elevation change: 200 feet

Seasons: All summer, whenever Tioga Road is open
Nearest facilities: Food and phones at While Wolf; gas at Crane Flat
Permits: None
Map: USGS Yosemite Falls quad

Finding the trailhead: On Tioga Road (CA 120), drive about 2 miles east of the White Wolf junction. The signed parking area is on the south side of the road, but the trail begins on the north side. Trailhead GPS: N37 51.04 / W119 36.53

The Hike

Cross Tioga Road carefully and head uphill through an almost pure red fir forest. The cones underfoot come from the occasional western white pine or mountain hemlock. Fir cones do not fall but decompose and release their seeds while still on the tree. Watch for odd leafless plants like pinedrops, brilliant red snow plant, and little saprophytic orchids on the forest floor. The sunny spots scattered here and there among the trees are dense with chinquapin—green and gold shrubs with spiny but delicious nuts—ready for eating in midsummer.

The trail tops a rise, drops again to pick up a creek lined with dozens of species of waist-high wildflowers, and turns left to follow the stream to Lukens Lake at 0.8 mile. The lake is shallow and grassy and warmer than most lakes in the Sierra, and it's reputed to be a good fishing spot. The moisture that nourishes the lush display of wildflowers means lots of mosquitoes, too, so take repellent. Keep to the trail to the left (south and west) side of the lake and follow the lakeshore around its northwest end, crossing the outlet stream, to a junction with the trail to White Wolf at 1.2 miles. This is a great place for a snack or a picnic, but camping is prohibited near the lake since it is much too close to

▶ **Theodore Lukens, for whom the lake is named, was at one time mayor of Pasadena, California.**

the road. When you have botanized, fished, or loafed to your heart's content, retrace your steps to the trailhead. It is possible to walk all the way around the lake, but the way is dense and mushy and the vegetation on the northeast side so fragile and easily damaged that you should return the way you came.

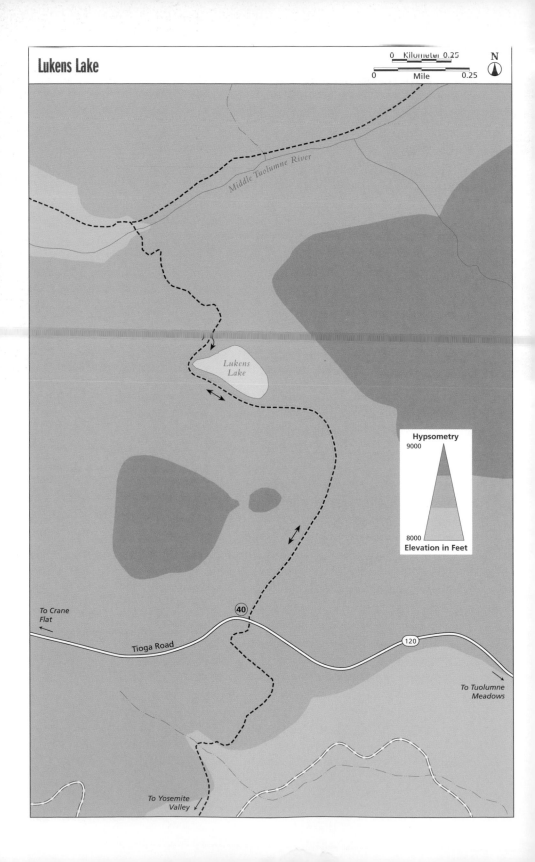

Lukens Lake is a favorite destination for wildflower lovers.

Miles and Directions

0.0 Lukens Lake Trailhead

0.8 Lukens Lake

1.2 White Wolf Trail junction

2.4 Return to Lukens Lake Trailhead

41 Ten Lakes

The Ten Lakes Basin contains only seven bodies of water large enough to be called lakes, along with an indeterminate number of smaller ponds. The trail climbs Ten Lakes Pass, and drops into the basin and skirts two of the ten lakes before climbing back out of the basin again. You can scramble to several other lakes on a layover day if you're not in a hurry. After leaving the basin, you make another descent into the isolated valley of the South Fork of Cathedral Creek, climb again to round a shoulder of Tuolumne Peak, then swing south to return to the Tioga Road via May Lake. Many people start at the Ten Lakes Trailhead, visit the lakes, then return the same way. But if you can arrange a car shuttle, this horseshoe-shaped loop makes an especially rewarding backpack through varied and beautiful country.

Start: Ten Lakes Trailhead
Total distance: 22.4-mile one-way shuttle
Hiking time: 2 to 6 days
Difficulty: Moderate
Elevation change: 3,300 feet
Seasons: All summer, whenever Tioga Road is open
Nearest facilities: Food, phones, and gas at Crane Flat and Lee Vining

Permits: Required; available in advance or at the Tuolumne Meadows Wilderness Center
Maps: USGS Falls Ridge, Ten Lakes, Tenaya Lake, and Yosemite Falls quads
Special considerations: This area holds snow later than most, so check with rangers to make sure the trail is passable in early summer.

Finding the trailhead: On Tioga Road (CA 120), drive about 20 miles east of Crane Flat or 26 miles west from Tuolumne Meadows. There is parking on both sides of the highway. The Ten Lakes Trail departs from the north side. You will need to leave another car or arrange to be picked up at the May Lake Trailhead, at the end of the spur road that heads north of Tioga Road along Snow Creek. Trailhead GPS: N37 51.09/W119 34.36

The Hike

From the parking area follow the trail that parallels the road west to the junction with the Yosemite Creek Trail at 0.1 mile. The trail heads northward through the forest over level ground, then emerges into sunshine. You soon begin to climb along the western slope above Yosemite Creek amid ceanothus and manzanita, hopping little mossy (and slippery) rivulets. A foaming white cascade tumbles down a shallow notch across the canyon to the east below Mount Hoffman. The trail reenters the forest and crosses several creeks, then meets the White Wolf Trail at 2.1 miles. Continue straight ahead (north) and, amid a patch of some truly gigantic lupines, cross a branch of Yosemite Creek that can present a challenge early in the year. The trail climbs relentlessly, working its way northeast to reach Half Moon Meadow at the base of an open granite ridge. There are a few marginal campsites at the northern end. Leaving the meadow, the path climbs very steeply between two little creeks and wonderful wildflower gardens. The grade lessens as the trail passes through a moist patch of sedges, then reaches the top of the ridge above Half Moon Meadow at the Grant Lakes junction at 5.9 miles. The Grant Lakes lie at the bottom of a flowery bowl and offer more solitude than you will find at Ten Lakes.

Cross over the open ridge called Ten Lakes Pass and pause to gasp at a stupendous panorama that extends from Mount Conness, past the great red Tioga Crest, across to Matterhorn Peak and the Sawtooth Ridge all the way to Tower Peak. The Grand Canyon of the Tuolumne River cuts a deep gash between the ridge just in front of you and the peaks behind. Now the trail drops down off the pass to the west, but don't put away your camera yet, for another grand vista soon appears. Here four of the (approximately) Ten Lakes descend from bowl to bowl, north to south down toward the Grand Canyon of the Tuolumne against a backdrop of more dramatic high peaks. You now drop steeply through willows, then slosh through a marshy spot to reach a stream connecting two of the lakes that can be tricky to cross early in the year. The southern shore of one of the larger Ten Lakes lies just beyond at 6.3 miles. There is plenty of camping here, but you will have lots of neighbors and a bear or two. This

Hike to the Ten Lakes Basin for classic glacial scenery.

is a popular spot for a layover where you can drop your pack and visit several of the other lakes above and below this one.

The route between this lake and the next one along the main trail is obscure. Watch for tree blazes and keep an eye on the topographic map to find the spot where the trail makes a steep rocky climb to a ridge high above the east side of the lake you just left. Now the trail swings southeast and passes fairly close to the shoreline of another lake at mile 8.2. This one also has good camping and is not usually as crowded as the first. Now descend through a forested gully, round a corner, and begin a steep drop down spectacular granite slabs decorated with some picturesque old junipers into the beautiful basin of the south fork of Cathedral Creek. There are a few campsites back off the trail where you can rest your aching knees and cool your feet after the long descent. The South Fork can be challenging to cross in early season because the water is deep and you can't see the bottom. Hiking poles are handy here. Once on the east side, at mile 10.4, the trail follows the creek for almost 2.0 miles before it switchbacks up the hillside, then climbs northward to round a shoulder of Tuolumne Peak, rising and falling over lots of little pockets where snow patches linger late into the summer. It drops through a narrow slot and turns a corner, where it follows a narrow ridge alongside a couple of tiny tarns on the south and an open panorama of the Cathedral Range to the north. Now the trail makes a long descent down the forested mountainside until it levels out in a boggy hollow filled with avalanche debris. There it meets a junction with the trail to Glen Aulin at 17.5 miles.

Turn right (south), cross a wide saddle, then begin a steep but stunning climb up a mostly open slope down which little creeks trickle through tiny gardens. Across the Murphy Creek drainage to the east are Polly Dome, Mount Conness, and the northern Sierra crest on the skyline. The path then drops briefly down the west side of the rocky ridge. When it enters the forest again, watch to the left for a glimpse of Raisin Lake, almost hidden behind rocks. This is a welcome stop for a swim after your long, hot climb. May Lake is not too much farther, but it is closed to swimming. Beyond Raisin Lake another short, steep set of switchbacks takes you up a slope, past a meadow with an ephemeral pond, then meets the northeast end of May Lake and skirts its shore to the May Lake High Sierra Camp, at 21.1 miles. From here drop down a rocky slope onto the flat forest floor, where after a few more minutes you reach the May Lake trailhead at the end of the Snow Flat Road.

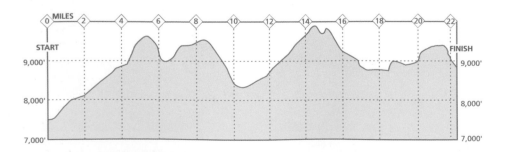

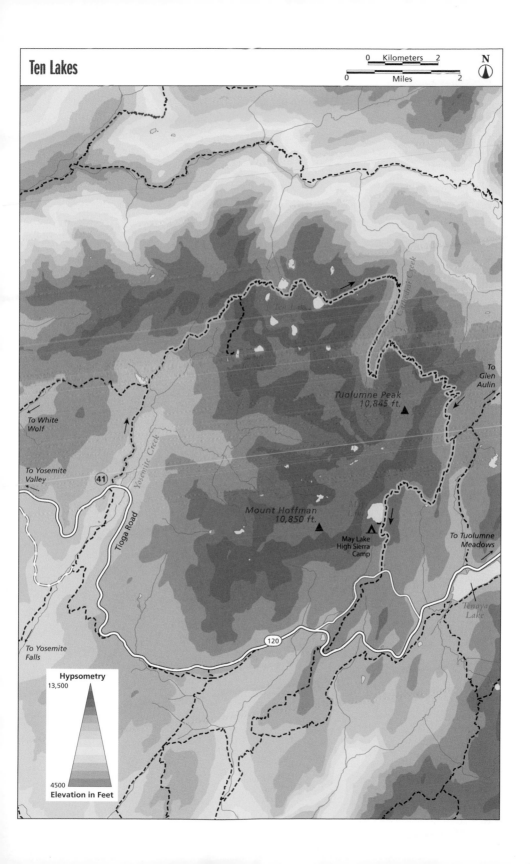

Ten Lakes

Ten Lakes

Cathedral Creek

To Glen Aulin

Tuolumne Peak
10,845 ft.

To White Wolf

Yosemite Creek

To Yosemite Valley

41

Tioga Road

Mount Hoffman
10,850 ft.

May Lake

May Lake High Sierra Camp

To Tuolumne Meadows

To Yosemite Falls

120

Tenaya Lake

Hypsometry

13,500

4500

Elevation in Feet

Miles and Directions

0.0 Ten Lakes Trailhead/parking lot/

0.1 Yosemite Creek Trail

2.1 White Wolf Trail junction

5.9 Grant Lakes junction

6.3 First of Ten Lakes

8.2 Second of Ten Lakes

10.4 Cathedral Creek Crossing

17.5 Glen Aulin junction

21.1 May Lake High Sierra Camp

22.4 May Lake Trailhead

Options: Grand Tour of the Grand Canyon of the Tuolumne—You can make a grand tour of almost the whole southern drainage of the Grand Canyon of the Tuolumne by turning north toward Glen Aulin at the junction at mile 17.5. From Glen Aulin you can follow the Tuolumne River down past Waterwheel Falls, through the Grand Canyon of the Tuolumne to Pate Valley, then climb out of the gorge to White Wolf. From there turn southeast to close the loop at the Ten Lakes Trailhead. You could also begin this big loop from White Wolf or from the Glen Aulin Trailhead. Lots of elevation change is involved, and it can be hot in the bottom of the canyon while the Ten Lakes Basin still has patches of snow, so check trail conditions before you go. You should allow a full week for this one since the distance is a bit over 50 miles and the terrain is rugged.

42 Soda Springs and Parsons Lodge

This is an easy exploration of the largest subalpine meadow in the Sierra with wildflowers galore, a good chance of seeing wildlife, and a taste of Yosemite history.

Start: Soda Springs Trailhead east of the Tuolumne Meadows Visitor Center
Total distance: 1.2 miles out and back, or as long as you want to make it
Hiking time: 1 hour to all day
Difficulty: Easy
Elevation change: Negligible

Seasons: All summer, whenever Tioga Road is open, though the going can be sloppy in June
Nearest facilities: Food and phones at Tuolumne Meadows; gas at Lee Vining
Permits: None
Maps: USGS Tioga Pass and Vogelsang Peak quads

Finding the trailhead: From the visitor center in Tuolumne Meadows, drive a few hundred yards east on Tioga Road to the signed trailhead on the north side of the road. Trailhead GPS: N37 52.20 / W119 22.13

The Hike

A wide, sandy trail heads right into the heart of enormous Tuolumne Meadows amid a riot of wildflowers: purple meadow penstemon and shooting stars, white pussytoes and yellow goldenrod. Off to the right (east) is long, sloping Lembert Dome, and farther beyond, the two red hulks of Mount Dana and Mount Gibbs. To their right is gray granite Mammoth Peak (not to be confused with Mammoth Mountain, the ski area farther to the south). Ahead, across the main channel of the river winding its sinuous way through the meadow, the path crosses a wood-and-stone footbridge. Pause here and turn around for a panoramic view of the Cathedral Range, with the spires of Cathedral Peak itself, then Echo Peak and the Cockscomb rising behind rounded Fairview Dome. To continue ahead, just beyond the bridge the trail intersects a gravel road on which you turn left (west) and proceed a few yards to a sign directing you to Soda Springs and Parsons Lodge to the right (north) up a little slope.

At 0.5 mile Parsons Lodge, built of local stone by the Sierra Club in 1915 and sold to the National Park Service in 1973, is open daily during the summer and contains exhibits about the history of the area. Next door the log-built McCauley Cabin houses park service volunteers who are eager to share local lore. Rest for a while on the rocks in front of the lodge to watch the activities of the marmot families who live in burrows nearby.

Now head toward the roofless log structure clearly visible to the east. Here naturally carbonated Soda Springs bubble out of the ground in dozens of places, staining the soil red-brown. This is a good place to see mule deer, especially mornings and evenings, as they come to lick the minerals deposited by the springs. You can spend

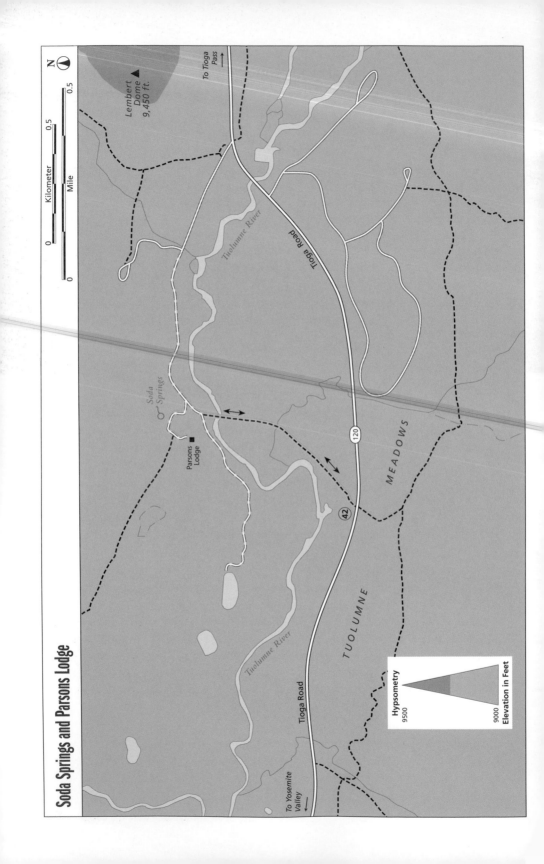

Soda Springs and Parsons Lodge

Lembert Dome
9,450 ft.

To Tioga Pass

Tuolumne River

Tioga Road

Soda Springs

Parsons Lodge

120

42

M E A D O W S

T U O L U M N E

Tuolumne River

Tioga Road

To Yosemite Valley

Kilometer

0   0.5

0   0.5

Mile

N

Hypsometry

9500

9000

Elevation in Feet

The ground bubbles with naturally carbonated water at Soda Springs.

a whole day wandering these meadows, using the well-marked trails to create your own loop, or you can return the way you came to Tioga Road.

Miles and Directions

- **0.0** Soda Springs Trailhead
- **0.5** Parsons Lodge
- **0.6** Soda Springs
- **1.2** Return to Soda Springs Trailhead

43 Dog Lake

This is an easy and popular out-and-back day hike through lodgepole pine forest to a lovely lake, tucked out of sight of Tuolumne Meadows behind Lembert Dome. It is at its most beautiful in late afternoon.

Start: Lembert Dome/Dog Lake Trailhead
Total distance: 2.8 miles out and back
Hiking time: 1 to 3 hours
Difficulty: Easy
Elevation change: 570 feet

Seasons: All summer, whenever Tioga Road is open
Nearest facilities: Tuolumne Meadows; gas at Lee Vining
Permits: None
Map: USGS Tioga Pass quad

Finding the trailhead: From the west drive Tioga Road (CA 120) eastward past the Tuolumne Meadows Visitor Center, store, and campground, all on the right. Just after crossing the bridge over the Tuolumne River, turn left into the Lembert Dome parking area. From the east (Tioga Pass) on Tioga Road, pass the turnoff to the wilderness center and Tuolumne Meadows Lodge on the left, then turn right into the Lembert Dome parking lot a few hundred yards beyond. Trailhead GPS: N37 52.38/W119 21.13

The Hike

Set out northward from the signed trailhead through lodgepole pines and cross an open rocky slab polished to a high sheen in places by glacial ice. If you look carefully, you can see the striations or scratches in the rock showing the direction in which the rivers of ice flowed. Reenter the forest, and at 0.2 mile meet a trail coming in from the stables to the west. A few yards beyond, a second trail from the stables joins this one. Keep straight ahead at both junctions. Climb steeply alongside the sheer face of Lembert Dome, then cross a little creek. The grade now becomes gentler. At 1.0 mile a trail cuts off to the right around the back side of Lembert Dome; continue straight ahead toward Dog Lake.

At 1.2 miles turn right onto the Dog Lake Trail, and at 1.4 miles reach an opening in the forest that perfectly frames the lake. Dog Lake is surrounded on three sides by lodgepole pine, but at the far east end a green meadow provides the foreground for the huge red bulks of Mount Dana and Mount Gibbs. The official mapped trail continues for about 0.5 mile along the south shore of the lake, but it is possible to circumnavigate the whole thing, adding about 1.5 miles to your hike. The meadow around the lakeshore, especially at the east and north ends, can be boggy, and it is very fragile, so travel with care. From the northeast end of the lake, there's a good view of Cathedral Peak poking up through the forest. Camping is not permitted here because the area is too delicate and too close to the road. Return the way you came.

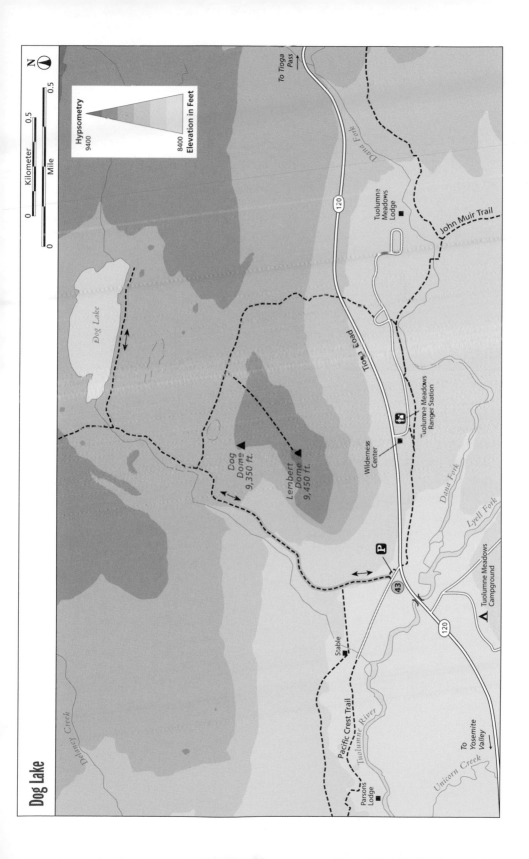

Dog Lake

N

Kilometer		
0	0.5	

Mile		
0	0.5	

Hypsometry

9400

8400

Elevation in Feet

To Tioga Pass

Dana Fork

120

Tuolumne Meadows Lodge

John Muir Trail

Tioga Road

Dog Lake

Delaney Creek

Dog Dome
9,350 ft.

Lembert Dome
9,450 ft.

Wilderness Center

Tuolumne Meadows Ranger Station

P

43

Dana Fork

Lyell Fork

Stable

Pacific Crest Trail

Tuolumne River

Parsons Lodge

Unicorn Creek

To Yosemite Valley

120

Tuolumne Meadows Campground

Mount Gibbs and Mount Dana are reflected in Dog Lake.

Miles and Directions

0.0 Lembert Dome/Dog Lake Trailhead

0.2 Trail from stables; keep right

1.0 Trail to Lembert Dome; keep left

1.2 Dog Lake Trail cutoff; turn right

1.4 Dog Lake

2.8 Return to Lembert Dome/Dog Lake Trailhead

44 Lembert Dome

Lembert Dome, among the premiere features of Tuolumne Meadows, is the huge, lopsided, smoothly polished mound of granite just north of Tioga Road. This hike takes you to the top of the dome, approaching from the west and returning to the east to make a loop. The views from the top are marvelous.

Start: Lembert Dome Trailhead
Total distance: 3.2-mile loop
Hiking time: 2 to 3 hours
Difficulty: Moderate
Elevation change: 870 feet
Seasons: All summer, whenever Tioga Road is open
Nearest facilities: Everything you need is in Tuolumne Meadows except gas at Lee Vining

Permits: None
Map: USGS Tioga Pass quad
Special considerations: Near the top of the dome, the going is steep and the rock is slick and smooth. You'll need good boots with lug soles, and if you're bothered by heights, don't try it. If you have doubts, remember that coming down a steep slope is more difficult than going up.

Finding the trailhead: From the west follow Tioga Road (CA 120) past the Tuolumne Meadows Visitor Center, store, cafe, and campground, all on the right. Just after crossing the bridge over the Tuolumne River, turn left into the Lembert Dome parking area. From the east (Tioga Pass) on Tioga Road, pass the turnoff to the wilderness center on the left, continue about a hundred yards, then turn right into the Lembert Dome parking area. Trailhead GPS: N37 52.38 / W119 21.13

The Hike

Set out northward, past the picnic tables and restrooms from the "Dog Lake/Lembert Dome Trailhead" sign beneath the lodgepole pines, then cross an open rocky slab where the route is marked by big boulders. The granite has patches polished to a high sheen by glaciers. If you look carefully, you can see the striations or scratches in the rock showing the direction in which the rivers of ice flowed.

At 0.2 mile a trail comes in from the stables to the west. A few yards beyond a second trail from the stables joins this one. Keep straight ahead at both junctions. Climb fairly steeply alongside the sheer face of Lembert Dome. The grade becomes gentler

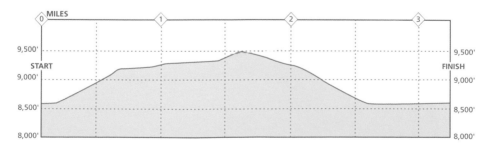

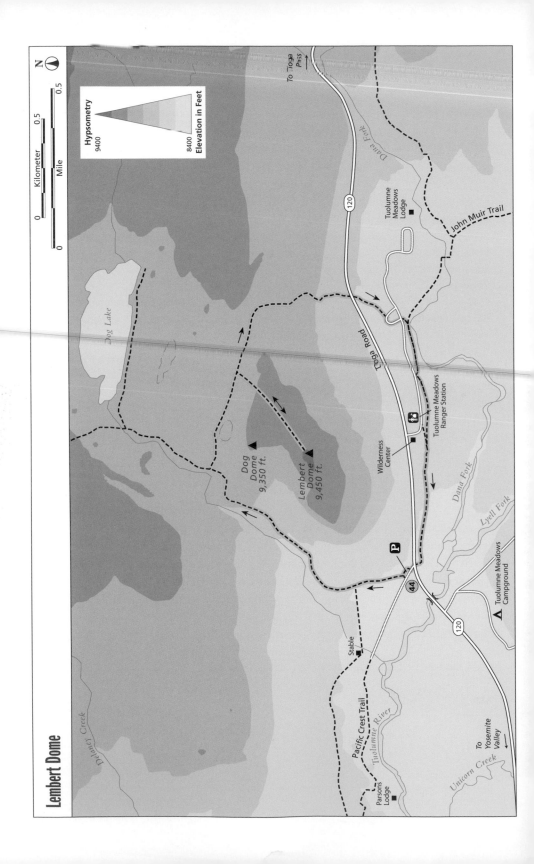

Lembert Dome

Hypsometry

Elevation in Feet

9400

8400

N

Kilometer
0   0.5

Mile
0   0.5

To Tioga Pass

Dana Fork

Tuolumne Meadows Lodge

120

John Muir Trail

Tioga Road

Tuolumne Meadows Ranger Station

Wilderness Center

Dog Lake

Dog Dome
9,350 ft.

Lembert Dome
9,450 ft.

Delaney Creek

P

44

Dana Fork

Lyell Fork

Tuolumne Meadows Campground

120

To Yosemite Valley

Stable

Pacific Crest Trail

Tuolumne River

Unicorn Creek

Parsons Lodge

as you cross a little creek. At 1.0 mile turn right (east) at another signed junction. The left fork goes on uphill to Dog Lake. Saunter along an almost flat path, passing a little pond at the base of the dome. At 1.7 miles is a junction not shown on the topographic map. You'll return to this point after visiting the summit. Turn right here and climb westward up a wooded ridge to a rocky saddle between Lembert Dome itself and a smaller bump known as Dog Dome. Follow the layered exfoliating granite slabs that form a natural stairway straight up the slope, then pick the easiest way to the top, at 2.0 miles. The slope is a little less steep toward the left (south) side of the dome.

When you have caught your breath, stroll around on top, where the footing is more level, to take in the view. You can see the high peaks of the north boundary country, the warm-red rocks of Mount Dana and Mount Gibbs on the eastern crest, and the Lyell Fork of the Tuolumne River flowing down from the Lyell Glacier to meet the Dana Fork in the broad green meadow. To the south the spires of the Cathedral Range pierce the sky, and to the west a series of rounded domes extend into the distance toward Yosemite Valley.

When you are ready, return to the last trail junction (2.3 miles) and follow the fairly steep switchbacks downhill to Tioga Road. Cross the road at 2.6 miles and continue on down to a parking lot on a small side road (the one that leads to Tuolumne

Examine glacial features like scratches and polish on Lembert Dome.

Meadows High Sierra Camp). Cross this road (south) and find a sign marking the John Muir Trail at 2.7 miles. Turn right and follow this alongside the road, then recross the Tioga Road to the Lembert Dome parking area.

Miles and Directions

0.0   Lembert Dome Trailhead

0.2   Trail from stables; keep right

1.0   Cutoff to Dog Lake; turn right

1.7   Trail to top of Lembert Dome

2.0   Summit of Lembert Dome

2.3   Return to trail junction; turn right

2.6   Cross Tioga Road

2.7   John Muir Trail sign; turn right

3.2   Return to Lembert Dome Trailhead

45 Young Lakes

The three Young Lakes lie in a subalpine lake basin with superb panoramic views of the Cathedral Range along the way. The hike starts out steeply but becomes more gradual as you climb. It's a good weekend backpack, but if you can, take an extra day to explore the high country beyond. You can make semi-loop of the hike since there is an alternate, though less scenic, trail to the west on which you can return.

Start: Young Lakes Trailhead at Lembert Dome picnic area

Total distance: 13.4 miles out and back

Hiking time: 1 day if you hurry; 2 days are better

Difficulty: Strenuous as a day hike, moderate as a backpack

Elevation change: 1,460 feet

Seasons: All summer, whenever Tioga Road is open

Nearest facilities: Food and phones in Tuolumne Meadows; gas in Lee Vining

Permits: None required for a day hike; available for overnights in advance or at the Tuolumne Meadows Wilderness Center

Map: USGS Tioga Pass quad

Finding the trailhead: From the west drive Tioga Road (CA 120) eastward past the Tuolumne Meadows Visitor Center, store, and campground, all on the right (south). Just after crossing the bridge over the Tuolumne River, turn left into the Lembert Dome parking area. From the east (Tioga Pass) on Tioga Road, pass the turnoff to the wilderness center and Tuolumne Lodge on the left. A few hundred yards beyond, turn right into the Lembert Dome parking lot and picnic area. You can also ride the Tuolumne Meadows shuttle to Lembert Dome (stop 4). If you plan to spend the night at Young Lakes, park along the road that roughly parallels the highway. Overnight parking is prohibited in the Lembert Dome lot. Be sure to stow all food and food containers in the bear-proof boxes along the road. Trailhead GPS: N37 32.58/W119 21.13

The Hike

Set out northward from the "Lembert Dome/Dog Lake Trailhead" sign through lodgepole pines, crossing an open rocky slab where the route is marked by big boulders. The granite has patches polished to a high sheen by glaciers. If you look carefully, you can see the striations or scratches in the rock showing the direction in which the rivers of ice flowed.

The trail reenters the forest, and at 0.2 mile a trail comes in from the stables to the west. A few yards beyond, a second trail from the stables joins this one. Keep straight ahead at both junctions. Climb fairly steeply alongside the sheer face of Lembert Dome, then cross a little creek as the grade becomes more gradual. At 1.0 mile keep left at a junction with the trail heading east around the back side of Lembert Dome. At 1.2 miles another trail to the right cuts off to Dog Lake, worth a short detour, especially in afternoon light. Your trail continues straight ahead, crossing the outlet stream from the lake and ascending a moderate slope for about a half mile to a pretty

Ragged Peak is reflected in the morning calm surface of the second Young Lake.

meadow where you hop or wade Delaney Creek. From the middle of the meadow you can see the great red peaks of Mount Gibbs and Mount Dana on the skyline, so different from the surrounding gray granite. Climb easily up a forested little ridge beyond the meadow around the west side of an unnamed granite dome, then emerge onto a meadowy terrace with twisted whitebark pines and little flower-lined streams trickling through.

The view from here must be one of the finest in the entire Sierra Nevada, with the whole Cathedral Range, including Unicorn, Echo, and Cathedral Peaks, spreading out before you. To the right is Mount Hoffman, geographic center of Yosemite; to the left is Mount Lyell, highest peak in the park, sheltering the Lyell Glacier. Leaving this perfect spot, the trail climbs a short distance over a sandy shoulder of Ragged Peak, the highest point on this hike, then descends to the Soda Springs Trail junction on the other side at 5.1 miles; turn right. The trail joining yours is an alternate route to Young Lakes from Tuolumne Meadows. Your trail continues northward, gradually curving to the east, skirting Ragged Peak, finally dipping into the basin containing the lowest of the three Young Lakes at 6.7 miles. There is plenty of good camping along the western side of this first lake, and most backpackers pitch their tents here, but the higher lakes are equally beautiful and less crowded. To reach them, follow the use trail that runs along the northern shore and scramble up alongside the little

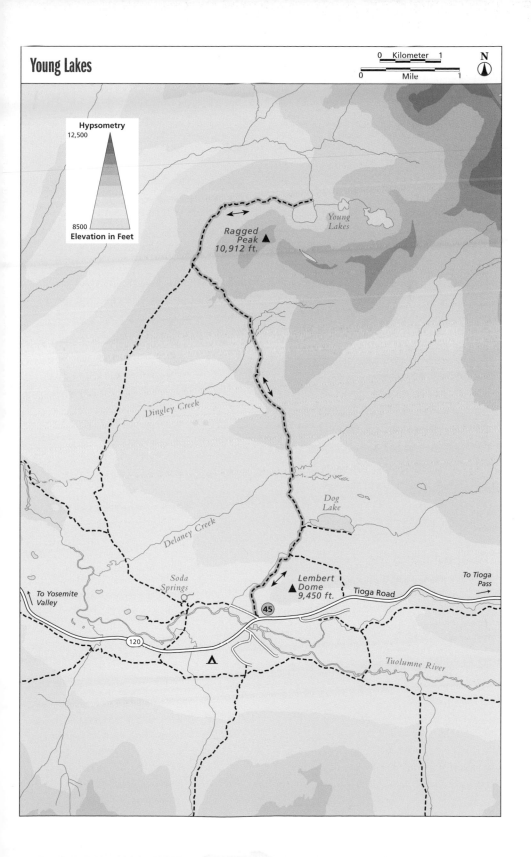

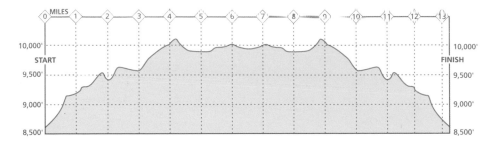

waterfall that connects the lakes. From the uppermost lake you can look down upon the lower ones, with snaggle-toothed Ragged Peak jutting up behind them.

On your return to Tuolumne Meadows, you can vary your hike by keeping right (west) instead of left at the trail junction 1.5 miles below Young Lakes. You will end up not far from Soda Springs, where you turn left (east) to follow a dirt road back to the trailhead. This route is heavily forested all the way, so you will miss the great views of the Cathedral Range on the way down unless you return the way you came.

Miles and Directions

0.0   Young Lakes Trailhead
0.2   Trails to stables; keep right
1.0   Trail to Lembert Dome; go straight ahead
1.2   Trail to Dog Lake; keep left
5.1   Soda Springs Trail junction; turn right
6.7   First Young Lake
13.4   Return to Young Lakes Trailhead

46 Gaylor Lakes

This is a steep but short day hike into a truly alpine environment where permanent snowfields lie in the shady folds of the mountains, and even in July you might have to skirt snow patches or wade through slush. Your reward is a grand open basin filled with masses of miniature belly flowers and the chirps and whistles of pikas and marmots among a scattering of pristine lakes and ponds.

Start: Gaylor Lakes Trailhead
Total distance: 3.0 miles out and back
Hiking time: 2 to 4 hours
Difficulty: Moderate
Elevation change: 600 feet
Seasons: All summer, whenever Tioga Road is open

Nearest facilities: Food and phones in Tuolumne Meadows; gas at Crane Flat and Lee Vining
Permits: None
Map: USGS Tioga Pass quad

Finding the trailhead: The trailhead is on Tioga Road (CA 120) immediately inside the eastern park entrance, on the west side of the road. Trailhead GPS: N37 54.36 / W119 15.30

The Hike

Follow the well-used path uphill through subalpine forest. The trail tops out on a broad, open saddle on broken metamorphic rock. Behind you massive red Mount Dana thrusts upward above Dana Meadows. Beyond a few clumps of windblown whitebark pine, the trail drops as steeply as it rose to the first of the Gaylor Lakes. It skirts the north edge of the lake, which seems to reach to the very lip of the shallow dish in which it sits. Beyond it the spiky tops of the Cathedral Range appear to be emerging from the surface of the lake itself.

Climb gradually north past Gaylor Peak, skirt the west end of another lake, swing around a ridge to the left, then climb to another ridgetop at the border of the park. There, at 1.5 miles, you'll find the old Great Sierra Mine, a failed silver-mining operation that commands another grand view. You can explore this lake basin for hours, or you can cross the low rise immediately west of Gaylor Peak to discover the Granite Lakes in another shallow bowl at the base of a classic glacial cirque.

There is a second route leading to the lakes that begins a few miles farther west on Tioga Road, but the trailhead is not obvious and the distance to the first lake is longer. The two trails do not meet in the lake basin, so if you want to make a longer shuttle hike, you will have to travel about a mile cross-country between the trails, or return the way you came.

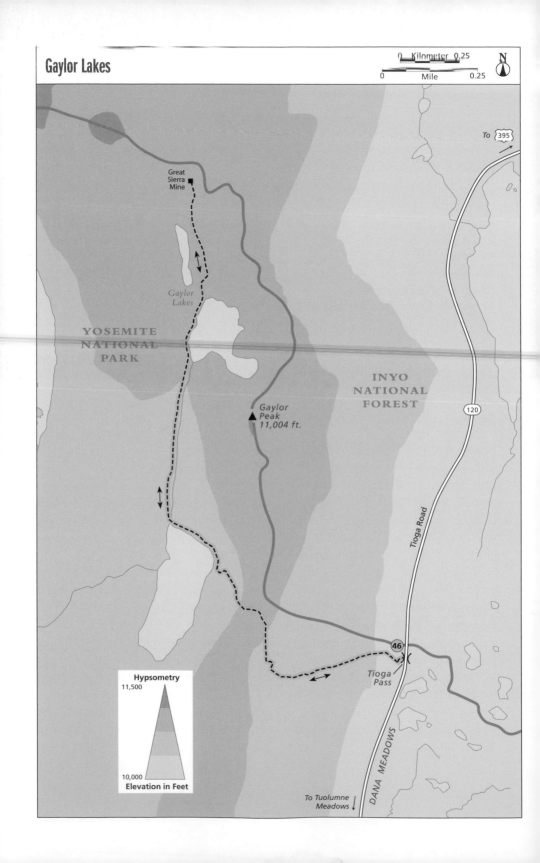

Gaylor Lakes

To 395

Great
Sierra
Mine

Gaylor
Lakes

YOSEMITE
NATIONAL
PARK

INYO
NATIONAL
FOREST

Gaylor
Peak
11,004 ft.

120

Tioga Road

Hypsometry

11,500

10,000

Elevation in Feet

46

Tioga
Pass

DANA MEADOWS

To Tuolumne
Meadows ↓

High alpine meadows surround Gaylor Lakes.

Miles and Directions

0.0 Gaylor Lakes Trailhead
1.5 Great Sierra Mine
3.0 Gaylor Lakes Trailhead

Honorable Mention

White Wolf to Harden Lake

This easy 6-mile round-trip stroll to Harden Lake is a favorite of wildflower lovers. It begins on a road now used only by service vehicles that winds gently downhill most of the way. The lake itself is not among the most scenic in Yosemite, but it makes a pleasant lunch or snack stop and is the usual turnaround point. It is the flower gardens along the bank of the Middle Fork of the Tuolumne River, almost tropical in their variety and profusion, that make this a popular hike. Your starting point, White Wolf Lodge, is itself set in a sunny meadow carpeted with flowers most of the summer. The route follows the paved road past the campground, tent cabins, and ranger station, then over the Tuolumne River, where the pavement ends. From here just follow the road, which eventually turns into trail, downhill, over occasional humps, ignoring any minor roads or trails branching off this one until you reach a spur trail at about 2.0 miles on the right directing you to Harden Lake, another 0.9 mile and partly uphill.

White Wolf Lodge and campground are less than a mile down a well-signed side road that heads north off the Tioga Road. The turnoff is 14 miles east of Crane Flat and 17 miles west of Tenaya Lake.

Hetch Hetchy

etch Hetchy Reservoir, begun in 1914, completed in 1923, then expanded in 1938, provides water and power for the City of San Francisco. For this reason, since September 11, 2001, park rangers at the entrance kiosk record license numbers of all vehicles entering and leaving the area. Before the dam captured and tamed the Tuolumne River, the Hetch Hetchy Valley was said to rival Yosemite itself in scenic beauty. John Muir's famous,

The O'Shaughnessy Dam flooded Hetch Hetchy Valley, said to have rivaled Yosemite Valley in beauty.

if fruitless, battle against the dam brought the need to preserve such wilderness trea
sures to the attention of the public and gave impetus to the growth of the National
Park Service and to the conservation movement as a whole. Even now a campaign
is under way to convince legislators to raze the dam, drain the reservoir, and allow
Hetch Hetchy to return to its original state. The area around the lake has the best
display of springtime wildflowers in the park. It's a great place to hike in early season
when the higher country is still under snow, and is pleasant in October when the
black oaks change color. In midsummer it's dry and hot. No swimming or boating is
allowed in the reservoir.

There are no overnight accommodations at Hetch Hetchy, except for a walk-
in backpack campground. You must have a wilderness permit to use it, and you
are limited to a one-night stay. The Hodgden Meadow Campground near the Big
Oak Flat entrance is the closest park campground and requires reservations. There
is also a concessionaire-operated USDA Forest Service campground on Evergreen
Road open on a first-come, first-served basis, and other accommodations in nearby
Groveland.

To reach the main Hetch Hetchy trailhead at O'Shaughnessy Dam, you must leave
Yosemite Park at the Big Oak Flat Entrance Station if you are coming from the
east, then reenter at the Hetch Hetchy Entrance Station about 8 miles up Evergreen
Road. From the west turn off the highway before you reach the main (Big Oak Flat)
entrance station. (See directions at the beginning of each hike.) Wilderness permits
are available at the Hetch Hetchy Entrance Station and the Big Oak Flat Entrance
Station. It's a good idea to ask about the condition of the road before you start out
because it washes out regularly and may be closed for repairs.

47 Wapama Falls

This is an out-and-back day hike along the controversial Hetch Hetchy Reservoir through a riotous show of springtime wildflowers past the base of one gentle waterfall to the crash and spray of a mighty one—at least in springtime when high country snows are melting.

Start: Trailhead at O'Shaughnessy Dam
Total distance: 5.0 miles out and back
Hiking time: 3 to 6 hours
Difficulty: Easy
Elevation change: 500 feet
Seasons: Mid-Apr through June

Permits: None
Nearest facilities: Food and accommodations at Evergreen Lodge near Camp Mather; phones, toilets, and water near the trailhead; gas at Crane Flat
Map: USGS Lake Eleanor quad

Finding the trailhead: Drive 1 mile west of the Big Oak Flat Entrance Station to Yosemite on CA 120. Turn right (north) on Evergreen Road and drive about 7 miles. At Camp Mather turn right (northeast) on Hetch Hetchy Road. Pass through the park entrance station in about a mile, then continue on for 8 miles more to where the road ends in a one-way loop. Partway around is the dam, and just beyond it, a parking area. Trailhead GPS: N37 56.48/W119 47.14

The Hike

Walk across the dam past some historical markers. On the far side at 0.1 mile, enjoy the troupe of acrobatic swallows swooping and diving before the entrance to a dark and dripping tunnel. Pass through the tunnel and continue along the level road skirting the lake; it's lined with live oak, bay trees, and poison oak, along with dozens of species of wildflowers, among them the unusual pink-and-yellow harlequin lupine. Little trickles of water seep from cracks in the rocks to nourish buttercups, monkey flowers, and columbines. In May, if you're lucky, you'll catch the spring migration of the little brown-and-orange California newts crossing the trail in such numbers that you must step carefully to avoid squashing them. The low elevation here also makes

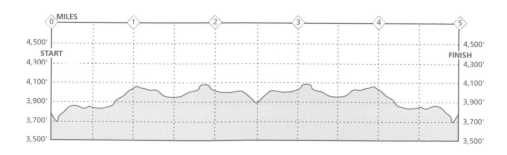

THE CALIFORNIA NEWT

A newt is a particular kind of salamander. Most of the year they live on land, hiding under leaves and rocks. They have rough skins, not at all slimy, but they need water to breed, and in springtime the males develop smooth skin and their tails become flattened vertically to make swimming more efficient. California newts (also known as "water dogs") are not as wary of sunlight as other salamanders, especially when it's mating time, so they are easier to spot than other species. They are poisonous to eat, so are avoided by most predators, and are themselves carnivorous, snapping up snails, worms, and insects. They are not dangerous to handle so long as you rinse your hands afterward. When startled, they throw back their heads and raise their tails to flash their bright orange undersides in a defense posture.

The spray from Wapama Falls sometimes floods the trail when high country snow melts in spring.

Wapama Falls

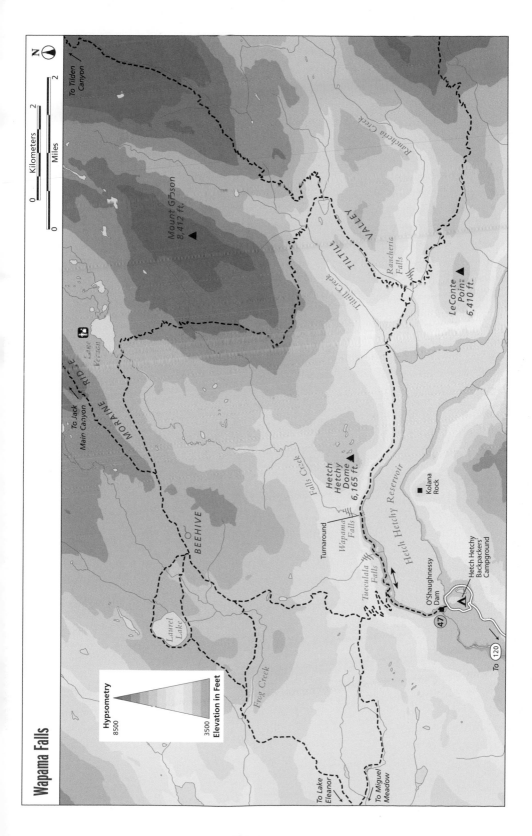

N

To Tilden Canyon

Kilometers
0   2

Miles
0   2

To Jack Main Canyon

MORAINE RIDGE

Lake Vernon

Mount Gibson
8,412 ft.

Rancheria Creek

BEEHIVE

Laurel Lake

Falls Creek

Frog Creek

Tiltill Creek

TILTILL VALLEY

Rancheria Falls

Hetch Hetchy Dome
6,165 ft.

LeConte Point
6,410 ft.

Turnaround

Wapama Falls

Tueeulala Falls

Hetch Hetchy Reservoir

Kolana Rock

O'Shaughnessy Dam

Hetch Hetchy Backpackers' Campground

(47)

To (120)

To Lake Eleanor

To Miguel Meadow

Hypsometry
8500

3500
Elevation in Feet

this a likely spot for snakes of several kinds, including rattlers. They are not aggressive, but they do not like to be handled or stepped on.

The road climbs fairly gently for awhile; then, at 0.9 mile, it continues on to the left, while the trail to the falls cuts to the right toward the lake. The route rises and falls and curves back and forth past more delicate little gardens, waterfalls, and pools while Kolana Rock broods darkly over the reservoir on the other side.

Farther along, Tueeulala Falls tumbles down over the trail. Early in the season you'll probably get your feet wet as you pass, but by mid-June the creek that feeds it is usually dry. The trail continues along the cliff above the lake, climbing and descending for a short distance more until at last, at 2.5 miles, the spray and thunder of Wapama Falls make themselves felt. Toward the bottom the fall splits into several sections, each of which is crossed on a separate footbridge. Sometimes the bridges are shin-deep underwater, though safe to wade; at other times the force of the falling torrent is so great that it is risky to cross. You can enjoy the falls from either side, or from the middle—if you crave a refreshing shower. Return the way you came.

Miles and Directions

- **0.0** O'Shaughnessy Dam Trailhead
- **0.1** Tunnel
- **0.9** Trail/road junction; turn right onto the trail
- **2.5** Wapama Falls
- **5.0** Return to O'Shaughnessy Dam Trailhead

48 Rancheria Falls

Lots of flowers, birds, bears, and reptiles are likely company on this popular springtime backpack. The route runs along the north shore of Hetch Hetchy Reservoir, past Tueeulala and Wapama Falls, where you can expect to be thoroughly drenched by spray, to campsites beside the spot where Rancheria Creek tumbles down a series of cascades into the lake. You can do it as a strenuous day hike, but there are lots of moderate ups and downs that make it more demanding than it looks. Rancheria Falls has always been a notorious hangout for "problem" bears, so keep your canister locked.

Start: Trailhead at O'Shaughnessy Dam
Total distance: 13.8 miles out and back
Hiking time: 6 hours to 2 days
Difficulty: Moderate
Elevation change: 1,400 feet
Seasons: Mid-Apr through June
Permits: None for a day hike; available for overnights in advance or at the Hetch Hetchy Entrance Station
Nearest facilities: Food and accommodations at Evergreen Lodge near Camp Mather; phones, toilets, and water near the trailhead; gas at Crane Flat

Maps: USGS Hetch Hetchy Reservoir and Lake Eleanor quads
Special considerations: Even though there are bridges over several sections of Wapama Falls where the trail crosses below it, you may still be wading chin-deep through fast-moving water. Be prepared for wet feet and carry some sort of pack cover, even if only a plastic bag, because the spray can be heavy enough to soak your pack and its contents. At the height of snow melt in spring, check with rangers before you begin to make sure you can get past the falls safely.

Finding the trailhead: Drive 1 mile west of the Big Oak Flat Entrance Station to Yosemite on CA 120. Turn right (north) on Evergreen Road for about 7 miles. At Camp Mather turn right (northeast) on Hetch Hetchy Road. Pass through the park entrance station in about a mile, then continue on for 8 miles to where the road ends in a one-way loop. Partway around is the dam, and just beyond it, a parking area. Trailhead GPS: N37 56.48 / W119 47.14

The Hike

Walk across the dam past some historical markers and on through a dark and dripping tunnel on an old gravel road lined with live oak, bay trees, and poison oak, along with dozens of species of wildflowers. Climb easily along the road for a while; then, at 0.9 mile, turn right, toward the lake, at a signed trail that cuts off from the road. The route rises and falls and curves back and forth past delicate little gardens, waterfalls, and pools while Kolana Rock broods darkly over the reservoir on the other side.

Farther along, Tueeulala Falls tumbles down over the trail, where you will get your feet wet in early season, though by mid-June the creek that feeds it is dry. The trail continues along the cliff above the lake, climbing and descending for a short distance more until, at 2.5 miles, the spray and thunder of Wapama Falls make themselves felt.

Rancheria Creek cascades into Hetch Hetchy Reservoir over Rancheria Falls.

Pick your way across the several bridges that span the multiple strands of the falls, sometimes sloshing through deep water, sometimes bracing yourself against potentially dangerous torrents, sometimes strolling by with perfectly dry feet. The trail gains some elevation above the lake and the base of the falls and makes its way around Hetch Hetchy Dome, occasionally climbing or dropping on switchbacks to avoid various obstacles. Occasional patches of shady oak forest alternate with stretches of sunny, sweaty trudging until the trail crosses a shady, unnamed creek on a little bridge, rounds a corner, and crosses more substantial Tiltill Creek on a bigger one. Finally, after one last hot, shadeless climb, it tops out on a shoulder from which there is a good view of Rancheria Creek roaring down a series of water slides to the reservoir. About a quarter mile beyond, at 6.9 miles, a sign marks the turnoff to the camping area near the river on your right. This is such a popular spot that it is especially important to pitch your tent at least 100 feet from the creekside and practice Leave No Trace camping techniques. When you are ready, retrace your steps to the dam and the parking lot.

▶ **Watch for congregations of all kinds of butterflies at mud puddles or damp spots along the trail. These are young males sucking up water and minerals, biding their time until the females, who emerge later, appear. This behavior is called "puddling."**

Rancheria Falls

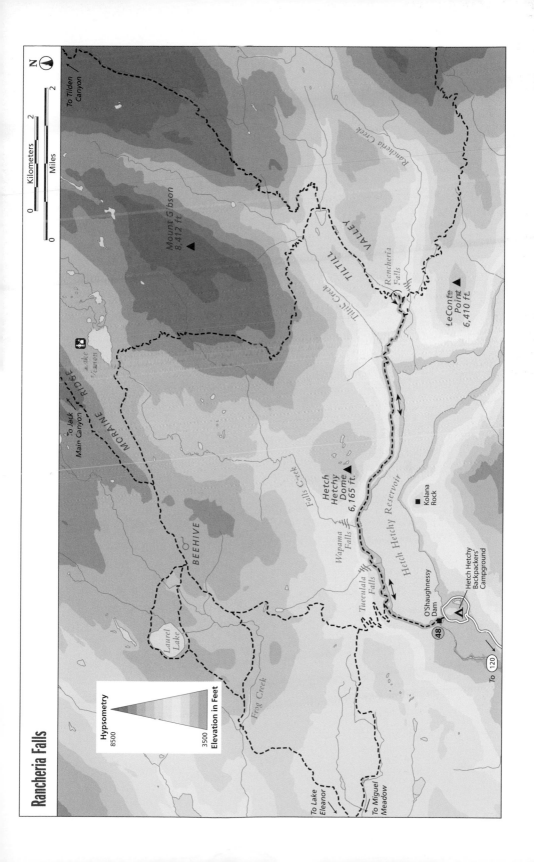

Hypsometry

Elevation in Feet

8500

3500

N

Kilometers
0   2

Miles
0   2

To Tilden Canyon

Rancheria Creek

Mount Gibson
8,412 ft

To Jack
Main Canyon

RIDGE

MORAINE

Lake Canyon

TILTILL VALLEY

Tiltill Creek

Rancheria Falls

LeConte Point
6,410 ft

BEEHIVE

Laurel Lake

Falls Creek

Hetch Hetchy Dome
6,165 ft.

Wapama Falls

Hetch Hetchy Reservoir

Kolana Rock

Frog Creek

Tueeulala Falls

O'Shaughnessy Dam

48

Hetch Hetchy
Backpackers'
Campground

To Lake Eleanor

To Miguel Meadow

To 120

Miles and Directions

0.0   O'Shaughnessy Dam Trailhead

0.9   Wapama Falls Trail cuts off to the right

2.5   Wapama Falls

6.9   Rancheria Falls Campground

13.8   Return to O'Shaughnessy Dam Trailhead

Option: Top of Rancheria Falls—To visit the top of the Rancheria Falls, continue on up the trail past the campground, keeping to the right at a junction with the trail to Tiltill Valley at about a quarter mile up. Just around the corner the bridge over the Rancheria Creek spans a rocky gorge where the stream is squeezed into the neck of a deep, narrow funnel that opens out just below the bridge, releasing water in a boiling, foaming rush down past the campground. This adds only about a half mile round-trip to the hike total.

49 Laurel Lake

This is a moderate, early season weekend hike with lots of wildflowers, birds, good camping, and a rare botanical treat at the end. Signs of the 2013 Rim Fire are evident, but many trees have been scorched only around the base, and the new openings in the forest allow sunlight to reach the floor to promote luxuriant new growth. The burned snags still standing make homes for woodpeckers, bluebirds, and lots of other animals. You can expect mosquitoes, too, but while you are swatting, keep in mind that some of the loveliest flowers here, like the delicate white rein orchid, are mosquito-pollinated.

Start: Trailhead at O'Shaughnessy Dam
Total distance: 16.2 miles out and back
Hiking time: 7 hours to 2 days
Difficulty: Moderate as a backpack, strenuous as a day hike
Elevation change: 2,700 feet
Seasons: Mid-Apr through June

Permits: None for a day hike; available for overnights in advance or at the Hetch Hetchy Entrance Station
Nearest facilities: Food and accommodations at Evergreen Lodge near Camp Mather; phones, toilets, and water near the trailhead; gas at Crane Flat
Maps: USGS Lake Eleanor and Kibbie Lake quads

Finding the trailhead: Drive 1 mile west of the Big Oak Flat Entrance Station to Yosemite on CA 120. Turn right (north) on Evergreen Road for about 7 miles. At Camp Mather turn right (northeast) on Hetch Hetchy Road. Pass through the park entrance station in about a mile, then continue on for 8 miles to where the road ends in a one-way loop. If you are day hiking only, you can park about halfway around the loop at the parking area just beyond the dam. If you are backpacking, you must park in the signed backpackers' parking lot near the beginning of the loop. This is an active bear area. Be sure to stow all food in the bear boxes provided. Trailhead GPS: N37 56.48/ W119 47.14

The Hike

Walk across the dam past some historical markers and on through a dark and dripping tunnel to emerge into sunlight on the old Lake Eleanor Road, lined with oak, bay trees, and poison oak, along with dozens of species of wildflowers. At 0.9 mile a trail cuts away from the road, leading to the right toward the reservoir, but you keep left along the road and climb the long, partly shaded switchbacks to a junction with the trail to Miguel Meadow at 3.6 miles. Keep right (north) and ascend beneath pines and incense cedars to a more level stretch that winds through an open rocky area lined with manzanita.

Reenter partly burned-over forest and climb past a couple of tiny emerald green meadows carpeted with white meadow foam and yellow monkey flowers and take

Rare pink azaleas line the shore of Laurel Lake.

time to enjoy views back down over the reservoir. After a steady climb of more than a mile, reach a long flat stretch of trail through waist-high bracken fern, then pass by another junction heading back to Lake Eleanor at 6.0 miles on an overgrown trail. At 6.8 miles you arrive at a soggy, sometimes buggy, but marvelously flowery meadow at Beehive junction. A piped spring partly protected by wooden planks (the water should be purified before drinking) is just a few yards from the junction, and there is decent camping in the forest on the other side of the trail.

Turn left (west) here at the sign pointing to Laurel Lake. The other fork goes on to Lake Vernon. At only 0.1 mile the trail splits, but both forks go to Laurel Lake. The left fork says Laurel Lake is 1.0 mile; the right one says Laurel Lake is 1.4 miles. Take the left fork. Not only is it shorter, but the right fork is overgrown with fallen trees and brush and in some places is frequently underwater. In another 0.2 mile downhill, cross Frog Creek, either hopping on rocks or wading carefully if the water is high. Wind moderately up and over a partly burned ridge to spot Laurel Lake ahead. Beautiful dense azalea shrubs line the lake almost all the way around, some a rare and delicate pink, a color unknown elsewhere in Yosemite and perhaps anywhere else in the Sierra. There are plenty of good campsites above the southwest shore. If you want to explore a bit further, continue on the trail along the lakeshore, crossing the outlet stream on a logjam to find a sign that says "Laurel Lake 6650 Feet" (though the map

Laurel Lake

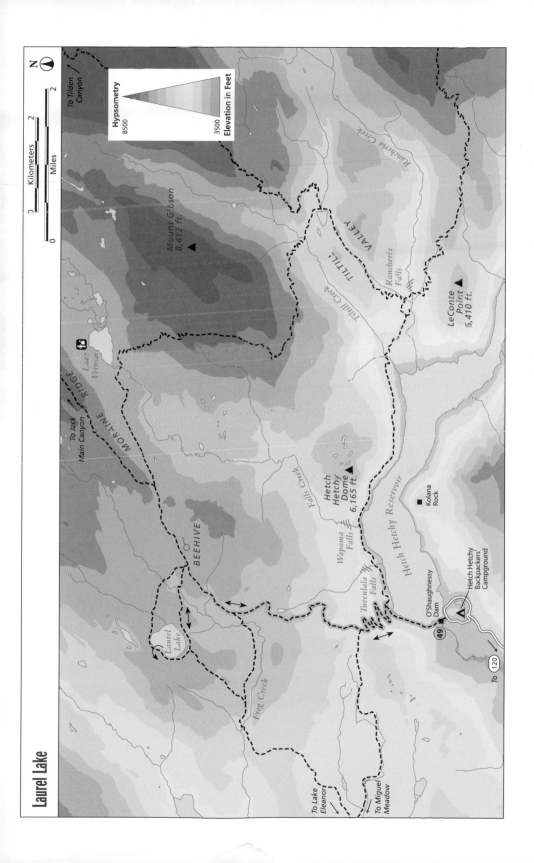

N

Kilometers
0   2

Miles
0   2

To Tilden
Canyon

Hypsometry
8500

3500
Elevation in Feet

To Jack
Main Canyon

MORAINE   RIDGE

Lake
Vernon

BEEHIVE

Laurel
Lake

Frog Creek

Falls Creek

Mount Gibson
8,412 ft.

Tiltill Creek

TILTILL
VALLEY

Rancheria Creek

Rancheria
Falls

LeConte
Point
5,410 ft.

Hetch
Hetchy Dome
6,165 ft.

Wapama
Falls

Tueeulala
Falls

Hetch Hetchy Reservoir

Kolana
Rock

O'Shaughnessy
Dam

Hetch Hetchy
Backpackers'
Campground

49

120

To 120

To Lake
Eleanor

To Miguel
Meadow

says 6,490 feet). Just beyond, find another junction with a trail to Lake Eleanor and one to "Wilmer" Lake (most maps and some signs call it "Wilma" Lake) and the continuation of the Beehive Trail. This is a good place to turn around. The sign here says "Beehive 2.8 Miles," so you can circumnavigate the lake if you like, but the numbers on the signs don't really add up, and continuing around the lake back to Beehive is difficult to follow and not very scenic.

Miles and Directions

0.0 Trailhead at O'Shaughnessy Dam

0.9 Lake Eleanor Road/trail junction

3.6 Miguel Meadow trail junction

6.0 Lake Eleanor cutoff

6.8 Beehive junction

6.9 Laurel Lake trail splits; turn left

8.0 Laurel Lake

8.1 Laurel Lake/Lake Eleanor/Beehive junction

16.2 Return to trailhead

Option: You can circumnavigate Laurel Lake, but it is not recommended and will add about 2 miles of overgrown, scratchy, sometimes marshy bushwhacking to your hike.

50 Lake Vernon and Tiltill Valley

Lake Vernon lies in a real subalpine setting at an elevation of only 6,568 feet, so this loop is a good way to get in a real High Sierra backpack while the higher country is still under snow. The wildflowers and waterfalls along the Hetch Hetchy Reservoir on the last leg of the trip are spectacular; there are Native American sites to investigate in Tiltill Valley, and good camping at Rancheria Falls.

Start: Trailhead at O'Shaughnessy Dam
Total distance: 26.7-mile loop
Hiking time: 2 to 4 days
Difficulty: Moderate
Elevation change: 3,000 feet
Seasons: Early May through early July and Oct
Permits: Required; available in advance or from the Hetch Hetchy Entrance Station

Nearest facilities: Food and accommodations at Evergreen Lodge near Camp Mather; phones, toilets, and water near the trailhead; gas at Crane Flat
Maps: USGS Hetch Hetchy Reservoir, Kibbie Lake, Lake Eleanor, and Tiltill Mountain quads

Finding the trailhead: Drive 1 mile west of the Big Oak Flat Entrance Station to Yosemite on CA 120. Turn right (north) onto Evergreen Road and drive about 7 miles. At Camp Mather turn right (northeast) onto Hetch Hetchy Road. Pass through the park entrance station in about a mile, then continue on for 8 miles to where the road ends in a one-way loop at O'Shaughnessy Dam and the parking area. Trailhead GPS: N37 56.48 / W119 47.14

The Hike

Walk across the dam past some historical markers and on through a dark and dripping tunnel to emerge into sunlight on the old Lake Eleanor Road, lined with live oak, bay trees, and poison oak, along with dozens of species of wildflowers. At 0.9 mile a trail cuts away from the road, heading to the right toward the reservoir. Stay on the road and follow the long, partly shaded switchbacks to a junction with the trail to Miguel Meadow at 3.6 miles. Keep right (north) and ascend beneath pines and incense cedars to a more level stretch that winds through an open, rocky area lined with manzanita. Stay alert and watch the ducks to avoid losing the trail.

Reenter burned-over forest and climb past a couple of tiny emerald green meadows carpeted with white meadow foam and yellow monkey flowers until you arrive at another junction heading back to Lake Eleanor at 6.0 miles, and keep right (north) again. Very soon you reach Beehive, at 6.8 miles. It is a soggy and mosquito-ridden meadow with a piped spring protected by wood planks. (The water should be purified before drinking.) Another path goes west to Laurel Lake from here. Keep right, heading northeast out of Beehive, gaining elevation steadily to reach yet another junction at 8.1 miles with the Jack Main Canyon Trail heading northeast to the top

Listen for the booming call of the blue grouse in the Tiltill Valley region.

of Moraine Ridge toward Wilmer Lake. Follow the right fork for a time, then drop down an open rocky slope and cross over a low hump to enter the Lake Vernon basin at 10.3 miles. There is some beautiful camping to be found on broad flat rock slabs along the northwestern shore of the lake.

Leaving Lake Vernon, head south, crossing Falls Creek, the lake's outlet stream, on a bridge. The route now climbs above the lake basin and looks out over splendid High Sierra scenery—wild and open glacier-scoured white granite, dotted with junipers. In springtime this section of trail reeks with the smell of onions. So many tiny, low-growing, almost transparent flowers sprout in the sandy soil at your feet that it's impossible to avoid stepping on some of them. The trail crosses over the top of this ridge, reenters forest, and hops a creek. It follows the ridge for a time, passes alongside a meadow, then swings left around its south end and crosses another creek. The route curves east and drops down the hot, south-facing slope through scratchy, overgrown ceanothus and manzanita for what seems like a long time before it once again reaches forest cover. Listen for the booming of male blue grouse announcing their territorial claims along this stretch. You are almost guaranteed to hear them in spring.

Continue the knee-jarring descent into Tiltill Valley and cross a creek. The trail sloshes along the north side of the soggy meadow, then rather abruptly turns south. A detour of a few yards eastward takes you to the only area near the meadow high and dry enough for camping. A big boulder at the upper end of the campsite has several bedrock mortars, smooth hollows in the rock where the native Miwok pounded their acorn meal.

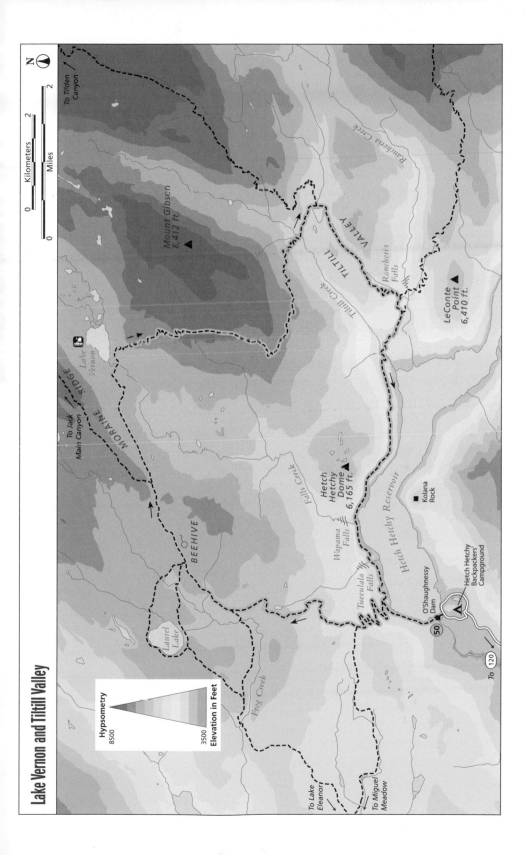

Lake Vernon and Tiltill Valley

Elevation in Feet

Hypsometry
8500
3500

N

Kilometers
0   2

Miles
0   2

To Tilden Canyon

Rancheria Creek

Mount Gibson
8,412 ft.

TILTILL VALLEY

Tiltill Creek

Rancheria
Falls

LeConte
Point
6,410 ft.

To Jack
Main Canyon

RIDGE

Lake
Vernon

MORAINE

BEEHIVE

Falls Creek

Hetch
Hetchy
Dome
6,165 ft.

Hetch Hetchy Reservoir

Kolana
Rock

Laurel
Lake

Frog Creek

Wapama Falls

Tueeulala Falls

O'Shaughnessy
Dam

50

To Lake Eleanor

To Miguel
Meadow

Hetch Hetchy
Backpackers'
Campground

120

To

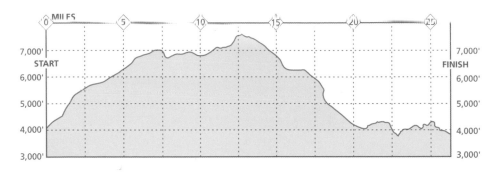

Back in the meadow's center, a trail to Tilden Lake and beyond cuts off to the east at 17.1 miles. The path is extremely mushy at the south side of the meadow, and there is no convenient way to get around it, but you can enjoy the lovely liquid song of red-winged blackbirds as you slosh along. Your boots will dry on the climb to the top of the ridge above the meadow. Pass through a notch and skirt a lovely little pond lined with azaleas and blooming with yellow pond lilies. There may be lots of mosquitoes, too. Now you'll drop down hot, dry switchbacks to meet a trail junction just above Rancheria Falls at 19.8 miles. Turn right (north) and head toward Hetch Hetchy Reservoir. The Rancheria Creek camping area, marked by a sign, is the last place you can camp along this loop. Beyond the campground the path switchbacks down to bridges across Tiltill Creek and a smaller, unnamed stream, then contours along the cliff above the reservoir to reach Wapama Falls at mile 24.2. You will probably be ready for the refreshing shower you'll get from the bridge beneath it. In little more than a half mile, wade the stream at the base of wispy Tueeulala Falls and continue on in and out of black and live oak forest to meet the junction at mile 25.8, where you once again pick up the old Lake Eleanor Road; turn left and follow it back through the tunnel to the O'Shaughnessy Dam trailhead.

Miles and Directions

0.0 Trailhead at O'Shaughnessy Dam

0.9 Lake Eleanor Road/trail junction

3.6 Miguel Meadow trail junction

6.0 Lake Eleanor cutoff

6.8 Beehive

8.1 Jack Main Canyon Trail junction

10.3 Vernon Lake

17.1 Tiltill Valley

19.8 Rancheria Falls junction

24.2 Wapama Falls

25.8 Lake Eleanor Road/trail junction

26.7 Return to O'Shaughnessy Dam Trailhead

51 Jack Main Canyon and Tilden Lake

This multiday loop hike has been included in the Hetch Hetchy section because it begins and ends there, but part of it extends into the remote north boundary country. Spring runoff in early season makes some sections of trail nearly impassable and many creek crossings extremely dangerous. On the other hand, if you wait too long, the beginning and end of the trip at the low elevations around Hetch Hetchy Reservoir can be hot and dry. Still, if the conditions are right, it's a great hike, with solitude guaranteed. Just be sure to check with the park service about trail conditions before setting out.

Start: Trailhead at O'Shaughnessy Dam
Total distance: 46.5-mile loop
Hiking time: 3 to 6 days
Difficulty: Moderate to strenuous, depending on how fast you take it
Elevation change: 5,500 feet
Seasons: Mid-July through Sept
Permits: Required; available in advance or from the Hetch Hetchy Entrance Station

Nearest facilities: Food and accommodations at Evergreen Lodge near Camp Mather; phones, toilets, and water near the trailhead; gas at Crane Flat
Maps: USGS Hetch Hetchy Reservoir, Kibbie Lake, Lake Eleanor, Tiltill Mountain, and Piute Mountain quads

Finding the trailhead: Drive 1 mile west of the Big Oak Flat Entrance Station to Yosemite on CA 120. Turn right (north) on Evergreen Road and drive about 7 miles. At Camp Mather turn right (northeast) on Hetch Hetchy Road. Pass through the park entrance station in about a mile, then continue on for 8 miles more to where the road ends in a one-way loop. Partway around is the dam, and just beyond it, a parking area. Trailhead GPS: N37 56.48 / W119 47.14

The Hike

Walk across the dam past some historical markers and on through a dark and dripping tunnel to emerge into sunlight on the old Lake Eleanor Road, lined with live oak, bay trees, and poison oak, along with dozens of species of wildflowers early in the year, though it is dry and dusty by midsummer. At 0.9 mile a trail cuts away from the road, heading to the right toward the reservoir. Stay on the road and follow the long, partly shaded switchbacks to a junction with the trail to Miguel Meadow at 3.6 miles. Keep right (north) and ascend beneath pines and incense cedars to a more level stretch that winds through an open rocky area lined with manzanita, where you must stay alert and watch the ducks to avoid losing the trail.

Reenter burned-over forest and climb past a couple of tiny meadows carpeted with white meadow foam and yellow monkey flowers until you arrive at another junction heading back to Lake Eleanor at 6.0 miles, and keep right (north) again. Very soon you reach Beehive, at 6.8 miles. It is a soggy and mosquito-ridden meadow with a piped spring protected by wood planks. The water should be purified before drinking. Another path goes west to Laurel Lake. Keep right, heading northeast out of Beehive, gaining elevation steadily to reach the junction with the Jack Main Canyon trail at 8.1 miles. Keep left here and climb Moraine Ridge, part of which is shaded, part open, grassy, and waterless, with heavy sand underfoot that makes uphill progress tedious. Drop down off the toe of Moraine Ridge on a section of trail known as the Golden Stairs into Jack Main Canyon, and along the way enjoy a glimpse of one of the Branigan Lakes to the east.

At the base of the stairs, meet Falls Creek, which drops into Hetch Hetchy Reservoir as Wapama Falls far below. It must be one of the most interesting and beautiful streams in Yosemite as it winds its way along the floor of Jack Main Canyon, cascading from pool to pool, widening out in lazy meanders, then roaring through narrow gaps in the canyon walls. There are plenty of good places to camp, the finest being on sunny rock slabs above one of the many small, unnamed lakes. The trail undulates over uneven ground that is sometimes very rocky, sometimes sloppy, sometimes completely underwater. At 15.1 miles a trail heads off to the east to connect with the Pacific Crest Trail (PCT) in a little more than 2.0 miles. **Option:** You can make a shorter loop using this route if you don't have time for the longer one or if the trail farther north at Wilma Lake is flooded.

To continue, keep left and ascend very gradually, passing through interesting, narrow slots that have trapped snowmelt lakes that have no inlets or outlets. Pass to the west of a long, wide meadow just below Wilma Lake. You can't reach the lake directly from here, but must continue north to the junction with the PCT at 18.1 miles, then cut back along the PCT to the south to reach the lakeshore. If the water is high, this section may be too deep and wide to negotiate.

Return to the main trail. Your trail and the PCT now coincide and continue north. Go through a gate and wander along the flat valley floor to 20.0 miles, where you leave the PCT again and turn right (east). Climb a ridge to meet the southern end of Tilden Lake at 21.7 miles, where Chittenden Peak squats beside the outlet. Tilden Lake is a classic glacial finger lake that has plenty of good camping on its southeast side. There are great views up the lake canyon, with Tower Peak at the far end. The trail follows the irregular shore for a while, then swings south through

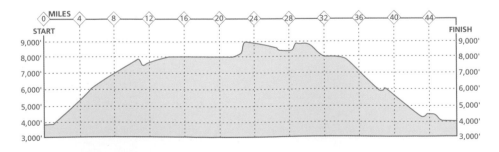

Tilden Lake is a classic glacial finger lake.

meadows and pools and climbs to meet the PCT again at 25.4 miles. Keep left here. The right fork goes back to Wilma Lake.

In a very short time, at 25.5 miles, leave the PCT as it goes east toward Stubblefield Canyon. Your trail goes right (southwest), dropping into a valley just west of main Tilden Canyon through more grassy, marshy meadows and ponds, then climbs to a junction with the trail back over to Jack Main Canyon at 28.1 miles. Just beyond are good views back to Tower Peak and the surrounding wilderness. Descend very gradually now through the forest to the south until you reach a ridge, where you descend more steeply over rocks through hot, open brush toward Tiltill Valley, which is now visible below with the Hetch Hetchy Reservoir beyond. At the end of a knee-knocking drop, splash through the meadow at Tiltill Valley to meet the trail back down to Rancheria Falls at 35.9 miles. Climb out of the basin, passing a very pretty lily pond. Drop down hot, dry switchbacks to meet a trail junction just above Rancheria Falls at 38.6 miles. Turn right (north) and head toward Hetch Hetchy Reservoir. The Rancheria Creek camping area, marked by a sign, is the last place camping is possible along this loop. Descend to cross Tiltill Creek on a bridge, then another little stream, and skirt the lake, bobbing up and down along the cliff above it to reach Wapama Falls at mile 44.0. You will probably be ready for the refreshing shower you might get from the bridge beneath it if it is early enough in the season to be flowing. A little more than a half mile beyond, wade or hop the stream at the base of gentler Tueeulala Falls and continue on in and out of black and live oak forest to meet the trail junction at mile 45.6, where

Jack Main Canyon and Tilden Lake

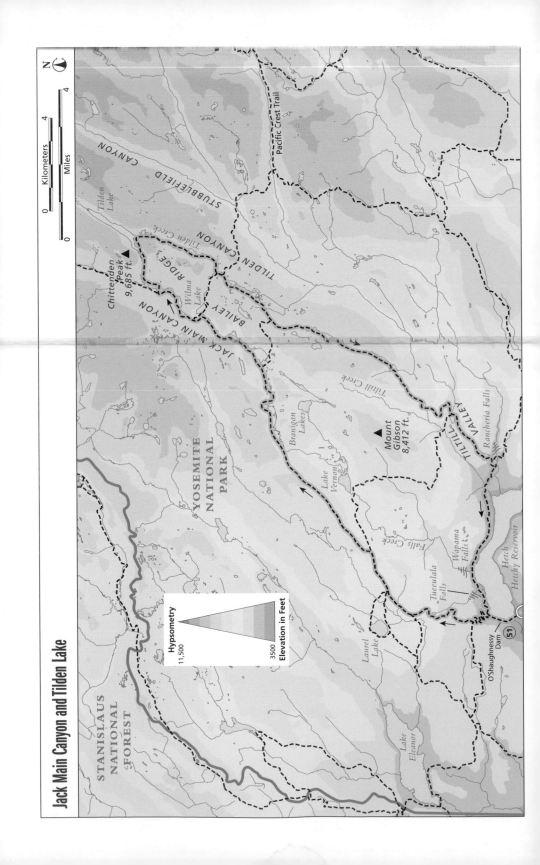

you once again pick up the Lake Eleanor Road; turn left and follow it back to the O'Shaughnessy Dam trailhead.

Miles and Directions

0.0   Trailhead at O'Shaughnessy Dam

0.9   Lake Eleanor Road/trail junction

3.6   Miguel Meadow trail junction; keep right

6.0   Lake Eleanor cutoff; keep right

6.8   Beehive

8.1   Jack Main Canyon Trail junction; go left

15.1   Jack Main Canyon

18.1   Wilma or Wilmer Lake

20.0   Tilden Creek Crossing; turn right, leaving the PCT

21.7   Tilden Lake outlet

25.4   Wilma Lake/PCT junction; keep left

25.5   Leave the PCT; stay right

28.1   Jack Main Canyon Trail junction

35.9   Tiltill Valley

38.6   Rancheria Falls junction

44.0   Wapama Falls

45.6   Lake Eleanor Road/trail junction; turn left

46.5   Return to O'Shaughnessy Dam Trailhead

Honorable Mention

Smith Meadow and Smith Peak

From the top of Smith Peak, you can get views of Hetch Hetchy Reservoir, Rancheria Falls, the Grand Canyon of the Tuolumne, and the high peaks of the north boundary country that you can't get from anywhere else in the park. There is year-round spring water flowing and a fabulous show of wildflowers in June. It's a fairly stiff climb from 4,200 feet at the trailhead to 7,800 feet at the summit, so it makes a good conditioning hike in fall or spring, though it's too hot in summer. Smith Meadow has pleasant camping if you want to spend the night. Much of the timber was burned in the Ackerson Fire of 1996, and again in the Rim Fire of 2013, so parts of the trail are quite overgrown with brush, but you can still find the trail if you're careful. The hike to the meadow is 5.0 miles one way, and the peak is 1.5 miles farther. You can get information and permits at the Hetch Hetchy Entrance Station off CA 120.

The North Boundary Country

This is Yosemite at its wildest. It is part of the largest roadless area in California and in the United States. The average elevation here is lower than in other parts of Yosemite, though the northeastern crest has some high peaks. The topography away from the crest appears to be more rolling, too, but the hiking is no less strenuous. The glaciers that shaped the land have gouged a series of parallel canyons that make east-west hiking exhausting. There is more

A hiker cools off in a high country pool.

open rock and fewer extensive stands of forest because the recent (in geologic terms) glaciers have scoured away most of the soil. When the snow melts in spring, these rocky canyons carry enormous volumes of water, at least partly because there is little soil to absorb it. Early in the year, even well into July, big sections of the trails may be completely submerged, and many stream crossings are high and dangerous. Trails are not as frequently patrolled or maintained, so you must be well prepared, must be skilled at route-finding, and must take special pains to find out about trail conditions before you start.

The shorter hikes that begin near US 395 on the eastern border of the park are popular, since most pass through part of the Hoover Wilderness, part of the Toiyabe and Inyo National Forests, which allow more commercial development than the National Park Service does. The forest service also stocks the hundreds of lakes with trout and permits hunting, so day hikers will meet lots of anglers, and in fall, a few hunters. Hikers who have penetrated farther than a day's journey into the park from any of its borders, or those who have entered from one of the more remote trailheads to the north, however, will only meet other hardy souls like themselves and a few through-hikers on the Pacific Crest Trail.

All the hikes in this section begin off US 395 or the Tioga Road (CA 120). Supplies and gas can be found in Lee Vining or Bridgeport on US 395, and in Tuolumne Meadows. Trailheads with small resorts like Mono Village, Saddlebag Lake, Lundy Lake, Virginia Pass, and Tioga Pass have cafes and limited groceries.

For hikes beginning outside Yosemite, get permits at the Mono Basin or Bridgeport USDA Forest Service ranger stations. They are good inside the park and are also subject to trailhead quotas.

52 Saddlebag Lake and 20 Lakes Basin

Saddlebag Lake is just outside Yosemite in the Hoover Wilderness and, like Lundy Canyon, is a favorite of Yosemite hikers. It is also a backdoor cross-country entrance into the park by way of McCabe Lakes. The region behind and including Saddlebag Lake is known as the 20 Lakes Basin, but is not identified by that name (or any other name) on the topographic map. The loop can be hiked in either direction, but the views are better if you proceed counterclockwise. The lakes are stocked with trout and are simply swarming with anglers. The little resort near the trailhead operates a shuttle boat that will drop you off at the far end of the lake and pick you up later at whatever time you specify, if you are in a hurry. It is inexpensive and saves you 1.5 miles each way.

Start: Saddlebag Lake Trailhead east
Total distance: 8.3-mile loop
Hiking time: 4 to 6 hours
Difficulty: Moderate
Elevation change: 500 feet
Seasons: All summer, whenever Tioga Road is open; however, high water, wet meadows, and deep snow sometimes make travel difficult early in the season

Nearest facilities: Cafe, store, and campground at Saddlebag Lake Resort; toilets and water at the trailhead
Permits: None for a day hike; available for overnights from the Mono Basin Visitor Center just outside Lee Vining at Mono Lake
Maps: USGS Dunderberg Peak and Tioga Pass quads

Finding the trailhead: From Tioga Road (CA 120), drive about a mile east of the Yosemite Park entrance and turn west onto Saddlebag Lake Road. Drive 2.5 miles over partly paved road to the south end of the lake. Follow the signs to the backpack parking lot near the (now closed) wilderness permit kiosk or to the day-use parking area at the end of the road. Trailhead GPS: N37 57.96/W119 16.22

The Hike

Walk toward the lake from the parking lot. A small sign just above the store/cafe/boat-launch area says "Saddlebag Lakes Loop." Follow the trail along the eastern shore of the lake on broken red-and-black rock. Little trickles year-round nourish gardens of bright yellow monkey flowers at the south end of the lake. While this entire basin is a veritable wonderland of wildflowers, the trail along the eastern shore is exceptionally aromatic, lined with sagebrush and pennyroyal. Directly ahead lies the Shepherd Crest, culminating in the sharp point of Sheep Peak, surprisingly white among the adjoining rusty crags. As you progress along Saddlebag's eastern shore, North Peak gradually appears from behind a nearby ridge; then the even-bigger Mount Conness, among the highest peaks in the park at 12,590 feet, is revealed. It shelters a small glacier at its base.

A decommissioned ranger station that looks like a little dollhouse surrounded by the round white heads of flowers known as ranger buttons stands near the end of the lake above the boat landing.

Just beyond the ranger station, at 2.2 miles, the trail splits. Follow the right (north) fork and climb easily past the sign announcing the entrance to the Hoover Wilderness. Just beyond, to the right of the trail, is little Hummingbird Lake. Above it are a few small campsites in the shelter of some whitebark pines. Cross the outlet from the lake over rather flimsy logs and continue climbing to Lundy Pass at 3.1 miles. Below soaring, rusty red-and-black cliffs lies Odell Lake, with an odd, little round island in the middle. Descend to the northwestern shore of the lake, then follow its outlet down a steep, narrow gorge to Helen Lake. This gorge holds some snow for most of the year, and in early season it may be too steep, icy, and dangerous to attempt.

The path around the eastern side of Helen Lake goes along a rocky and precipitous slope to the outlet where a sign at 3.9 miles points the way to Lundy Canyon, straight ahead. Turn left (west), crossing Helen Lake's outlet on logs. Follow a use trail, not shown on the topographic map, around the west side of the lake. It's quite distinct and passes several little ponds, waterfalls, and meadows spangled with alpine wildflowers. Climb a beautifully ice-polished ridge and follow ducks to look out upon

Mount Conness provides a backdrop for Saddlebag Lake.

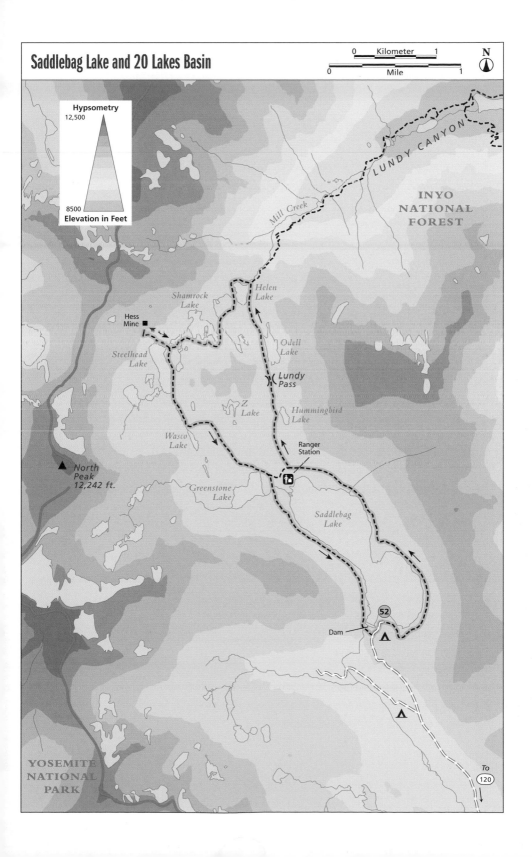

Saddlebag Lake and 20 Lakes Basin

0 Kilometer 1

0 Mile 1

N

Hypsometry

12,500

8500

Elevation in Feet

LUNDY CANYON

INYO
NATIONAL
FOREST

Mill Creek

Helen
Lake

Shamrock
Lake

Hess
Mine

Odell
Lake

Steelhead
Lake

Lundy
Pass

Z
Lake

Hummingbird
Lake

Wasco
Lake

Ranger
Station

North
Peak
12,242 ft.

Greenstone
Lake

Saddlebag
Lake

52

Dam

YOSEMITE
NATIONAL
PARK

To
120

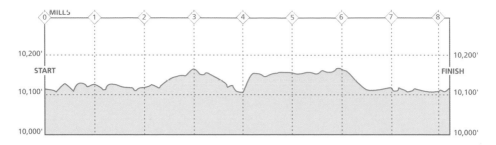

one of the prettiest views in the Sierra. Shamrock Lake below has an irregular, rocky shoreline and several picturesque islands, all trimmed with perfect arrangements of gnarled whitebark pine and brilliant, magenta mountain pride penstemon. Beyond, North Peak provides a majestic backdrop. The trail descends round the west side of Shamrock to another small, unnamed lake. Here a very short, steep path drops down to the right to meet an old mining road running past Steelhead Lake, at 4.9 miles. The road ends about 100 yards to the right at the abandoned Hess Mine.

The flat ridge above the mine between North and Sheep Peaks is a fairly easy cross-country route into Yosemite via McCabe Lakes. Your present route turns left, crossing an outlet from the lake on a log, and follows the road southward along the main outlet from Steelhead Lake. A low, flat isthmus separates Wasco from Saddlebag Lake, and several use trails leave the road to cross to the west side of the basin, at 6.6 miles. Some of these fade out partway across the meadow and some arrive at the creek connecting the two lakes, at a place where it is impossible to cross. Follow any (or none) of these paths to wherever you can ford easily and pick up the trail on the other side, heading south along the western shore of Saddlebag Lake, then hike the rough, rocky path along the mountainside to the dam, at 6.7 miles. You can cross on the top of the dam if the spillway is closed, or if it is open, follow a trail downstream and over a bridge to meet Saddlebag Lake Road, on which you turn left and proceed to your car.

Miles and Directions

- **0.0** Saddlebag Lake Trailhead east
- **2.2** North end of Saddlebag Lake; trail splits; follow right fork
- **3.1** Cross Lundy Pass
- **3.9** Helen Lake/Lundy Canyon junction; turn left
- **4.9** Steelhead Lake
- **6.6** North end of Saddlebag Lake; keep right
- **6.7** Dam at Saddlebag Lake Trailhead western shore; turn left onto road
- **8.3** Return to Saddlebag Lake Trailhead east

53 Lundy Canyon

Lundy Canyon is part of the Hoover Wilderness. It does not actually belong to Yosemite, but it can be used as a route into the park via a short cross-country connection. At any rate, it is well known to those who love Yosemite and is included here because it is the most beautiful canyon in the area, with the finest wildflower display, the most brilliant fall colors, and the greatest number of waterfalls. You can do it as an out-and-back day hike, just sample a short portion of the valley, or make a shuttle hike into 20 Lakes Basin if you can arrange a ride.

Start: Lundy Canyon Trailhead in the Lundy Campground

Total distance: 10.8 miles out and back

Hiking time: All day

Difficulty: Strenuous if you go all the way to Saddlebag Lake

Elevation change: 2,000 feet

Seasons: Summer through fall

Nearest facilities: Lundy Lake Resort

Permits: None for a day hike; available for overnights at the Mono Basin Visitor Center, just outside Lee Vining at Mono Lake

Map: USGS Dunderberg Peak quad

Finding the trailhead: From US 395 take the Lundy Lake turnoff 7 miles north of Lee Vining. Drive west 5 miles to the far end of Lundy Lake. When the road forks just below the lake, keep right. The left fork ends at the dam. Pass the tiny general store and continue for about a mile on a narrow, bumpy road through a primitive campground to where the road makes a one-way loop. Trailhead GPS: N38 01.20/W119 15.42

The Hike

Begin along the northeast slope of Lundy Canyon above Mill Creek on colorful red, black, and white rock. A very active population of beavers has dammed the lower part of the creek in several places, but eventually the slope becomes too steep and the stream too rapid for their dams as it drops over the first of several sets of waterfalls. The trail crosses the creek amid riotously blooming flower gardens under dense quaking aspen, whose brilliant golden foliage more than compensates for lack of blooms in late September.

Cross another branch of the creek on logs and come to the remains of an old trapper's cabin. Once the trail is out in the open again, waterfalls flow down the cliffs on all sides of the canyon above the aspen groves. The low, contorted shapes of these trees hint of the violence of snow and rockfall that occur here in winter.

The trail now begins to climb the slope above the canyon. Ignore any apparent trails that cut away from the main route and continue upward to the southwest for 2.0 miles, then due south, zigzagging up a very steep and rough, slaty slope. Partway to the top of the ridge, the trail meets Mill Creek and climbs close alongside

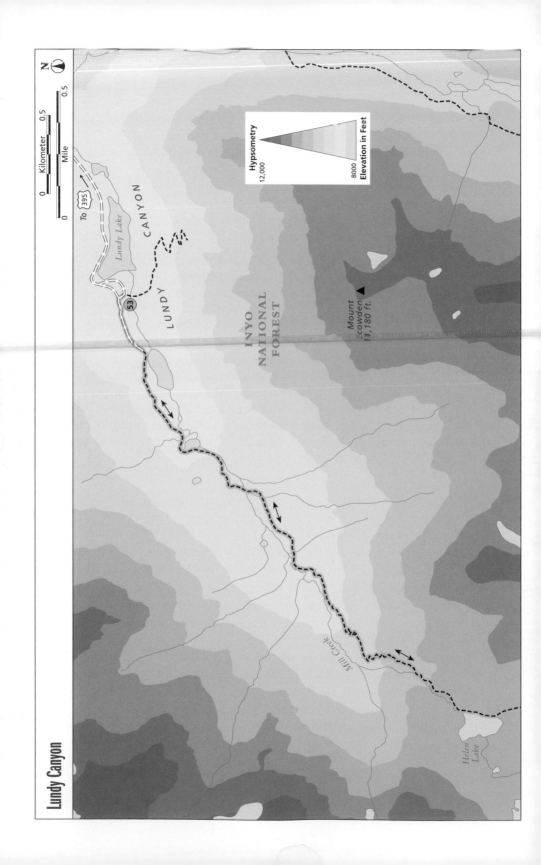

Lundy Canyon

N

Hypsometry

12,000

8000
Elevation in Feet

0   Kilometer   0.5

0   Mile   0.5

To 395

Lundy Lake

53

LUNDY   CANYON

INYO NATIONAL FOREST

Mount Scowden
11,180 ft.

Mill Creek

Helen Lake

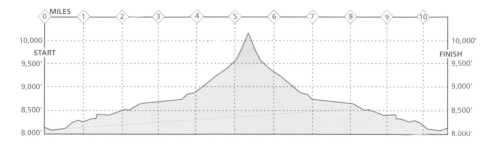

it as it tumbles down a gully. The top of this gully holds snow until quite late in the year. If the trail is mostly snow-covered or icy, do not continue upward without crampons or an ice axe. At last the trail tops a rise and enters the 20 Lakes Basin (though it is not named on the map). A very short distance farther, Mill Creek rushes through a narrow slot, behind which lies Helen Lake. Beyond, North Peak rises above a permanent snowfield, and just behind it Mount Conness shades the Conness Glacier.

With wildflowers, fall colors, and waterfalls, Lundy Canyon is among the most beautiful approaches to Yosemite from the east.

You can return this way, descending the rocky gully very cautiously, or you can continue on down into the basin, exploring the lakes and skirting big Saddlebag Lake, where you can leave a car or arrange to be picked up. There is camping in the upper part of Lundy Canyon as well as in the 20 Lakes Basin, but no fires are allowed.

Miles and Directions

0.0 Lundy Canyon Trailhead
5.4 Helen Lake
10.8 Return to Lundy Canyon Trailhead

54 Green Creek

The Green Creek drainage offers high drama and great photos because of its vivid, red-and-white metamorphic rocks; intensely blue lakes; green forests; and in fall, golden aspen groves. It is a fairly steady uphill pull to the crest of the ridge, but there are plenty of excuses to stop and plenty of places to camp all the way up if you want to spend the night.

Start: Green Creek Trailhead
Total distance: 11.6 miles out and back
Hiking time: All day or overnight
Difficulty: Strenuous as a day hike, moderate as a backpack
Elevation change: 3,200 feet
Seasons: Fine hiking all summer; late Sept to mid-Oct for fall foliage

Nearest facilities: Groceries, gas, phones, and accommodations in Bridgeport
Permits: None for a day hike; available for overnights at the USDA Forest Service ranger station in Bridgeport
Map: USGS Dunderberg Peak quad

Finding the trailhead: From US 395 turn west on Green Creek Road 21 miles north of Lee Vining, 4.7 miles south of Bridgeport. Follow the dirt road for about 10 miles to the trailhead parking area on the right, just before entering the Green Creek Campground. Trailhead GPS: N38 06.32 / W119 16.45

The Hike

The trail rambles alongside Green Creek through dense quaking aspen groves and lots of water-loving wildflowers at first, then climbs steeply beside a series of noisy cascades. A sign marks the entrance to the Hoover Wilderness as you continue to ascend steadily to a junction with the West Lake Trail at 2.0 miles. Take the left fork south past the northwest corner of Green Lake, usually lined with anglers. The forest service stocks these lakes, but the park service does not plant trout anymore, so the fishing is more challenging beyond the Yosemite Park border. There are plenty of good campsites around the lake, but you'll have lots of neighbors.

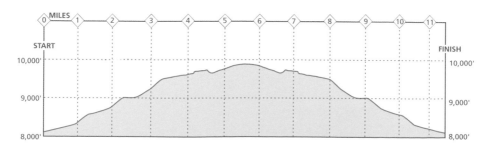

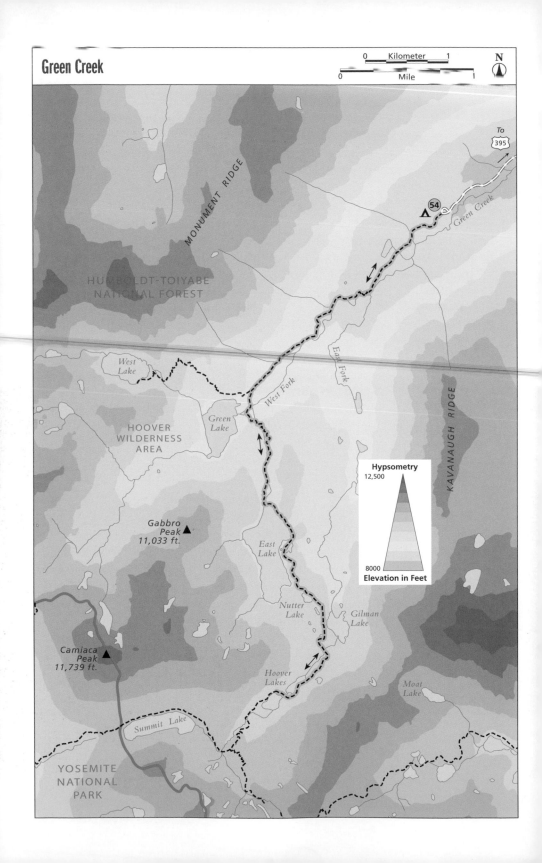

Green Creek

0 Kilometer 1

0 Mile 1

N

To 395

Green Creek

54

MONUMENT RIDGE

HUMBOLDT-TOIYABE
NATIONAL FOREST

East Fork

West Lake

West Fork

KAVANAUGH RIDGE

HOOVER
WILDERNESS
AREA

Green Lake

Hypsometry

12,500

8000

Elevation in Feet

Gabbro
Peak
11,033 ft.

East Lake

Nutter
Lake

Gilman
Lake

Camiaca
Peak
11,739 ft.

Hoover
Lakes

Moat
Lake

Summit Lake

YOSEMITE
NATIONAL
PARK

Cross the stream connecting Green Lake to East Lake and climb the steep switch-backs alongside it, crossing again where it flows out of East Lake, largest in the basin at 3.5 miles. There is a small, artificial dam that probably made the lake bigger than it was originally. There is plenty of camping near the dam. The trail follows the shore-line very closely for a time, then clambers over more open rocky ridges above the lake. Just beyond, beautiful little Nutter Lake appears below the trail at the base of a smooth rock outcrop, trimmed with red mountain heather in summer and scarlet Sierra bilberry in fall. After the trail passes a small, unnamed pond, Gilman Lake appears down in a pocket to the left (east) at 4.5 miles. A faint, unmarked spur leads down to the lakeside. You will find more solitude here than at some of the other lakes, since it is off the trail.

Cross the Gilman Lake inlet very carefully. The rocks are smooth and slimy here and have soaked many a backpacker and gear. Ascend through a subalpine forest of lodgepole and whitebark pine; graceful, droopy mountain hemlock; and tall, straight, dignified silver pines. These last, with their reddish bark in more or less regular square plates, are widely scattered and relatively uncommon.

All but small patches of trees are left behind as the rocky path reaches the south-eastern shore of the lower Hoover Lake, then crosses a rocky isthmus connecting the

Metamorphic rocks surround Hoover Lakes in Green Creek Canyon.

two lakes to the northwest side of the upper one at mile 5.8. There are a few isolated campsites in clumps of trees near the lakes, but for the most part camping here is bleak and exposed. Between the two Hoover Lakes you can hear water flowing from the upper to the lower lake. Return the way you came.

Miles and Directions

0.0 Green Creek Trailhead

2.0 Green Creek/West Lake Trail junction

3.5 East Lake

4.5 Gilman Lake

5.8 Hoover Lakes

11.6 Return to Green Creek Trailhead

55 Virginia Lakes Basin

This is a high-elevation out-and-back hike through a cluster of timberline lakes. It is actually outside the Yosemite border, but is a convenient and very scenic route to many more hikes in the north boundary country of the park and beyond.

Start: Virginia Lakes Trailhead
Total distance: 6.6 miles out and back
Hiking time: 3 to 6 hours
Difficulty: Moderate
Elevation change: 1,260 feet
Seasons: Summer through fall

Nearest facilities: Store, cafe, lodge, and phone at the largest of the Virginia Lakes
Permits: None for a day hike; available for overnights from the USDA Forest Service ranger station in Bridgeport
Map: USGS Dunderberg Peak quad

Finding the trailhead: From US 395 at Conway Summit north of Mono Lake, take Virginia Lakes Road west for 6 miles. Beyond the pack station the road forks: to the left is a small lodge, store, and cafe; to the right is the USDA Forest Service Trumbull Campground, and beyond that, the marked trailhead and hikers' parking lot. Trailhead GPS: N38 02.58/W119 15.49

The Hike

The trail begins climbing gradually around the north shore of Blue Lake. A long, cascading waterfall flowing from Cooney and Moat Lakes above feeds into it at the far end. There is nothing subtle about this scenery. While most of the basin containing the brilliant sapphire of the lake is gray granite, Dunderberg Peak to your right (north) is red, and Black Mountain to the left (south) is—you guessed it—black. White snow patches and green clumps of forest make this basin a favorite with color photographers. *Note:* Camping is prohibited at Virginia, Blue, and Red Lakes.

The rocky slope beside Blue Lake is home to a colony of pikas, busy little earth-colored creatures related to rabbits, which scamper over the rocks of the high country all summer, cutting plant material to store in their burrows under the rubble for winter use. The bundles of grass they carry as they scurry over the talus makes them

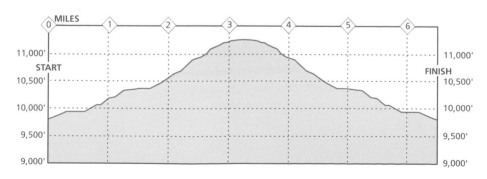

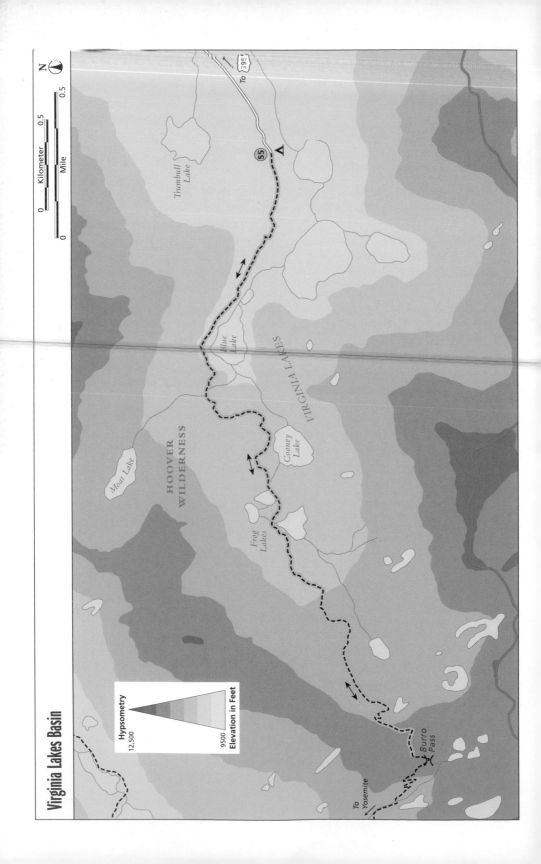

Virginia Lakes Basin

Trumbull Lake

55

To 395

Blue Lake

VIRGINIA LAKES

Cooney Lake

HOOVER WILDERNESS

Moat Lake

Frog Lakes

Burro Pass

To Yosemite

Hypsometry

12,500

9500

Elevation in Feet

N

Kilometer
0   0.5

Mile
0   0.5

Pikas, or rock rabbits, are abundant in rock piles in the high country.

appear to have huge green mustaches. You can hear their sharp chirps of alarm as you approach, but they become invisible when immobile. If you stand quietly for a few minutes until they decide you are not dangerous, they will resume their activities.

As the trail climbs, it passes an old miner's log cabin, crosses the outlet from Moat Lake, then ascends through forest to the north shore of Cooney Lake. After gaining the shelf above the lake, it flattens out as it crosses a creek and winds through the open meadow basin containing the Frog Lakes, at 1.8 miles. The gnarled whitebark pines that mark timberline are left behind now as you climb toward the head of the canyon, passing one last stark unnamed lake before puffing up the few remaining steep switchbacks, sometimes through late-lying snowfields, to the pass at 3.3 miles. This pass is unnamed on the USGS topographic maps but is known as "Burro Pass" to locals. (There is another "real" officially named Burro Pass to the west near Matterhorn Peak, so don't get the two confused.) Whatever its name, it is actually just a broad, flat bench. Make sure to cross over to the west side for a look around before turning back or you will miss the dramatic multicolored panorama that includes the Sawtooth Range to the north behind Summit Lake. If you have come for only a day hike, return the way you came. Or, to finish at the Green Creek Trailhead, see Option below.

A series of lakes connected like a string of beads is known as Paternoster Lakes.

Miles and Directions

0.0 Virginia Lakes Trailhead
1.8 Frog Lakes
3.3 "Burro" Pass
6.6 Virginia Lakes Trailhead

Option: Green Creek/Virginia Canyon Shuttle—If you can leave one vehicle or get a ride to either the Green Creek or Virginia Lakes Trailhead, you can explore two spectacular canyons in one hike and avoid retracing your steps. Hike up the Virginia Lakes Trail to "Burro" Pass at 11,100 feet, then head northwest, dropping down to the trail that connects Summit Lake with the Green Creek Trail, about a mile away. Turn right at the junction and drop down into Green Creek Canyon toward Hoover Lakes and finish at the Green Creek Trailhead. The total distance is a little more than 10.0 miles.

56 Matterhorn Canyon and the Sawtooth Range

This is a long semi-loop shuttle hike beneath the spectacular Sawtooth Range, where you will cross three high passes and visit dozens of high country lakes, while experiencing more solitude (except at the very beginning and end of the hike) than you'll find in most other regions of Yosemite.

Start: Barney Lake Trailhead in Mono Village
Total distance: 39.0-mile one-way shuttle
Hiking time: 5 to 7 days
Difficulty: Moderate to strenuous, depending on how much time you take
Elevation change: 4,800 feet
Seasons: All summer and early fall

Nearest facilities: Groceries, cafe, campground, and phones at Mono Village
Permits: Required; available from the USDA Forest Service ranger station in Bridgeport
Maps: USGS Buckeye Ridge, Dunderberg Peak, Falls Ridge, Matterhorn Peak, and Twin Lakes quads

Finding the trailhead: From Bridgeport turn west off US 395 onto Twin Lakes Road and follow it about 13 miles to its end at Mono Village. Supervised overnight parking is available (and recommended) for a fee. Drive to the kiosk in front of the campground for a parking permit and directions to the backpackers' lot. Behind the kiosk yellow markers on the trees indicate the way to Barney Lake. Leave a second car (or arrange to be picked up) at the Green Creek Trailhead, 4.7 miles south of Bridgeport, 10 miles southeast of US 395. Trailhead GPS: N38 08.85 / W119 22.69

The Hike

Follow the yellow signs in the trees marking the trail directly through the campground on a road until you reach a meadow. Climb over a chain blocking the way, and in a few minutes turn right at a trail sign and leave the road. Pass through a forest of Jeffrey pine, pausing at mile 0.2 at a big wilderness sign with maps and trail rules. Soon you enter an aspen grove, which opens out onto a glorious panorama of Robinson, Eagle, Victoria, and Hunewell peaks as well as the Sawtooth Range. In the foreground is a field of big, yellow mule's ears, blue lupine, and in early season, purple irises. After passing the mouth of Little Slide Canyon coming in from the south, enter another aspen grove and climb moderate switchbacks up through flowery gardens, crossing several little runnels to reach Barney Lake at 4.0 miles. The lake is overused around its edges, and camping is prohibited there, but if you cross the outlet stream on logs, you will find beautiful campsites among the junipers above its eastern shore.

Skirt Barney Lake's west shore, watching for pikas in the rock piles and signs of beavers at the upper end of the swampy area at the head of the lake. Cross Robinson Creek and begin switchbacks uphill, sometimes through graceful mountain hemlocks, sometimes over open rock. At 6.3 miles meet the junction with the Peeler

Lake Trail, which goes off to the northwest. Your trail turns left, winds around a few big rocky outcrops, then drops into a basin, first passing a little pond with improbably blue-green water, then past the north edge of lower Robinson Lake. Camping here is often too damp and buggy for comfort. The trail crosses an isthmus between the two lakes, climbs a few switchbacks, cuts through a gap where snow often lingers late in the season, then reaches Crown Lake at 8.0 miles. Backed by Crown Point, the lake is stunning, but the only camping nearby is at its north end on sandy spaces among the rocks.

The trail skirts Crown Lake for a short distance before switchbacking up the slope to the west, past little pocket meadows with tiny lakes and miniature gardens, to a junction with the Rock Island Pass Trail at 8.7 miles. Keep left as your trail curves gently southward and continue up a narrowing gully, often partly snow-filled, to a false summit. Just beyond this is another sparkling little lake in a meadow. The true Mule Pass at 10.1 miles is another 100-foot climb where you enter Yosemite at 10,400 feet. The Sawtooth Ridge spreads out along the horizon with Matterhorn Peak at its far end. The trail descends, then rises to cross a low saddle, then drops down a gulch into the Piute Creek drainage, bottoming out at 9,400 feet. Follow the creek, climbing gently past numerous cascades through a carpet of dwarf bilberry, brilliant green in summer, glowing red in fall. There are several good campsites here along the creek.

Continue to climb moderately, heading straight for Matterhorn Peak until the sparse whitebark pine gives out altogether, the route curves south, and you easily cross Burro Pass at 13.3 miles. At 10,600 feet, this is the highest point on the route.

The trail descends along the west side of the big bowl at the head of Matterhorn Canyon, then eases down very gently alongside Matterhorn Creek past some spectacular avalanche areas—the velocity of the snow was so great here that trees were flattened all the way down one side of the canyon and halfway up the other. Be sure to glance backward now and then as you descend. The jagged Sawtooth Ridge on the horizon back at the head of the canyon is spectacular. There are small campsites for the first couple of miles in the canyon, but after you have passed Quarry Peak, the walls narrow and camping becomes more difficult.

You cross Matterhorn Creek three times before reaching the junction with the Pacific Crest Trail at 19.5 miles, then follow it left, almost due south, leaving the stream and climbing fairly steeply out of the canyon. The trail levels out, then drops a bit before entering a big meadow, at the far end of which lies Miller Lake at 21.0 miles, where the trail turns sharply northeast. This is a good, shallow, warm lake for swimming, and there is good camping in the timber across the meadow from the trail.

From the lake the route gently undulates, passing a couple more little ponds; goes through a gate; and makes a last steep, sandy climb out of the basin. Then it drops steeply on dusty switchbacks to cross Spiller Creek just before its confluence with Return Creek in Virginia Canyon at 25.3 miles. Now you leave the Pacific Crest Trail and walk up Virginia Canyon, gaining elevation very gradually, passing more

You will find more solitude in Matterhorn Canyon than in most other parts of Yosemite.

avalanche chutes on the way. Cross to the east side of Return Creek one last time to find the Virginia Pass Trail junction on the far side, at 29.3 miles. There is a small, mediocre campsite just upstream.

Now climb the steep, forested slope to Summit Pass at 30.3 miles, leaving Yosemite at the top at 10,250 feet. Skirt the northern shore of Summit Lake, which is very beautiful but often very windy. Since the shore is also quite fragile, camping is discouraged near the lake, though there are a few small, protected sites past its east end. The trail drops below the lake along a flowery creek, rock-hops over another shallow stream, and turns left (north), climbing a little until it meets the Green Creek Trail junction at 31.6 miles. Continue on down Green Creek to Hoover Lakes at 32.6 miles, passing between the two on a narrow strip of broken rock, beneath which you can hear water flowing from the upper to the lower lake. Drop down to follow along the rim of the bowl containing Gilman Lake, crossing the slippery rocks at its inlet.

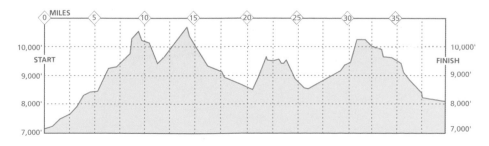

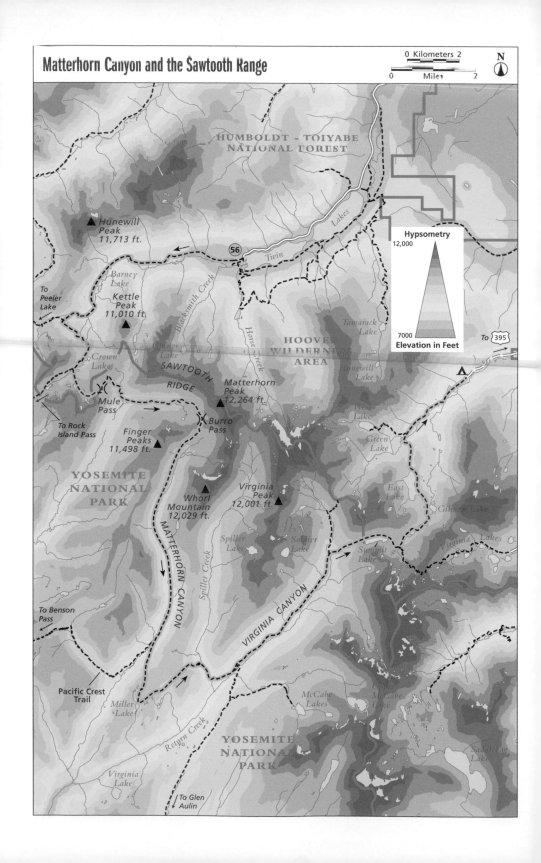

Matterhorn Canyon and the Sawtooth Range

0 Kilometers 2

0 Miles 2

N

Hypsometry

12,000

7000

Elevation in Feet

HUMBOLDT - TOIYABE NATIONAL FOREST

Twin Lakes

▲ Hunewill Peak 11,713 ft.

56

Barney Lake

Kettle Peak 11,010 ft. ▲

Blacksmith Creek

Horse Creek

Tamarack Lake

To Peeler Lake

HOOVER WILDERNESS AREA

To 395

Crown Lake

SAWTOOTH RIDGE

Matterhorn Peak 12,264 ft. ▲

Hunewill Lake

Mule Pass

Burro Pass

To Rock Island Pass

Finger Peaks 11,498 ft. ▲

Peeler Lake

Green Lake

YOSEMITE NATIONAL PARK

Whorl Mountain 12,029 ft. ▲

Virginia Peak 12,001 ft. ▲

East Lake

Gilman Lake

MATTERHORN CANYON

Spiller Creek

Spiller Lake

Soldier Lake

Summit Lake

Virginia Lakes

To Benson Pass

VIRGINIA CANYON

Pacific Crest Trail

Miller Lake

Return Creek

McCabe Lakes

Upper McCabe Lake

Virginia Lake

YOSEMITE NATIONAL PARK

Saddlebag Lake

To Glen Aulin

Pass a small, unnamed pond, then pretty Nutter Lake, to reach East Lake, largest in the basin, at 35.9 miles. There is plenty of camping near the dam at its outlet, as there is at Green Lake, just below, though you will have to share the shore with plenty of other campers and anglers. At mile 36.7 turn right (northeast) at a junction with the West Lake Trail, and reach the Green Creek Trailhead at 39 miles.

Miles and Directions

0.0 Barney Lake Trailhead

4.0 Barney Lake; turn right to skirt its western shore

6.3 Peeler Lake Trail junction; turn left

8.0 Crown Lake

8.7 Rock Island Pass Trail junction; turn left

10.1 Cross Mule Pass (Yosemite park boundary)

13.3 Cross Burro Pass

19.5 Pacific Coast Trail/Benson Pass Trail junction; keep left

21.0 Miller Lake; trail turns sharply northeast

25.3 Return Creek, turn left, up-canyon

29.3 Virginia Pass Trail junction; keep right

30.3 Summit Pass (Yosemite park boundary)

31.6 Green Creek Trail; turn left

32.6 Upper Hoover Lake

35.9 Pass the eastern shore of East Lake

36.7 Green Lake/West Lake Trail junction; keep right

39.0 Green Creek Trailhead

57 Benson Pass-Northeast Yosemite Grand Tour

This extended backpack loop is probably the most challenging hike in the book. Not only is the distance long and the changes in elevation extreme (between 4,400 and 10,000 feet), but your window of opportunity is narrow. The high north country may still have lots of snow while the low point in Pate Valley can be hot. Still, for most of the way, you'll have solitude and a good sampling of remote Yosemite in all its variety.

Start: Glen Aulin Trailhead in Tuolumne Meadows
Total distance: 58-mile lollipop
Hiking time: 5 to 9 days
Difficulty: Strenuous
Elevation change: 6,800 feet
Seasons: Summer through early fall

Nearest facilities: Tuolumne Meadows
Permits: Required; available in advance or from the Tuolumne Meadows Wilderness Center
Maps: USGS Dunderberg Peak, Falls Ridge, Matterhorn Peak, Ten Lakes, and Tioga Pass quads

Finding the trailhead: From the west follow Tioga Road (CA 120) past the Tuolumne Meadows Visitor Center, store, cafe, and campground, all on your right. Just after crossing the bridge over the Tuolumne River, turn left (north) into the Lembert Dome parking area. From the east (Tioga Pass), follow the Tioga Road past the turnoff to the wilderness center on your left and continue about a hundred yards to the Lembert Dome parking area on your right. You can also ride the Tuolumne Meadows shuttle bus to Lembert Dome (stop 4). Overnight parking is prohibited in the parking lot, so you must park along the paved road parallel to Tioga Road. The road turns right at a closed gate, where your hike begins. Trailhead GPS: N37 52.44 / W119 21.30

The Hike

Go through the gate and follow the road (closed to vehicles) through the meadow, keeping right and climbing a small rise where the road splits. From the top of the rise, head toward the ramshackle log structure partially containing Soda Springs at mile 0.5. Just beyond is Parsons Lodge, a stone building with historical exhibits. There the path splits at mile 0.6, where you turn right to a big "Glen Aulin Trail" sign where the trail meets the road a few yards beyond. Turn left and walk through flowery meadows and lodgepole pine forest on footing that is heavy and dusty from lots of horse and foot traffic. Ford Delaney Creek at mile 1.2. A trail heading north to Young Lakes cuts off to the right at mile 1.6, but your route stays left, northwest. In less than a mile, you emerge from behind a low ridge to behold the spectacular Cathedral Range with the Tuolumne River in the foreground. The next couple of miles along the trail presents one incredible photo op after another. After passing through a short stretch of forest, climb around a low shoulder of rock and keep watch on your left for the Little Devil's Postpile, an unusual volcanic feature much younger than the surrounding rock.

A hiker takes a rest in Spiller Creek, a stop on one of Yosemite's longest loops—the Grand Tour.

The trail turns sharply right and drops down a short, steep notch, and very soon reaches a pair of footbridges across the Tuolumne River, at 3.5 miles. From this point on the river picks up speed and cascades over a series of falls. As you descend, you can enjoy views up Cold Canyon to Matterhorn Peak and Mount Conness on the northern boundary of the park. The trail dives into and out of deep forest lined with Labrador tea and corn lily, then emerges again into sunlight on cobblestones or smooth granite marked with ducks. Finally it meets a junction with the May Lake/ McGee Lake Trail at 5.0 miles. A few more steep, slippery switchbacks lead down to a bridge and back to the other side of the river. Few hikers can resist the urge to stop on the bridge to snap a photo or simply gape at the frothy White Cascade splashing into a pool in front of the Glen Aulin High Sierra Camp. You have come 5.2 miles.

Head northward across Cold Creek from the High Sierra Camp, still on the Pacific Crest Trail (PCT), partly through open forest, partly through meadow, up Cold Canyon, with Mount Conness at its head. The McCabe Lakes junction, at 12.2 miles, is not shown correctly on the topographic map, but if you stay left, following the PCT, you'll be on track. At 13.2 miles keep left again, following Return Creek in Virginia Canyon downstream, dropping to cross Spiller Creek, then climbing fairly steeply up some dusty switchbacks. Pass through a gate and make another sandy descent, cross a low rise, pass a couple of shallow ponds, then emerge into the meadow bordering Miller Lake. It's a nice warm lake for swimming, and there is good camping in the timber across the meadow from the trail. Leaving the lake, the trail swings back northward, crossing a shoulder with views to the Sawtooth Ridge, then drops steeply

Benson Pass-Northeast Yosemite Grand Tour

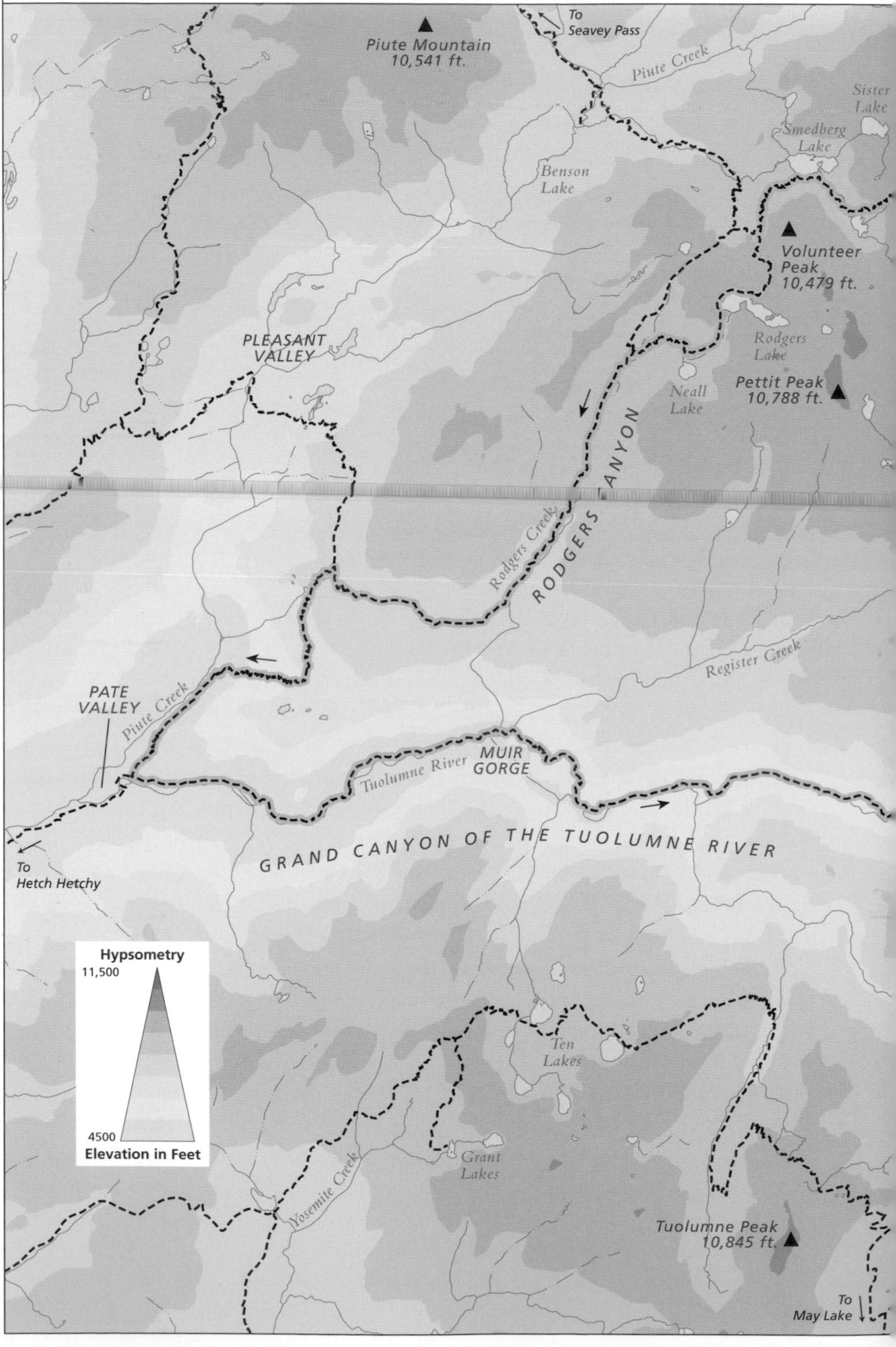

Piute Mountain
10,541 ft.

To
Seavey Pass

Piute Creek

Sister
Lake

Smedberg
Lake

Benson
Lake

Volunteer
Peak
10,479 ft.

Rodgers
Lake

PLEASANT
VALLEY

Neall
Lake

Pettit Peak
10,788 ft.

RODGERS CANYON

Rodgers Creek

PATE
VALLEY

Piute Creek

Register Creek

MUIR
GORGE

Tuolumne River

GRAND CANYON OF THE TUOLUMNE RIVER

To
Hetch Hetchy

Hypsometry

11,500

4500

Elevation in Feet

Ten
Lakes

Yosemite Creek

Grant
Lakes

Tuolumne Peak
10,845 ft.

To
May Lake

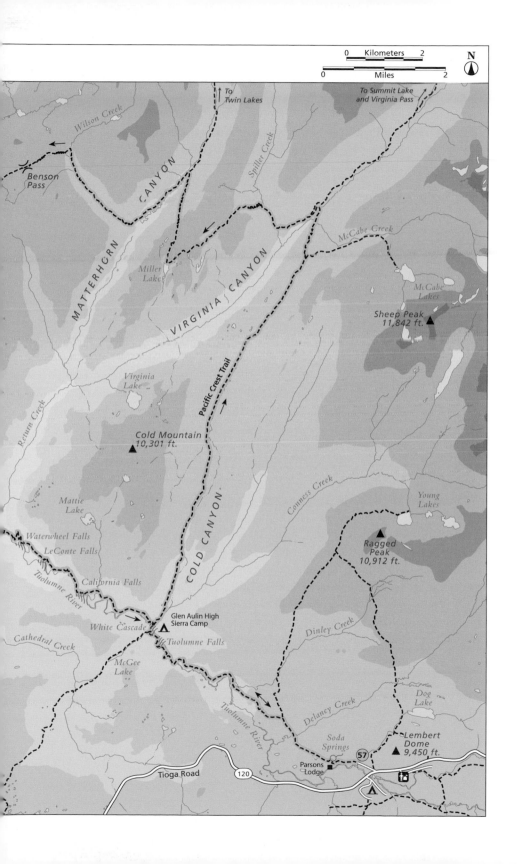

To
Twin Lakes

To Summit Lake
and Virginia Pass

Wilson Creek

Spiller Creek

MATTERHORN CANYON

Benson
Pass

McCabe Creek

Miller
Lake

VIRGINIA CANYON

McCabe
Lakes

Sheep Peak
11,842 ft. ▲

Return Creek

Virginia
Lake

Pacific Crest Trail

Cold Mountain
10,301 ft. ▲

Conness Creek

Young
Lakes

Mattie
Lake

COLD CANYON

Waterwheel Falls

Ragged
Peak
10,912 ft. ▲

LeConte Falls

Tuolumne River

California Falls

Glen Aulin High
Sierra Camp △

White Cascade

Tuolumne Falls

Dinley Creek

Cathedral Creek

McGee
Lake

Tuolumne River

Dog
Lake

Delaney Creek

Soda
Springs

Lembert
Dome
▲ 9,450 ft.

57

Tioga Road   120

Parsons
Lodge

△

into Matterhorn Canyon, at 19.0 miles, in a flowery meadow where there is more good camping. The PCT makes a sharp dogleg here, cutting back southwest, crossing Matterhorn Creek, and following its broad meandering course downstream for more than a mile. The trail swings northwest, climbing along Wilson Creek, which it crosses several times before it turns west and climbs switchbacks to wide, grassy Benson Pass at mile 22.8. Descend fairly gradually from the pass and wade the outlet of Smedberg Lake at the edge of a meadow. The lake lies at the foot of blocky Volunteer Peak. There is good camping at the lake; the best sites are on the shore opposite the trail.

After leaving Smedberg Lake, reach a junction at the steep west base of Volunteer Peak, at 26.5 miles. Here you leave the PCT, which cuts off in a westerly direction toward Seavey Pass. Continue south, climb an open grassy hump, and descend to Rodgers Lake at the base of flat-topped, red Regulation Peak, with pointed West Peak to the south. Continue descending a short spur to Neall Lake in a little hollow fringed by forest. Camping is best near the lake's outlet.

Soon after leaving Neall Lake, meet a junction in Rodgers Canyon at 30.1 miles, turn left (south), and follow along the meandering creek through a broad meadow. The grade steepens as you head down Rodgers Canyon toward the Tuolumne River Canyon. Eventually the trail swings west and leaves Rodgers Creek, your last source of water for a while if the season is late. Cross a low saddle, then meet the Piute Creek junction at 34.9 miles. Turn left (west) and tighten your boots for the long, long, knee-bashing, toe-squashing descent to the river. As you lose elevation, the vegetation changes to ponderosa pine, incense cedar, and black oak in the places where there is still some tree cover, and it can become uncomfortably hot. At last you reach the cool green pools and refreshing cascades along the Tuolumne, at 39.5 miles, at the upper end of Pate Valley. Your route goes upstream to the left, but there is camping downstream in the lower part of the valley. Watch out for rattlesnakes in this low country.

From the upper end of Pate Valley, turn left (east) to follow the Tuolumne upstream, crossing Rodgers Creek on a bridge, then Register Creek over rocks at the base of a pretty cascade at mile 43.5. The trail now climbs steeply up out of the drainage of Register Creek, detouring over a smooth, polished boulder above the steep, impassible canyon walls of Muir Gorge. The trail remains above the river for a long, up-and-down dry spell before rejoining its north shore again and following it gradually up through the Grand Canyon of the Tuolumne to cross the footbridge over Return

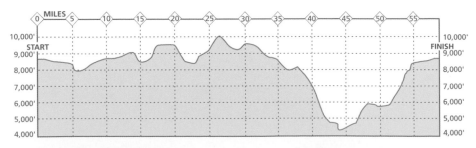

Creek at 48.4 miles. Begin the switchbacks that take you up alongside the Tuolumne's most exciting section of cascades and falls, one after another, up stairstep after stairstep of roaring river, including the fabulous Waterwheels at mile 50.2, then LeConte and California Falls, and back up to Glen Aulin High Sierra Camp at mile 52.8, where you retrace your steps to the trailhead.

Miles and Directions

0.0 Glen Aulin Trailhead

0.5 Soda Springs

1.2 Ford Delaney Creek

1.6 Young Lakes Trail Junction; keep left

3.5 Cross the Twin Bridges

5.0 McGee Lake Trail junction; turn sharp right, downhill

5.2 Glen Aulin High Sierra Camp

12.2 McCabe Lakes junction; stay left

13.2 Virginia Canyon/Return Creek; hairpin turn to the left, south, then sharp north again at Miller Lake

19.0 Matterhorn Canyon; another sharp left turn (south)

22.8 Benson Pass

26.5 Rodgers Lake junction; keep straight ahead, south

30.1 Rodgers Canyon; turn left

34.9 Piute Creek; turn left

39.5 Pate Valley; turn left, upstream along the Tuolumne

43.5 Cross Rodgers Creek, then Register Creek

48.4 Cross Return Creek

50.2 Waterwheel Falls

52.8 Glen Aulin High Sierra Camp

58.0 Return to the Glen Aulin Trailhead

58 McCabe Lakes

This out-and-back overnight hike takes you to Upper and Lower McCabe Lakes in their beautiful cirque at the base of Sheep Peak by way of Green Creek, just outside the northeast boundary of Yosemite. If you prefer, you can begin and end the hike within the park by way of Glen Aulin High Sierra Camp.

Start: Green Creek Trailhead
Total distance: 30.4 miles out and back
Hiking time: 2 to 4 days
Difficulty: Moderate
Elevation change: 2,500 feet
Seasons: Summer through early fall

Nearest facilities: Gas, groceries, and phones in Lee Vining and Bridgeport
Permits: Required; available in advance or from the USDA Forest Service ranger station in Bridgeport
Maps: USGS Dunderberg Peak, Tioga Pass, Matterhorn Peak, and Falls Ridge quads

Finding the trailhead: From US 395 turn west on Green Creek Road 21 miles north of Lee Vining, 4.7 miles south of Bridgeport. Follow the dirt road for about 10 miles just past the Green Creek Campground to the parking area. Trailhead GPS: N38 06.32 / W119 16.45

The Hike

The trail rambles alongside Green Creek through dense quaking aspen groves and lots of water-loving wildflowers at first, then climbs steeply beside a series of noisy cascades. A sign marks the entrance to the Hoover Wilderness as you continue to ascend steadily to a junction with the West Lake Trail at 2.0 miles. Take the left fork south past the northwest corner of Green Lake, usually lined with anglers. There are plenty of good campsites around the lake, but you'll have lots of neighbors.

Cross the stream connecting Green Lake to East Lake and climb the steep switchbacks alongside it, crossing again where it flows out of East Lake, largest in the basin at 3.5 miles. There is a small, artificial dam that probably made the lake bigger than it was originally. There is plenty of camping near the dam. The trail follows the shoreline very closely for a time, then clambers over more open rocky ridges above the lake. Just beyond, beautiful little Nutter Lake appears below the trail at the base of a smooth rock outcrop, trimmed with red mountain heather in summer and scarlet Sierra bilberry in fall. After the trail passes a small, unnamed pond, Gilman Lake appears down in a pocket to the left (east) at 4.5 miles. A faint, unmarked spur leads down to the lakeside. You will find more solitude here than at some of the other lakes, since it is off the trail. Cross the Gilman Lake inlet carefully on slippery rocks. Ascend through a subalpine forest of lodgepole and whitebark pine, graceful mountain hemlock, and tall, dignified silver pines.

All but small patches of trees are left behind as the rocky path skirts the lakeshore of the lower Hoover Lake on one side of the steep, shaly base of the ridge at 5.8 miles. The two Hoover Lakes are separated by a narrow strip of broken rock, beneath which you can hear water flowing from the upper to the lower lake under your feet, as the trail follows this narrow isthmus to the north side of the upper lake. There are a few isolated camping sites in clumps of trees near the lakes, but for the most part, camping here is bleak and exposed. The trail crosses the inlet to the upper lake and toils up a sunny slope to a junction with the Virginia Lakes Trail at 6.2 miles. Continue to the right up to a flower-filled gully along a gurgling creek to Summit Lake. The views here are stupendous, and this seems a natural place to camp, but it is usually very windy, and the few sheltered spots among the whitebark pines are carpeted with very fragile and slow-growing vegetation, easily trampled and destroyed. Much of the area near the lake is closed to camping. Continue on along the north shore of the lake to a sign that marks the Yosemite boundary at Summit Pass, at 7.2 miles, the highest point on this hike. From here switchback steeply downhill into Virginia Canyon and arrive at the Virginia Pass Trail junction at Return Creek, at 8.2 miles. You can make a detour to Virginia Pass by turning right (north) and following Return Creek upstream, then scrambling up a steep slope to the pass, an extra 1.6 miles each way.

Evidence of winter avalanches remains in Virginia Canyon.

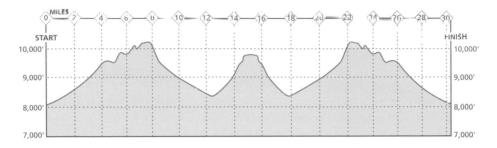

To continue on to McCabe Lakes, cross the creek and follow the trail to the left. A mediocre campsite can be found just off the trail to the right. You can usually rock-hop the creek, but there is a big log to cross on downstream if the water is high. Soon the forest opens as you very gradually descend along Return Creek, passing massive Excelsior Peak on your left. The slopes above the canyon for the next couple of miles have been scarred by repeated avalanches. Notice how, in some cases, the force was so great that trees were flattened not only down the side of the slope but also across the canyon floor and even a short distance up the other side. The height of the new little trees in the avalanche path gives a hint of how recently the last slide occurred.

The trail eventually nears the creek, where it flows over sculpted granite in picturesque cascades and falls. There are some campsites nearby. It's a great place for lunch, a snack, a nap, or a swim. Just beyond is the junction with the Pacific Crest Trail (PCT), at 12.2 miles. Turn left (south) here and follow the PCT for a short distance, climbing steeply. At a junction at 13.2 miles, turn left (east), leaving the PCT. Continue climbing, more gently now, up a wooded slope through an occasional meadow to Lower McCabe Lake, with Sheep Peak as its backdrop, at 15.2 miles. There is good camping on both sides of the outlet. Be sure to pitch your tent away from the lakeside to avoid trampling. You can scramble to Upper McCabe for better views by following the green slope to the west uphill along an inlet stream to an intermediate small lake, then crossing the low ridge to the northwest to reach the largest of the lakes. Return the way you came.

Miles and Directions

0.0   Green Creek Trailhead

2.0   Green Creek/West Lake Trail junction

3.5   East Lake

4.5   Gilman Lake

5.8   Upper Hoover Lake

6.2   Green Creek/Virginia Lakes Trail junction

7.2   Summit Pass (Yosemite park boundary)

8.2   Return Creek

12.2 PCT junction

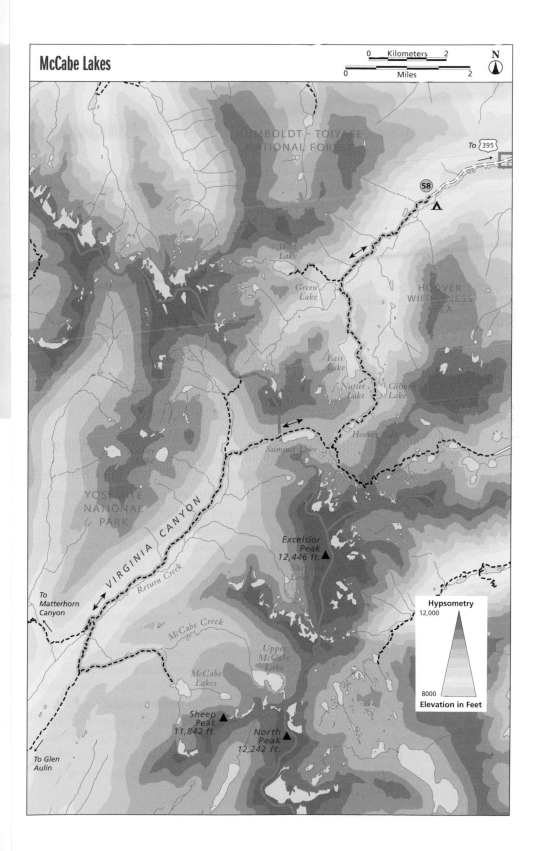

McCabe Lakes

0 Kilometers 2
0 Miles 2

N

HUMBOLDT - TOIYABE
NATIONAL FOREST

To 395

58

West
Lake

Green
Lake

HOOVER
WILDERNESS
AREA

East
Lake

Nutter
Lake

Gilman
Lake

Hoover Lake

Summit Lake

Soldier
Lake

YOSEMITE
NATIONAL
PARK

V I R G I N I A   C A N Y O N

Return Creek

Excelsior
Peak
12,446 ft.

Shepherd
Lake

To
Matterhorn
Canyon

McCabe Creek

Upper
McCabe
Lake

McCabe
Lakes

Sheep
Peak
11,842 ft.

North
Peak
12,242 ft.

To Glen
Aulin

Hypsometry
12,000

8000
Elevation in Feet

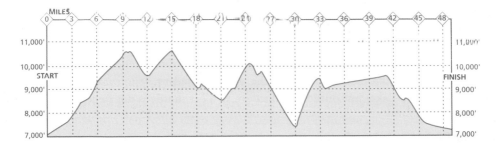

is usually too damp and buggy for comfort. The trail crosses an isthmus between the two lakes, climbs a few switchbacks, cuts through a gap where snow often lingers late in the season, then reaches Crown Lake at 8.0 miles. Backed by Crown Point, the lake is stunning, but the only camping nearby is at its north end on sandy spaces among the rocks.

The trail skirts Crown Lake for a short distance before ascending switchbacks up the slope to the west, past little pocket meadows with tiny lakes and miniature gardens, to a junction with the Rock Island Pass Trail at 8.7 miles. Keep left as your trail curves gently southward and continue up a narrowing gully, often partly snow-filled. Just below the top is another sparkling little lake. The trail flattens out a bit just before reaching 10,400-foot Mule Pass, at 10.1 miles, and entering Yosemite. The Sawtooth Range spreads out along the horizon with Matterhorn Peak at its far end. The trail descends, then rises to cross a low saddle, then drops down a gulch into the Piute Creek drainage, bottoming out at 9,400 feet. Follow the creek, climbing gently past numerous cascades through a carpet of dwarf bilberry, brilliant green in summer, glowing red in fall. There are several good campsites here along the creek.

Continue to climb moderately, heading straight for Matterhorn Peak until the sparse whitebark pines give out altogether, the route curves south, and you easily cross Burro Pass at 12.8 miles. At 10,600 feet, this is the highest point on the route.

The trail descends along the west side of the big bowl at the head of Matterhorn Canyon, then eases down very gently alongside Matterhorn Creek past some spectacular avalanche chutes. There are small campsites for the first couple of miles in the canyon, but after you have passed Quarry Peak, the walls narrow and camping becomes more difficult. You cross Matterhorn Creek three times before reaching the junction with the Pacific Crest Trail (PCT) at 19.0 miles. The PCT makes a sharp dogleg here, and you follow to the right (southwest), crossing Matterhorn Creek and continuing downstream for more than a mile. The trail swings northwest, climbing along Wilson Creek now, which it must cross several times before it turns west and climbs switchbacks to wide, grassy Benson Pass. Descend gradually and wade across the inlet of Smedberg Lake at the edge of a meadow, backed by blocky Volunteer Peak. There is good camping at the lake, but the best is on the shore opposite the trail.

Leaving Smedberg, reach Rodgers Lake junction at the base of Volunteer Peak at 26.5 miles. Now make a short climb through forest to another junction at 27.1

Smedberg Lake is one of the most remote lakes in Yosemite.

miles and turn right (north) toward Benson Lake, dropping down to cross and then follow the stream connecting Smedberg and Benson Lakes. Leave the stream to cross a rocky shoulder and descend to a boggy flat blooming with corn lilies, onions, wild geraniums, and other water-loving flowers, to meet the spur trail to Benson Lake at 30.1 miles. This is a big lake in a beautifully ice-polished rocky bowl. It is surprisingly popular for such a remote spot, probably because of its good camping and beautiful beach at the end nearest the trail.

Leaving the lake, the trail climbs up open manzanita-covered slopes heading toward the pointed beacon of Piute Mountain, directly ahead. Near the peak it swings northeast, climbs more steeply along the cascading stream, then levels out beside the first of several little lakes to Seavey Pass, a rather long, open ridge, studded with shining domes and tarns. A short distance down the north side of Seavey Pass, the PCT leaves your route and heads off down Kerrick Canyon, at 33.5 miles. Turn right and begin climbing easily along Rancheria Creek, which you soon cross in a meadow that is tinged pale lavender in July with shooting stars and little elephant heads. Continue upward out of the meadow through a beautiful rocky gorge that opens once again into another wide, sandy, grassy area. Arndt Lake, just off the trail to the east, feeds this meadow and its several little ponds.

Meet the Buckeye Pass junction at 38.7 miles. Walk northward along the edge of Kerrick Meadow, then turn right at a junction at 39.7 miles, toward Peeler Lake, at whose northwest shore you leave Yosemite at 40.2 miles. There is good camping and lots of human activity at this lake beneath the scenic backdrop of Crown Point. Cross

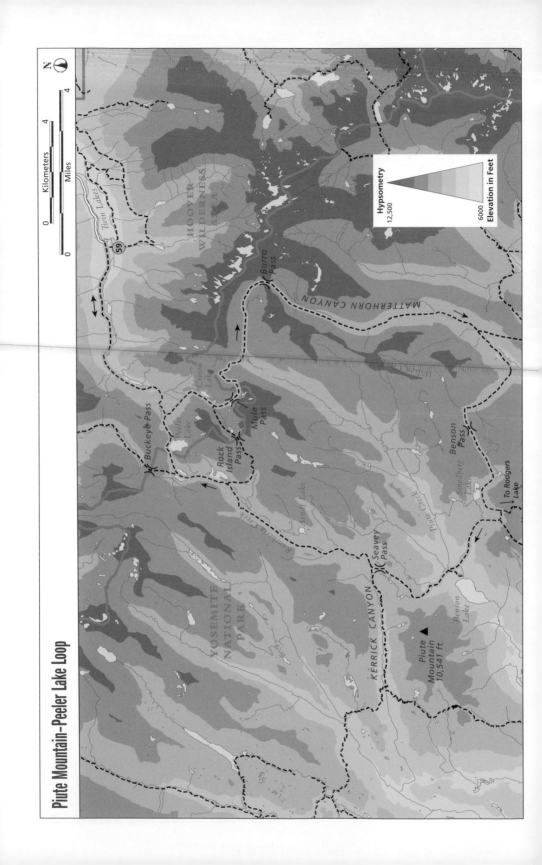

Piute Mountain–Peeler Lake Loop

Hypsometry

12,500

6000

Elevation in Feet

Kilometers

0   4

0   4

Miles

N

HOOVER WILDERNESS AREA

Twin Lakes

Buckeye Pass

Peeler Lake

Rock Island Pass

Crown Lake

Mule Pass

Robinson Creek

Smedberg Lake

Benson Pass

To Rodgers Lake

Benson Lake

Piute Creek

Seavey Pass

KERRICK CANYON

Piute Mountain 10,541 ft.

YOSEMITE NATIONAL PARK

Rancheria Creek

Matterhorn Canyon

Burro Pass

MATTERHORN CANYON

11,526

59

the inlet stream and climb around a rock ridge, then drop, winding through rocks, to a junction with Robinson Creek at 40.7 miles. Here you turn left (northeast) and descend switchbacks to Barney Lake at 44.7 miles. Then retrace your steps to Twin Lakes and the trailhead.

Miles and Directions

0.0 Barney Lake Trailhead

4.0 Barney Lake; turn right to skirt its western shore

6.3 Peeler Lake Trail junction; turn left

8.0 Crown Lake

8.7 Rock Island Pass Trail junction; turn left

10.1 Cross Mule Pass (Yosemite park boundary)

12.8 Cross Burro Pass

19.0 PCT junction; keep right

26.5 Rodgers Lake junction

27.1 Benson Lake junction; turn right

30.1 Benson Lake spur

33.5 Kerrick/Rancheria junction; turn right

38.7 Buckeye Pass junction

39.7 Peeler Lake Trail junction; turn right

40.2 Peeler Lake

40.7 Robinson Creek junction; turn left

44.7 Barney Lake

48.7 Return to Barney Lake Trailhead at Twin Lakes

Two Famous Trails

The John Muir and Pacific Crest Trails traverse some of the most spectacular high country anywhere. Both pass through Yosemite, and for a time they become one and the same.

The John Muir Trail follows the crest of the Sierra Nevada for roughly 211 miles between Yosemite Valley, at a mere 4,000 feet, and Mount Whitney, at around 14,500 feet in Sequoia National Park. It begins in Yosemite at Happy Isles, swings northeast to pass through Tuolumne Meadows, then turns south to leave the park at Donohue Pass. The trail was scouted by Theodore Solomons and named in honor of John Muir, who did so much to preserve the wild country of the Sierra Nevada for the public to enjoy. Congress appropriated the funds to begin the trail in 1915, and it was completed in 1938.

The entire trail takes anywhere from 3 to 6 weeks to finish, although the Yosemite section takes only a few days. It is enjoyable in either direction, but I describe it here beginning at Happy Isles. In this direction you do have more uphill, but starting low gives you a chance to adjust to higher elevations gradually. There is no trailhead at Donohue Pass, so if you plan to hike only the Yosemite section, you will have to divide it into two parts: Tuolumne to Donohue Pass, and Tuolumne to Yosemite Valley (or vice versa).

The Pacific Crest Trail, dedicated in 1993, is part of the National Trails System authorized by Congress in 1968. It begins at the Mexican border and runs through the most scenic parts of the western states for 2,650 miles to the Canadian border. Hiking the entire trail takes a long summer season, but you can sample one of its finest sections as it goes through Yosemite from Donohue Pass in the south to Dorothy Lake Pass on the northern park border in about 2 weeks.

Most PCT through-hikers begin in Mexico and hike north, following the summer snowmelt to reach Canada in fall. They usually reach the northern part of Yosemite by June and frequently find the deep snow and swift, high river crossings challenging or, at worst, impossible. The Yosemite section is described here in the usual south-to-north direction, but wait until mid-July for the most rewarding, least frustrating experience. The Pacific Crest Trail Association has lots of good information about current trail conditions and trip planning. You can contact them at 1331 Garden Hwy., Sacramento, CA 95833, (916) 285-1846, or online at www.pcta.org. For more John Muir Trail information, visit www.nps.gov/yose/planyourvisit/wildpermits.htm.

60 The John Muir Trail

Start: John Muir Trailhead at Happy Isles
Total distance: 34.3 miles one way
Hiking time: 4 to 6 days
Difficulty: Moderate
Elevation change: 7,500 feet
Seasons: Summer through early fall
Nearest facilities: Yosemite Village and Tuolumne Meadows; gas at Lee Vining
Permits: Required; apply in advance, see "Wilderness Permits" in the Introduction, and see "Special considerations" here
Maps: USGS Half Dome, Koip Peak, Merced Peak, Tenaya Lake, and Vogelsang Peak quads

Special considerations: You need only one wilderness permit for the entire John Muir Trail, but Yosemite now limits the number of permits valid for *exiting* Yosemite via Donohue Pass to 45 people per day: 15 of these will be available for the Lyell Canyon trailhead 24 weeks in advance, and 10 are available on a first-come, first-served basis. Permits for the remaining 20 people are available for the Happy Isles Trailhead to Little Yosemite Valley, Glacier Point to Little Yosemite Valley, and Sunrise Lakes Trailhead, and all of these can be reserved in advance.

Finding the trailhead: Leave your car in the hikers' lot east of Curry Village and ride the shuttle bus to Happy Isles (stop 16), or follow the signs along the footpath to Happy Isles where you cross the bridge over the Merced; turn right and follow the river upstream to the trailhead sign on the left. Trailhead GPS: N37 43.51 / W119 33.33

The Hike

The trail climbs gently on an eroded asphalt path through black oak and ponderosa pine forest among enormous lichen-draped boulders. In about a half mile, across the thundering Merced on your right, watch for 370-foot Illilouette Fall tucked back in its deeply cut gorge in the Panorama Cliff. The trail now steepens briefly, then suddenly descends to the Vernal Fall Bridge at 0.8 mile. Upstream, Vernal Fall is perfectly framed by maple, alder, and various conifers as it drops 317 feet over the lower step of the Giant Staircase.

Cross the bridge to the south side of the river and turn left, upstream. Just beyond, at mile 0.9, meet the Mist Trail, an alternate route to the top of Nevada Fall. The John Muir Trail (JMT) turns right and in a few yards continues straight ahead at the junction with a lateral trail on the right for horses only that leads back to the stables. The JMT switchbacks moderately but relentlessly uphill, providing you with plenty of excuses to rest and admire the scenery on the way. To the northeast across the river gorge, the rounded back side of Half Dome comes into view, along with Mount Broderick, Liberty Cap, and finally, 594-foot Nevada Fall. Beyond the excellent viewpoint at Clark Point where a lateral trail cuts left to meet the Mist Trail, the JMT passes beneath a dripping rock overhang decorated with delicate hanging gardens of ferns, columbines, and monkey flowers. At 3.3 miles the Panorama Trail, leading back to Glacier Point, joins this one from the right (south). The trail drops a bit, hops a couple of little creeks, then emerges into a wide sunny expanse of smooth granite at the top of Nevada Fall. Here, at 3.5 miles, amid crowds of humans and panhandling squirrels, cross to the north shore of the river on a footbridge. There is an outhouse here, and just beyond, the junction with the upper end of the Mist Trail. Continue upstream, climbing the well-defined trail over inlaid rocks. The way soon levels out and passes from sunlight into shade, and the Merced changes from a rushing, raging torrent to become quiet, dark, and deep.

At 4.3 miles the JMT cuts off to the left to reach busy Little Yosemite Valley at mile 4.8, your first camping opportunity. From the campground climb the well-beaten path toward Half Dome along with the crowd of hikers heading for the summit. The Half Dome Trail junction is at 5.3 miles. Turn right (east), and at 5.8 miles keep right again at the Sunrise Lakes junction and ascend along Sunrise Creek. At 7.7 miles meet a junction with a lateral trail to Echo Valley. Keep left (north) here and very soon arrive at a second junction, at 7.8 miles, where the JMT turns right (east). Climb gently, then steeply, to a ridgetop where there are views of the Cathedral Range, then descend to the big meadow and Sunrise High Sierra Camp at 12.3 miles. There is a backpack camping area here and some emergency supplies. Now follow the trail, eastward at first, then northward, skirting the meadow's edge to meet the trail to Merced Lake at 13.2 miles. Continue straight ahead into the forest, cross Echo Creek, then skirt the creek on its east side through aptly named Long Meadow. Veer northwest and climb toward Columbia Finger, rounding its base and reaching an open, rocky saddle. Here one of those awe-inspiring Yosemite vistas bursts upon you. The grand, sweeping, sculptured granite of Cathedral Peak, Echo Peak, and Matthes Crest looks like the spine of the world. Descend the hillside to the meadow below Cathedral Peak. At the end of the meadow, the trail drops over Cathedral Pass, revealing another knock-your-socks-off view. The spire of Cathedral Peak rises above a green meadow filled with flowers and the impossibly blue Upper Cathedral Lake, embellished with windblown pines and backdropped by the park's northern ranges. Descend the pass and cross the marshy meadow to Upper Cathedral Lake at 16.3 miles.

Drop down through forest to a spur trail to Lower Cathedral Lake at mile 16.8. The lower lake is a half mile to the west and is well worth a detour since Cathedral Peak is seen head-on from the lakeside and appears as a single, needlelike spire. From the lower lake cutoff, the trail rounds the end of the ridge on which Cathedral Peak is perched, then descends through forest to a junction with the trail to Tuolumne Meadows, just after crossing Budd Creek and before reaching the Tioga Road at 20.7 miles.

The trail passes behind the Tuolumne Meadows Visitor Center, Tuolumne Village, and the Tuolumne Meadows Campground, in case you need supplies or information. It passes several junctions leading to the Tioga Road and the other facilities to the north, then passes the rear entrance to the campground, the Elizabeth Lake Trailhead, and a second campground turnoff at 22.4 miles. Follow along the north shore of the Lyell Fork of the Tuolumne River until you meet a junction where the Pacific Crest Trail (PCT) joins the JMT at 23.1 miles near the Tuolumne Meadows Lodge.

Nevada Fall sits near the beginning of the John Muir Trail.

Follow the PCT/JMT southeast to a footbridge over the Dana Fork, ignoring the cutoff back to the Lodge, and cross the bridge, then turn left and follow the river upstream, pausing to enjoy the wildflower gardens along the shore. Ignore another cutoff to the left toward Gaylor Lakes just a short distance beyond. The route bends slightly to the right, crosses a low rise alongside a marshy area, and reaches the twin bridges over the Lyell Fork at 24.7 miles. This is surely one of the most sublime vistas in Yosemite, with the clear turquoise river winding toward you through the green meadow. Soon after you leave the twin bridges, another path leads back to the Tuolumne Meadows Campground, but you keep left on the JMT through lodgepole pine forest and over open rock to 25.4 miles, where the Rafferty Creek Trail heads uphill to the right, toward Vogelsang. Cross the bridge over the creek on your left and continue through forest and meadows until a glorious view of Lyell Canyon opens up and you rejoin the Tuolumne River, which you will now be following almost all the way to its headwaters, the Lyell Glacier, tucked beneath the shaded crest of Mount Lyell, the highest peak in Yosemite at 13,114 feet.

At 27.7 miles keep left at a fork with another trail to Vogelsang. Just beyond the point where Kuna Creek drops down from the Kuna Crest to join the Lyell Fork from the east, the trail begins to climb, winding among avalanche debris. Views of the river snaking away to the north down the canyon get better and better as you gain elevation. Cross the river on a bridge and arrive at Lyell Base Camp. It's a busy place, used by climbers preparing to tackle the mountain. There are plenty of good campsites here, and plenty of bears.

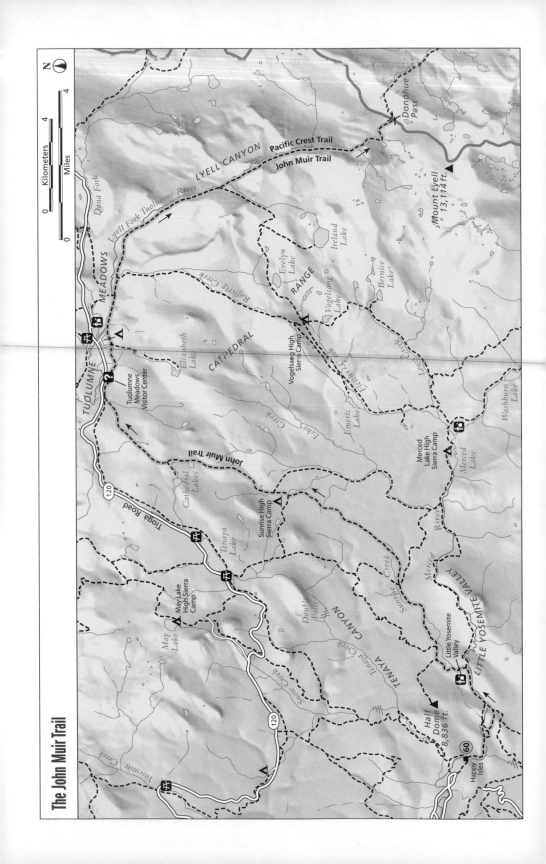

The John Muir Trail

N

Kilometers
0   4

Miles
0   4

Dana Fork

Lyell Fork Tuolumne River

LYELL CANYON

Pacific Crest Trail

John Muir Trail

Donohue Pass

Mount Lyell
13,114 ft.

TUOLUMNE

MEADOWS

Tuolumne
Meadows
Visitor Center

Rafferty Creek

Elizabeth
Lake

CATHEDRAL

RANGE

Evelyn
Lake

Ireland
Lake

Vogelsang
Lake

Bernice
Lake

Vogelsang High
Sierra Camp

Lewis Creek

Fletcher Creek

Echo Creek

Emeric
Lake

Washburn
Lake

Merced Lake High
Sierra Camp

Merced
Lake

Tioga Road

120

John Muir Trail

Cathedral
Lakes

Tenaya
Lake

Sunrise High
Sierra Camp

Sunrise Creek

Merced River

May Lake
High Sierra Camp

May
Lake

Snow Creek

Tenaya Creek

Donohue
Falls

TENAYA CANYON

LITTLE YOSEMITE VALLEY

Little Yosemite
Valley

Yosemite Creek

120

Half
Dome
8,836 ft.

60

Happy
Isles

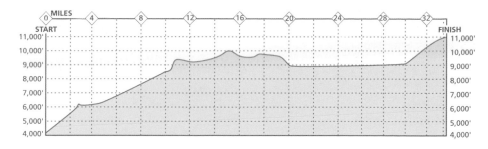

The trees begin to disappear as you climb beyond the camp, and from here on you get superb views up the canyon to the peaks and glaciers. One of the finest of these is from the outlet of a little lake at the end of a flowery meadow. This outlet can be tricky to cross at high water. Just past this crossing there is a rocky little rise sheltered by whitebark pines that could be used as a last, and simply exquisite, campsite before the pass. Climb another little rise, turn left (east), and cross the outlet of another tarn, not as difficult as the last one. Now work your way up over open granite, negotiating snow patches that often remain until midsummer to Donohue Pass and the Yosemite park boundary at 11,000 feet. Beyond, the John Muir and Pacific Crest Trails descend through an open rocky basin toward Rush Creek in the Ansel Adams Wilderness.

Miles and Directions

0.0 Happy Isles Trailhead

0.8 Cross the Vernal Fall Bridge

3.3 Panorama Trail junction; keep left

3.5 Top of Nevada Fall; cross the bridge

4.8 Little Yosemite Valley

5.3 Half Dome Trail junction; turn right

5.8 Sunrise Lakes Trail junction; turn right again

7.7 Echo Valley Trail junction; keep left

7.8 Sunrise High Sierra Camp Trail; turn right

12.3 Sunrise High Sierra Camp

13.2 Merced Lake Trail junction; continue straight ahead

16.3 Upper Cathedral Lake

16.8 Spur trail to Lower Cathedral Lake

20.7 Tuolumne Meadows Trail junction near Tioga Road; turn right

22.4 Turnoff to Tuolumne Meadows Campground

23.1 JMT and PCT meet

24.7 Twin Bridges over the Lyell Fork

25.4 Rafferty Creek Trail junction; turn left across the bridge

27.7 Vogelsang High Sierra Camp cutoff; keep left

34.3 Donohue Pass

61 The Pacific Crest Trail

Start: Yosemite park boundary at Donohue Pass

Total distance: 79.4 miles one way

Hiking time: 6 to 10 days

Difficulty: Strenuous

Elevation change: 4,500 feet

Seasons: Summer and early fall

Nearest facilities: Tuolumne Meadows; gas at Crane Flat and Lee Vining

Permits: Required in advance; check www.pcta .org and www.nps.gov/yose/planyourvisit/wild permits.htm for details

Maps: USGS Koip Peak, Vogelsang Peak, Tioga Pass, Tenaya Lake, Falls Ridge, Matterhorn Peak, Piute Mountain, Tiltill Mountain, and Tower Peak quads

Finding the trailhead: This Pacific Crest Trail (PCT) hike is described from border to border of Yosemite. There are no trailheads at either end. The only road the trail crosses is at Tuolumne Meadows. GPS at Donohue Pass: N37.45.39/W119 14.55

The Hike

From Donohue Pass at 11,000 feet, work your way down over open granite, negotiating snow patches that often remain until midsummer, crossing the outlet of a little tarn, and descending to the outlet of a second tarn where the ford can be tricky at high water. There is a small, exquisite campsite near the ford facing Mount Lyell, highest peak in the park at 13,114 feet, and its rapidly shrinking glacier. The forest begins to thicken as you wind your way down to Lyell Base Camp, on the other side of a bridge at 2.7 miles. It's a busy place with lots of good campsites, and lots of bears. Wind down through avalanche debris to the long, blooming meadow along the meandering Lyell Fork to a junction at mile 6.8 where a trail coming down from Vogelsang High Sierra Camp joins this one. The trail continues alongside the river for a time, then gradually swings away from it to make its way through forest and meadow, then back into forest to meet Rafferty Creek. Cross it on a bridge to find a junction with another route to Vogelsang at mile 11.1. Turn right. Ignore a side trail that cuts off to the left toward the Tuolumne Meadows Campground and swing right to reach the twin bridges over the Tuolumne at mile 11.7, where you will find one of the most sublime vistas in Yosemite. Leaving the bridges, head north over the dusty trampled trail to the "John Muir Trail" sign at a road, across from which is the Dog Lake parking lot. Ignore several spur trails that cut off to your right toward Gaylor Lakes and the Tuolumne Meadows Lodge, keeping left. Turn right only when you can see the sign and the road at mile 12.4.

Walk along this secondary road heading west until it meets the Tioga Road. Continue west along the Tioga Road for less than a half mile until you can see the Lembert Dome parking lot on the north side. Cross Tioga Road to the parking lot, turn

Dorothy Lake Pass above Dorothy Lake marks the point where the PCT leaves Yosemite.

left (west), and continue along the road that parallels Tioga Road to the Glen Aulin Trailhead. It begins at the closed gate at 13.0 miles. Go through the gate and follow the road (closed to vehicles) through the meadow, keeping right and climbing a small rise where the road splits. From the top of the rise, head toward the ramshackle log structure partially containing Soda Springs at mile 13.5. Just beyond is Parsons Lodge, a stone building with historical exhibits. There the path splits; you turn right to a big "Glen Aulin Trail" sign, then turn left. Walk through flowery meadows and lodgepole pine forest on footing that is heavy and dusty from lots of traffic. Ford Delaney Creek at mile 14.2, then ignore a trail that cuts off to the right toward Young Lakes at mile 14.4. In less than a mile, you emerge from behind a low ridge to behold the spectacular Cathedral Range with the Tuolumne River in the foreground. After passing through a short stretch of forest, climb around a low shoulder of rock and keep watch on your left for the Little Devil's Postpile, an unusual volcanic feature much younger than the surrounding rock.

The trail turns sharply right and drops down a short, steep notch, and very soon reaches a pair of footbridges across the Tuolumne at mile 16.3. From this point on the river picks up speed and cascades over a series of falls. It twice dives into and out of deep forest lined with Labrador tea and corn lily, then emerges again into sunlight on cobblestones and smooth granite marked with ducks. Finally it meets a junction with the McGee Lake Trail at 17.8 miles. A few more steep, slippery switchbacks lead down to a bridge and back to the other (north) side of the river. Few hikers can resist the urge to stop on the bridge to snap a photo or simply gape at the frothy White

Cascade splashing into a pool in front of the High Sierra Camp. You have come 18.0 miles. The High Sierra Camp (just a minute or two out of your way across the bridge over Cold Creek on your right) has a few emergency supplies and snacks for sale for a few hours each afternoon. You should also fill up with piped potable water there since the next few miles are sometimes dry by midseason.

Head northward across Cold Creek from the High Sierra Camp, hiking partly through open forest, partly through meadow, up Cold Canyon, with Mount Conness at its head. The McCabe Lakes junction, at 25.0 miles, is not shown correctly on the topographic map, but if you stay left, following the PCT, you will be on track. At 26.0 miles keep left again, following Return Creek in Virginia Canyon downstream, dropping to cross Spiller Creek, then climbing fairly steeply up some dusty switchbacks. Pass through a gate and make another sandy descent, cross a low rise, pass a couple of shallow ponds, then emerge into the meadow bordering Miller Lake. It's a nice warm lake for swimming, and there is good camping in the timber across the meadow from the trail. Leaving the lake, the trail swings back northward, crossing a shoulder with views to the Sawtooth Ridge, then drops steeply into Matterhorn Canyon at 30.8 miles in a flowery meadow where there is more good camping. The PCT makes a sharp dogleg here, cutting back southwest, crossing Matterhorn Creek, and following its broad meandering course downstream for more than a mile. The trail swings northwest, climbing along Wilson Creek, which it crosses several times before it turns west and climbs switchbacks to wide, grassy Benson Pass at mile 40.4. Descend fairly gradually from the pass and wade the outlet of Smedberg Lake at the edge of a meadow. The lake lies at the foot of blocky Volunteer Peak. There is good camping at the lake; the best sites are on the shore opposite the trail.

After leaving Smedberg Lake, reach a junction at the steep western base of Volunteer Peak at 52.5 miles. The fork of the trail continues south, but the PCT heads west toward Seavey Pass. You meet a second Seavey Pass junction at 53.1 miles. Head north toward Benson Lake, dropping down to cross and then follow the stream connecting Smedberg and Benson Lakes. Leave the stream to cross a rocky shoulder and descend to a boggy flat blooming with corn lilies, onions, and wild geraniums, to meet the spur trail to Benson Lake at 55.5 miles. This is a big lake in a beautifully ice-polished rocky bowl. It is surprisingly popular for such a remote spot, probably because of its good camping and beautiful beach at the end nearest the trail.

Leaving the lake, the trail climbs up open manzanita-covered slopes, heading toward the pointed beacon of Piute Mountain directly ahead. Near the peak it swings northeast, climbs more steeply along the cascading stream, then levels out beside the first of several little lakes to Seavey Pass, a rather long, open ridge studded with shining domes and tarns. A short distance down the north side of the pass, reach a junction with Kerrick Canyon at 58.9 miles.

Turn left (west) down the shady floor of Kerrick Canyon, pass an avalanche chute, and proceed to the junction with the Bear Valley Trail, at 62.5 miles. Switchback up out of the gully and follow a roller-coaster route, then drop down steeply into the

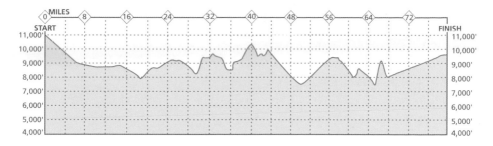

next valley, wading Thompson and Stubblefield Creeks in Stubblefield Canyon, then labor your way up and down over Macomb Ridge. Finally, cross Tilden Creek and meet the Tilden Canyon/Wilma Lake junction at 68.2 miles. Turn right (north) here and proceed a very short distance to a second junction at 68.3 miles, toward Wilma Lake. The trail follows very close to the southwest shore of the lake and crosses a short stream that connects the lake to Falls Creek. Through much of July this is a soggy morass, and earlier in the year it may be so deeply flooded that it is impassable.

Once on the west side of Falls Creek, turn right (north) at the junction at 70.3 miles. Soon you pass through a gate and wander along the flat valley floor to 72.2 miles, where a trail cuts off to the right (east) to the shore of Tilden Lake. A visit to this lake is worth a detour, and there is good camping at the southwest shore of this long, narrow finger of water, with Tower Peak above its far end.

Back on the PCT, continue north, passing Chittenden Peak, then a pretty water-fall, and level out to follow miles of grassy meadow. Pass briefly through forest, then into the even wider expanse of Grace Meadow. Ascend out of the meadow at its north end to reach the Dorothy Lake/Bond Pass junction at 78.7 miles. Turn right (east) here and skirt Dorothy Lake in its broad meadow to reach the park boundary at Dorothy Lake Pass, at 79.4 miles.

Miles and Directions

0.0	Donohue Pass
2.7	Lyell Base Camp
6.8	Joins trail from Vogelsang High Sierra Camp
11.1	Rafferty Creek Bridge; turn right
11.7	Twin Bridges over the Tuolumne; turn left
12.4	Turn right into Dog Lake parking lot
13.0	Glen Aulin Trailhead
13.5	Soda Springs
14.2	Ford Delaney Creek
14.4	Young Lakes Trail junction; keep left
16.3	Cross Twin Bridges
17.8	McGee Lake Trail junction; turn right
18.0	Glen Aulin High Sierra Camp

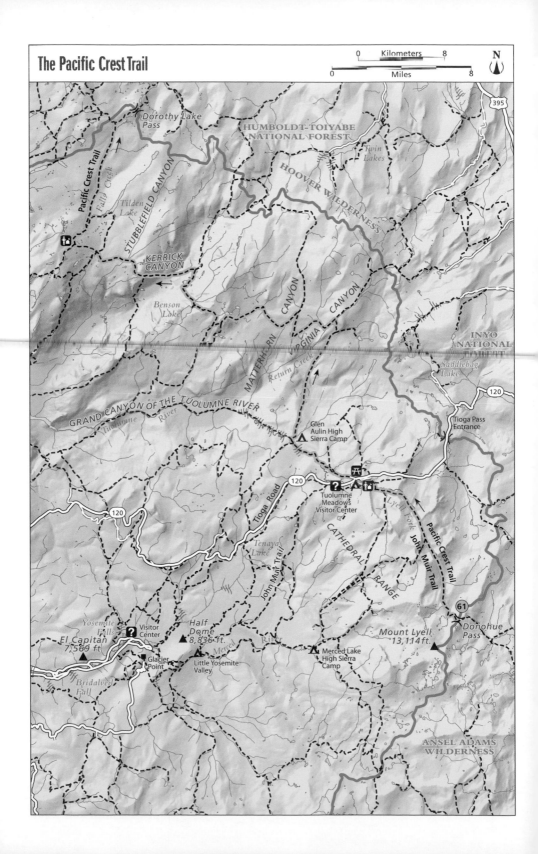

The Pacific Crest Trail

Dorothy Lake Pass

HUMBOLDT-TOIYABE NATIONAL FOREST

Twin Lakes

HOOVER WILDERNESS

Pacific Crest Trail

Falls Creek

Tilden Lake

STUBBLEFIELD CANYON

KERRICK CANYON

Benson Lake

MATTERHORN CANYON

VIRGINIA CANYON

Return Creek

INYO NATIONAL FOREST

Saddlebag Lake

GRAND CANYON OF THE TUOLUMNE RIVER

Tuolumne River

120

Tioga Pass Entrance

Glen Aulin High Sierra Camp

Tioga Road

120

? Tuolumne Meadows Visitor Center

Lyell Fork

Pacific Crest Trail / John Muir Trail

120

Tenaya Lake

John Muir Trail

CATHEDRAL RANGE

61

Yosemite Falls

Visitor Center

Half Dome 8,836 ft.

Merced River

Mount Lyell 13,114 ft.

Donohue Pass

El Capitan 7,569 ft.

Glacier Point

Little Yosemite Valley

Merced Lake High Sierra Camp

Bridalveil Fall

ANSEL ADAMS WILDERNESS

25.0	McCabe Lakes junction; keep left
26.0	Return Creek
30.8	Matterhorn Canyon
40.4	Benson Pass
52.5	Smedberg Lake junction
53.1	Seavey Pass junction
55.5	Spur trail to Benson Lake
58.9	Kerrick Canyon
62.5	Bear Valley Trail
68.2	Tilden Canyon/Wilma Lake junction
68.3	Second Wilma Lake junction
70.3	Jack Main Canyon
72.2	Tilden Lake junction
78.7	Dorothy Lake/Bond Pass junction
79.4	Dorothy Lake Pass

Appendix A: Further Reading

Barrett, S. A., and E. W. Gifford. *Miwok Material Culture.* Yosemite, CA: Yosemite Natural History Association, 1933.

Browning, Peter. *Place Names of the Sierra Nevada.* Berkeley, CA: Wilderness Press, 1991.

Gaines, David. *Birds of the Yosemite Sierra.* Oakland, CA: California Syllabus, 1977.

Glazner, Allen F., and Greg M. Stock, *Geology Underfoot in Yosemite National Park.* Helena, MT: Mountain Press Publishing Company, 2010.

Grater, Russell K. *Discovering Sierra Mammals.* Yosemite, CA: Yosemite Natural History Association and Sequoia Natural History Association, 1978.

Harmon, Will. *Leave No Trace.* Guilford, CT: Globe Pequot, 1997.

Harvey, H. Thomas, Howard S. Shellhammer, and Ronald E. Stecker. *Giant Sequoia Ecology. Scientific Monograph Series No. 12.* Washington, DC: US Department of the Interior, 1980.

Huber, N. King. *The Geologic Story of Yosemite National Park. US Geological Survey Bulletin 1595.* Washington, DC: US Department of the Interior, 1987.

Johnson, Verna R. *Sierra Nevada.* Boston: Houghton Mifflin Company, 1970.

Laws, John Muir. *The Laws Field Guide to the Sierra Nevada.* Berkeley, CA: Heyday Books, 2007.

Paruk, Jim. *Sierra Nevada Tree Finder.* Yosemite, CA: Yosemite Natural History Association, 1997.

Preston, Gilbert. *Wilderness First Aid.* Guilford, CT: Globe Pequot, 1997.

Sax, Joseph L. *Mountains without Handrails.* Ann Arbor: University of Michigan Press, 1980.

Schneider, Bill. *Bear Aware.* Guilford, CT: Globe Pequot, 2004.

Schneider, Bill, and Russ Schneider. *Backpacking Tips.* Guilford, CT: Globe Pequot, 2005.

Storer, Tracy I., and David Lucas. *Sierra Nevada Natural History.* Berkeley: University of California Press, 2004.

Swedo, Suzanne. *Wilderness Survival.* Guilford, CT: Globe Pequot, 2006.

Weeden, Norman. *A Sierra Nevada Flora.* Berkeley, CA: Wilderness Press, 1996.

Wenk, Elizabeth. *Wildflowers of the High Sierra and John Muir Trail.* Birmingham, AL: Wilderness Press, 2015.

Whitney, Stephen. *The Sierra Nevada: A Sierra Club Naturalist's Guide.* San Francisco: Sierra Club Books, 1979.

Wiese, Karen. *Sierra Nevada Wildflowers.* Guilford, CT: Globe Pequot, 2000.

Woodmencey, Jim. *Reading Weather.* Guilford, CT: Globe Pequot, 1998.

Zwinger, Ann H., and Beatrice E. Willard. *Land above the Trees.* New York: Harper & Row, 1972.

Appendix B: Hiker's Checklist

Always make and check your own checklist!

If you've ever hiked into the backcountry and discovered that you've forgotten an essential, you know that it's a good idea to make a checklist and check the items off as you pack so that you won't forget the things you want and need. Here are some ideas:

Clothing
❏ Dependable rain parka
❏ Rain pants
❏ Windbreaker
❏ Thermal underwear
❏ Shorts
❏ Long pants or sweatpants
❏ Wool cap or balaclava
❏ Hat
❏ Wool shirt or sweater
❏ Jacket or parka
❏ Extra socks
❏ Underwear
❏ Lightweight shirts
❏ T-shirts
❏ Bandana(s)
❏ Mittens or gloves

Footwear
❏ Sturdy, comfortable boots
❏ Lightweight camp shoes

Bedding
❏ Sleeping bag
❏ Foam pad or air mattress
❏ Ground sheet (plastic or nylon)
❏ Dependable tent

Hauling
❏ Backpack and/or day pack

Cooking
❏ 1-quart container
❏ 1-gallon water container for camp use (collapsible)
❏ Backpack stove and extra fuel
❏ Aluminum foil
❏ Cooking pots
❏ Bowls/plates
❏ Utensils (spoons, forks, knife)
❏ Pot scrubber
❏ Matches in waterproof container

Food and Drink
❏ Cereal
❏ Bread
❏ Crackers
❏ Cheese
❏ Trail mix
❏ Margarine
❏ Powdered soups
❏ Salt/pepper
❏ Main course meals
❏ Snacks
❏ Hot chocolate
❏ Tea

❏ Powdered milk

❏ Drink mixes

Photography

❏ Camera and batteries

❏ Filters

❏ Lens brush/paper

Miscellaneous

❏ Bear-proof canister

❏ Sunglasses

❏ Map and compass

❏ Sewing kit

❏ Toilet paper

❏ Pocketknife

❏ Sunscreen

❏ Good insect repellent

❏ Lip balm

❏ Flashlight with good batteries and a spare bulb

❏ Candle(s)

❏ First-aid kit

❏ Your FalconGuide

❏ Survival kit

❏ Small garden trowel or shovel

❏ Water filter or purification tablets

❏ Plastic bags (for trash)

❏ Soap

❏ Towel

❏ Toothbrush

❏ Fishing license

❏ Fishing rod, reel, lures, flies, etc.

❏ Binoculars

❏ Waterproof covering for pack

❏ Watch

❏ Hiking poles

Hike Index

About the Author

Suzanne Swedo has taught natural science seminars for the Yosemite Association in Yosemite National Park for thirty years. During the same period, she has conducted wilderness survival, outdoor skills, and natural history outings as founder and director of W.I.L.D., an international and domestic adventure travel company. She has also led nature and wilderness trips for various educational organizations including the University of California Extension, the National Outings Program of the Sierra Club, Wilderness Institute, Pacific Wilderness Institute, and Outdoor Adventures.

RICK SMITH PHOTO

Suzanne has demonstrated wilderness skills in a ten-week television series, *Alive and Well,* and served as a survival consultant for Warner Brothers Television. Her writings on travel and the outdoors have appeared in publications such as the *Los Angeles Examiner* and *California Maga-zine.* Other books for FalconGuides are *Wilderness Survival, Hiking California's Golden Trout Wilderness, Hiking the Hawaiian Islands,* and *Best Easy Day Hikes Yosemite National Park.*

American Hiking Society

Because you

hike.

We're with you
every step of the way

As a national voice for hikers, **American Hiking Society** works every day:

- Building and maintaining hiking trails
- Educating and supporting hikers by providing information and resources
- Supporting hiking and trail organizations nationwide
- Speaking for hikers in the halls of Congress and with federal land managers

Whether you're a casual hiker or a seasoned backpacker, become a member of American Hiking Society and join the national hiking community! You'll enjoy great member benefits and help preserve the nation's hiking trails, so tomorrow's hike is even better than today's. We invite you to join us now!

American Hiking Society